ROMANTICISM

The Culture of the Nineteenth Century

The Cultures of Mankind

GREEK CULTURE: The Adventure of the Human Spirit
Edited by Alice von Hildebrand

ROMAN CULTURE: Weapons and the Man
Edited by Garry Wills

MEDIEVAL CULTURE: The Image and the City
Edited by Ruth Brantl

RENAISSANCE CULTURE: A New Sense of Order
Edited by Julian Mates and Eugene Cantelupe

THE AGE OF REASON: The Culture of the Seventeenth Century
Edited by Leo Weinstein

THE ENLIGHTENMENT: The Culture of the Eighteenth Century
Edited by Isidor Schneider

ROMANTICISM: The Culture of the Nineteenth Century
Edited by Morse Peckham

TWENTIETH-CENTURY CULTURE: The Breaking Up
Edited by Robert Phelps

Romanticism

The Culture of the
Nineteenth Century

Edited by Morse Peckham

George Braziller · *New York*

Copyright © 1965, by Morse Peckham

Published simultaneously in Canada by Ambassador Books, Ltd., Toronto

All rights reserved
For information, address the publisher,
George Braziller, Inc.
One Park Avenue, New York 16

Library of Congress Catalog Card Number: 65-23181

First Printing

Printed in the United States of America

ACKNOWLEDGMENTS

The editor and publisher have made every effort to determine and credit the holders of copyright of the selections in this book. Any errors or omissions may be rectified in future volumes. The editor and publisher wish to thank the following for permission to reprint the material included in this anthology:

Atlantic—Little, Brown and Company—for "To the Reader" from Baudelaire's *The Flowers of Evil,* tr. by Stanley Kunitz in *Selected Poems 1928–1958* by Stanley Kunitz. Copyright ©, 1958, by Stanley Kunitz. Reprinted by permission of the publisher.

The Clarendon Press, Oxford—for selections from *The Poetical Works of William Wordsworth,* ed. by E. De Selincourt & H. Darbishire. Reprinted by permission of the publisher.

The Hogarth Press, Ltd.—for "The Drunken Boat" from *Selected Verse Poems of Arthur Rimbaud,* tr. by Norman Cameron. Reprinted by permission of the publisher.

New Directions—for a selection from *Sentimental Education* by Gustave Flaubert, "Brentano translation." Copyright ©, 1957 by New Directions. Reprinted by permission of the publisher.

Oxford University Press, Inc. and Faber & Faber Ltd.—for a selection from *Goethe's Faust, Parts I and II,* tr. by Louis MacNeice. Copyright 1951 by Louis MacNeice. Reprinted by permission of the publishers.

Random House, Inc.—for "Voyage to Cythera" and "The Voyage" from *Poems of Baudelaire, Les Fleurs du Mal,* by Charles Baudelaire, tr. by Roy Campbell. Copyright 1952 by Pantheon Books, Inc. Reprinted by permission of Random House, Inc.

Henry Regnery Company—for a selection from *Beyond Good and Evil* by Friedrich Nietzsche, tr. by Marianne Cowan. Copyright 1955. Reprinted by permission of the publisher.

Frederick Ungar Publishing Co., Inc.—for selections from *The Sufferings of Young Werther* by Goethe, tr. by B. Q. Morgan. Reprinted by permission of the publisher.

University of California Press—for "Hérodiade" from *Selected Poems* by Stéphane Mallarmé, tr. by C. F. MacIntyre. Reprinted by permission of the publisher.

PREFACE

There is an obvious absurdity in attempting to create a relatively brief anthology of nineteenth-century writing, painting, and architecture. But it would be just as absurd to create a large anthology. My first principle of selection is to confine myself to what I describe in the Introduction as the Romantic tradition. After all, quantitatively, the biggest cultural event in the nineteenth century was the spread of Enlightenment ideas. The development of those ideas which led to what we can recognize as modern was the creation of a small, embattled, and alienated minority, which was often misunderstood even by its admirers, and for the most part still is. I have conceived this tradition as a series of attempts to solve a central problem, each solution leading to new problems, with the most satisfactory solution yet, to my mind, having been achieved by Nietzsche, who concludes this volume.

Only eight lyric poems are presented in their entirety. The rest of the material consists of excerpts. All the material has been selected to reveal vital stages in the discovery and solution of the central problem. It is not intended to be representative of the work of the authors selected, though it sometimes is. Omitted passages have been indicated by centered dots. It is my hope that the excerpts are presented in a sufficiently stimulating context to persuade the reader to turn to the complete works, many of which are now neglected by the cultivated reading public. Most of the works excerpted here I have read repeatedly in their entirety, and my admiration for all of them grows with each reading.

The paintings and works of architecture have been selected to illuminate and symbolize some of the attitudes and problems presented in the literary and philosophical excerpts.

Finally, I have been motivated by the conviction that the next great task of twentieth-century culture is to understand what happened during the nineteenth century. The current revival of interest in all sorts of artists and writers who have long been neglected suggests that I am not alone in this conviction.

Morse Peckham

Philadelphia, November 30, 1964.

Contents

Part I   Analogism

Part II   Transcendentalism

Part III   Objectism

Part IV   Stylism

Part V   The Triumph of Romanticism

List of Illustrations

16. Karl Friedrich Schinkel, *Project for a Mausoleum*, interior. Schinkel Museum, Berlin.

Numbers 1–16 follow page 113

GROUP II

17. Eugène Delacroix (1798–1863), *Abduction of Rebecca*, 1846. The Metropolitan Museum of Art, Wolfe Fund, 1903.
18. Thomas Couture (1815–1879), *Romans of the Decadence*, 1847. The Louvre, Paris.
19. John Martin (1789–1854), *Manfred on the Jungfrau*, 1837. Courtesy of the Museum and Art Gallery, Birmingham, England.
20. Joseph Mallord William Turner (1775–1851), *Fire at Sea*, c. 1834. Courtesy of the Trustees, The National Gallery, London.
21. Honoré Daumier (1808–1879), *The Laundress*, 1861(?). The Louvre, Paris.
22. Harvey Lonsdale Elmes (1814–1847), *St. George's Hall*, Liverpool, 1842–1856.
23. Harvey Lonsdale Elmes, *St. George's Hall*, Liverpool.
24. Richard M. Upjohn (1802–1878), *Greenwood Cemetery*, Brooklyn, 1861. Photo: Wayne Andrews.
25. Ludwig Ferdinand Hesse (1795–1876), *Orangery*, Potsdam, 1851–1856.
26. Isaac Holden (d. 1884), *Pennsylvania Hospital*, Philadelphia, 1836–1841.
27. Thomas U. Walter (1815–1887), *Debtors' Wing, Moyamensing Prison*, Philadelphia, 1835.
28. Alexander Jackson Davis (1803–1892), *Harral House*, Bridgeport. Photo: Wayne Andrews.

Numbers 17–28 follow page 187

GROUP III

29. Ford Madox Brown (1821–1893), *Work*, 1852–1865. Reproduced by courtesy of Manchester City Art Galleries, England.
30. Arnold Böcklin (1827–1901), *The Isle of the Dead*, 1880. The Metropolitan Museum of Art, Reisinger Fund, 1926.
31. Dante Gabriel Rossetti (1828–1882), *Mnemosyne*, 1879. Courtesy of the Delaware Art Center, Samuel and Mary R. Bancroft Collection.

Numbers 29–46 follow page 233

GROUP IV

51. Paul Cézanne (1839–1906), *Still Life with Apples,* 1890–1900. Museum of Modern Art, Lillie P. Bliss Collection.
52. Paul Gauguin (1848–1903), *Tahitian Landscape,* c. 1891. The Minneapolis Institute of Arts.
53. Georges Seurat (1859–1891), *Young Woman Powdering Herself,* 1889–1890. Courtesy of the Courtauld Institute Galleries, London.
54. Odilon Redon (1840–1916), *Mystery.* The Phillips Collection, Washington, D.C.
55. Gustave Moreau, *Thomris and Cyrus,* Musée Gustave Moreau.
56. Philip Webb (1831–1915), *The Red House,* Bexley Heath, Kent, 1859.
57. Henry Hobson Richardson (1838–1886), *Watts Sherman Residence,* Newport, 1874–1876. Photo: Wayne Andrews.
58. Henry Hobson Richardson, *Allegheny County Court House,* Pittsburgh, 1884–1886.
59. Richard M. Hunt, *Biltmore,* Asheville, 1896.
60. Richard M. Hunt, *The Marble House,* Newport. Photo: Wayne Andrews.
61. John Carrère (1858–1911) and Thomas Hastings (1860–1929), *Hotel Ponce de Leon,* St. Augustine, 1885–1888.
62. Antonio Gaudí (1852–1926), *Casa Vicens,* Barcelona, 1878–1880.
63. Charles Rennie Mackintosh (1868–1928), *Glasgow School of Art,* 1897–1899.

Numbers 47–63 follow page 311

The Dilemma of a Century:
The Four Stages of Romanticism

When does the nineteenth century begin? It is much easier to say than it used to be. The cultural leaders of the time certainly knew when it had begun and what marked that beginning. It was only in the later nineteenth century and the first half of the twentieth that the question became obscured by the quarrel over the meaning of the term "Romanticism." That maddening and confusing word still has a fearful variety of meanings, and always will; but there is a growing agreement among cultural historians to limit its historical sense to a period that began in the late eighteenth century, when a small number of cultural leaders throughout Europe almost simultaneously, but at first quite independently, began to feel that they had arrived at a way of viewing the world which was profoundly different from any world-view that had ever appeared before. And they also felt that this new *Weltanschauung* (the Germans had to coin a new term to express what they were experiencing) forced them to see everything — philosophy, religion, the arts, history, politics, society — down an entirely new perspective.

Men have always had world-views, or metaphysics; it is impossible to cross a crack in the sidewalk without a metaphysic. But such metaphysics had been unconscious; that is, there had been no language in which to discuss them. There were arguments about this or that view of the world as it affected some aspect of human behavior; but these were arguments about metaphysics as truths which described the character and structure of the world. But the new way of thinking, the Romantic way, looked at itself from right angles; saw itself creating a world-view because the very character of the mind's relation to the world required it to have a metaphysic. At the same time, however, there was a conviction, at first but faint though deeply disturbing, that any world-view told the mind nothing about the world, but merely told it something about the mind. Any metaphysic was seen not as derived from the nature of the world but rather as derived from the nature of the mind and projected onto the world. A single step was taken, and all the world was changed. All previous world-views had assumed that the mind had access, whether through revelation from God or from study of the world, to the real nature and character, the true essence, of what was not the mind; and this assumption was unconscious. Or more precisely, the assumptiveness of this assumption was not verbalized or, apparently, experienced. The new attitude was not a simple assertion that we cannot know the world. Rather, it realized that we cannot know whether we know it or not. For all we know, a metaphysic may be a reliable description of the world; but there is no way to know that we know. For we are always inside a metaphysical system; we can get outside of one system only by gliding, whether we are aware of it or not, into another.

But the same position was arrived at in various ways, whether it was put in philosophical terms or not. One of the best indications of a profound cultural change is the emergence of new social roles. From this point of view, the fact that Romanticism developed a genuinely new social role is in itself almost sufficient evidence that the nineteenth century was experiencing a cultural earthquake, a convulsion at the profoundest levels of being. By itself, the new role, in all of its varieties, is enough to suggest that no profounder change had occurred in human life since the development of urbanism or "civilization" in the fourth millennium B.C. The essence of the new role is that it was an anti-role and that it was designed to symbolize the difference between role and Self. To play a role is to act according to the cultural conventions of a particular category of situations. For men before Romanticism, when one played a role there was, so to speak, nothing of the personality left over. To be sure, there was "self-consciousness," but it consisted merely of role-rehearsal and criticism of how well one had played or was playing the role. For the vast majority of human beings in our cultural tradition, and so far as I can tell, in all others, this is still the on-going state of affairs. But to the original tiny group of Romantics and to a steadily growing portion of the population ever since, role-playing did leave something over. So true was this, that these men played roles only for the sake of isolating what they called the Self, the sense of identity, the only subjectively perceived quality of experience common to the playing of all roles. And this was precisely analogous to the new attitude toward metaphysics. Roles were seen not as modes of behavior derived from the natural world, or dictated by a divine being, or inherent in man's relation to his world, but as something that man imposes on the world, something that serves only to carry out a given human intention, something, therefore, with the character of a mask. Masks and metaphysics — ultimately, they are identical. Man cannot live without such masks, but the vital, the essential, quality of experience came to be the realization of what the mask concealed. But since that hidden element was inaccessible, it was necessary to create an anti-role, a role that was different from all other roles in that it could not be integrated into the social structure of interlocking roles.

Today most people, even at the higher levels of culture, live according to the metaphysics of the Enlightenment, which reached its first climax of attempted realization in what a recent historian has called the Age of Revolutions. The American and the French Revolutions were simply the most conspicuous and sensational examples of revolutionary attempts all over western Europe. The Enlightenment can be reduced to one principle: The adaptation of the organism to the environment is properly the basis of all scientific and moral decisions; the aim was to make every scientific decision a moral one, and every moral decision a scientific one. Thus, it was thought, moral decisions can be grounded upon the real structure of nature, and this of course implied a metaphysic that asserted that the structure of the mind was identical with the structure of nature. Because, however, of man's ignorance and stupidity and his religious and political tyranny, the structure of society was out of line. The revolutionary effort of the late eighteenth century was designed to correct that fault, to line up mind, society, and nature into one unitary system.

But at the same time there was a conservative Enlightenment, best represented by Edmund Burke. He saw mind, society, and nature as an organic system that had gradually developed, and thus he saw the revolutionary effort as something that was bound to damage and even destroy the exquisitely complex and delicate interdependence of

the three elements of reality. Reform, not revolution, was the answer
to the social difficulties of the times. From the same metaphysic and
with the same values of adaptational effort two diametrically opposed
positions emerged; one justified the slaughter of the rich and powerful;
the other, the suppression of the poor and weak. To a few men of the
day (Wordsworth, the English poet, for one), it became apparent
that some other force was at work in the mind. Not an unconscious
force — Burke's organicism included that — but some force, some character of the human mind which called into doubt the fundamental
assumption of the Enlightenment: the isomorphism, or structural
identity, of mind and nature. No matter how cunningly fitted together
mind and nature might be, they were nevertheless utterly different in
their character. The structure of one was not identical with the structure
of the other. The mind could not know nature. Society, then, was but
an extension or instrument of the mind, a means of adaptation. But
that adaptation could not be perfect, must always be, perhaps, very
imperfect indeed. It was an adjustment of mind to nature, but it violated,
for that very reason, both. The role was a violation of the Self.

What, then, was the Self? How could it be defined? How could it be
talked about? What was the evidence for its existence? Since the basic
human desire was for structure, for order, or, to put it in other terms,
for meaning and the sense of value, the essence of the Self was precisely
that desire. Meaning was not immanent in nature, was not something that
the mind found in the world; it was something the mind imposed on the
world. And for this notion there was, in the experience of the pioneer
Romantics, felt evidence. For many of them the failure of the Enlightenment metaphysic was revealed by the course of the French Revolution,
which shifted from Utopian liberation to tyrannous oppression, *without
shifting its ground,* without changing its metaphysic. Ultimately there was
no difference between the revolutionary and the reactionary. This perception was like a new Fall of Man. The world suddenly lost its value;
life lost its meaning; the individual no longer had a source for his sense
of identity and a ground for his desire for order and structure. Even
before the French Revolution, a few individuals had had this experience.
The nineteenth century may almost be said to have begun with Goethe's
Sorrows of Young Werther.

Werther committed suicide, and his creator, Goethe, thought he would
lose his sanity. Rebirth, restoration, rediscovery of value for these men

came from within, came from, they felt, the ultimate depths of the mind itself, from its very nature and structure. At a stroke mind was sundered from nature, Subject from Object, the Self from the role, which was seen at best as the means of realizing the Self, and at worst, as the instrument whereby nature violated the Self. The Romantic experienced a sense of profound isolation within the world and an equally terrifying alienation from society. These two experiences, metaphysical isolation and social alienation — they are of course two different modes of the same perception — were the distinguishing signs of the Romantic, and they are to this day. To symbolize that isolation and alienation and simultaneously to assert the Self as the source of order, meaning, value, and identity, became one task of the Romantic personality. To find a ground for value, identity, meaning, order, became the other task. This anthology is designed to illustrate what I believe to be the four basic stages in the development of this second task. But it will help to glance first at some of the solutions to the social symbolization of this task in what I have called the various kinds of Romantic anti-role.

The first, though it is initially found in *Werther,* is generally called the Byronic Hero. It is a way of symbolizing precisely that utter loss of meaning and value which so many people experienced — and continue to experience — when the Enlightenment collapsed. The Byronic hero appears in numerous forms, the wanderer, the outcast, the Wandering Jew, the mysterious criminal whose crime is never explained. The normal development for the emerging Romantic type in the nineteenth century was from pre-Enlightenment Christianity to Enlightenment, and then to the stage of the Byronic hero, a stage which can well be called Negative Romanticism, for it negates all value and all meaning, both within the bounds of the individual and outside of it. The tremendous appeal of Byron's poems throughout Europe and America shows how widespread was the feeling, even though few understood the sources of the malaise which was responsible for it. Jack London's Wolf Larsen is an early twentieth-century instance.

The first stage of recovery and the first true or positive Romantic anti-role is that of the Poet-Visionary. The word often used at the time was "mystic," but what it represents is so profoundly different from traditional mysticism that it is evident that the term was employed simply because no other word was available. Indeed, it was so hard to understand at the time that "mystic" meant not much more than "incomprehensible."

Actually it referred to an effort to bridge the gap between Subject and Object, between Self and World, by a peculiar mode of perception which enables one to, as Wordsworth put it, "see into the life of things." Even Kant, in his aesthetic, had suggested that there is a mode of perception which enables us to experience the *Ding-an-sich,* the world-in-itself. It expresses the conviction that there is an order and meaning immanent in the natural universe, even though the understanding cannot reach it, even though we cannot say anything about it. It is the pure experience of value which arises from so intense an observation of the natural world that all roles, all mental categories, disappear. It is the pure revelation of truth, though what that truth is cannot be stated. And it was felt to be the peculiar task and privilege of the poet, the artist, to communicate that experience in the work of art. This is the source of the tremendous valuation given to art in the Romantic tradition, of the redemptive character of art; for in the act of creating the work of art, the artist both repeats and embodies, and also makes possible for himself and others the act of seeing through and past, of dissolving, all purely human or role-playing perceptions which mask the world, as the rational part of the mind does, so that the value immanent in the self reaches out and touches the value immanent in the world. This tradition still survives, though in an extraordinarily desiccated form, in the most modern aesthetics, and more vitally in such painters as Malevich and Klee.

But even while this Visionary Artist was developing, another anti-role was emerging, perhaps the most important of the various Romantic anti-roles: the Bohemian. Even today it is probably impossible, and certainly very difficult, to become a genuinely modern man — a Romantic of the twentieth century — without going through Bohemianism. Paris is the classic locale of Bohemianism, but it actually started in Germany, or even, in a mild sort of way, in England, with the experiments in living of Wordsworth and Coleridge in the last decade of the eighteenth century. All the essential ingredients of Bohemianism were as visible in the first decade of that century as they are today. Perhaps the key lies in the Bohemian's fascination with alcohol and drugs, for these are the means of shifting and changing consciousness, of putting the mind through permutations of perceptions which for the square, who is always boxed in by his social role, are impossible. Similar is the interest in sexual experimentation, in nonbourgeois modes of living, in indifference to middle-class standards of dress, furnishings, cleanliness; W. H. Auden warns against people who bathe too often. And this interest in the deliberate distortion of the senses and of the ways of relating to society is closely related to the aims of the Visionary Artist. Hence the Bohemian invariably makes art the center of his life, and the excuse for his deliberate offensiveness. And so he is constantly involved in unstable anti-institutions which reveal a new and, of course, at last the *true* nature or task of painting or poetry or music or philosophy. He publishes his manifestoes, his little magazine; he starts his ephemeral publishing house. And then he wanders off to a new little group or emerges as the dedicated artist who cannot be bothered with even a minimal Bohemian role.

The 1820's and the 1830's saw the emergence of two more anti-roles: the Virtuoso and the Dandy. It was Baudelaire who first saw the true significance of the Dandy. But even so, the full meaning of this anti-role has rarely been realized. And less comprehended is the anti-role of the Virtuoso. Yet the two greatest painters of the twentieth century have realized magnificently the essence of these two roles. Matisse gave the Dandy his full freedom; and Picasso did the same great task for the Virtuoso. Wallace Stevens has gone beyond them, for he is at once Dandy and Virtuoso. Some light on the related nature of these two roles can be gained from the realization that Stevens was both poet and successful businessman, while Matisse and Picasso exploited the business of being painters with a success that can make the most hardheaded middle-class anti-Romantic businessman, with his devotion to Enlightenment laissez-faire and free trade, blush with shame and envy.

The Visionary Artist avoided role-playing; the Bohemian defied it; but the Virtuoso and the Dandy transcended it, the one by fantastic mastery, the other by irony. Paganini was the first great Virtuoso, and for decades the anti-role model and the ideal. That he took something from the Byronic hero appears in the legend that he had gained his mastery of the violin by selling his soul to the devil, a Virtuoso theme that Thomas Mann uses in his *Doktor Faustus,* a study of a great twentieth-century Virtuoso composer. The Virtuoso explodes the role, then, from within. He symbolizes the uniqueness of the Self as the source of value by transforming the role into a source of unimagined splendor, order, power, and beauty. One such role exploded and transformed by the Romantic type was that of traveler. The great English Romantic Virtuoso traveler was Richard Burton, the translator of the *Arabian Nights,* who also extended the Virtuoso anti-role into sexual experience. From the

Virtuoso traveler emerged that most remarkable Romantic manifestation, the mountain climber, whose superhuman effort finally culminated in the conquest of Mt. Everest. The essence of the Virtuoso, then, is the symbolization of the inadequacy of society to meet the demands of the Self, and this inadequacy the Virtuoso reveals by a superhuman control and release of energy in an activity which, to the socially adapted, can only be pointless. "Why did you climb Everest?" "Because it was there." The word for the Virtuoso is "sublime."

The Dandy, on the other hand, transforms the role not by excess but by irony. The role of the highest status in European society is that of the aristocratic gentleman of leisure. By willfully playing this role better than those born and trained to it, the Dandy reveals the pointlessness of the socially adapted. He makes a mode of life designed to symbolize social status into a work of art designed to symbolize nothing at all, or nothing that the society values. It is an anti-role because it is purely gratuitous, because, indeed, it is pure, utterly free from self-interest. He erects play into a creed. But this, of course, ironically reveals the triviality of society: The social type with the highest status spends his life in play and pettiness. The Dandy, then, offers perfection and elegance without content, without social function. By stealing the clothes of society, he reveals its nakedness. But at the same time he symbolizes his own demands for a greater exquisiteness and order and perfection than society can achieve. And this explains the irritation of society with the Dandy, its efforts to deprive him of his value and his ironic authority, the moral nastiness with which England relished the downfall of Oscar Wilde.

One of the most perplexing qualities of the Romantic tradition is its historicism, which is most obvious in its architecture. But an examination of that reveals the Historian as a final Romantic anti-role. For this reason I have included photographs of some of the most — to modern taste — horrendous examples of nineteenth-century architecture; for the capacity to respond to such works, to penetrate through our modern notions of taste, is perhaps the ultimate test of whether one has truly grasped the spirit of Romantic culture. It is by no means enough to say that nineteenth-century architects imitated historical styles; for in the first place, they did not imitate them. Rather, they manipulated the historical styles with an extraordinary freedom and architectural imagination. Even when, toward the end of the century, they were less concerned with free fantasies on historical styles than with designing according to the principles of those styles, they were not imitating. Far from it. In an odd way, the buildings of the late nineteenth and early twentieth centuries are better examples of particular styles than the originals from which they were derived. Thus Ralph Cram's nave in St. John the Divine Church in New York City is one of the greatest Gothic naves ever designed, more beautiful, in some ways, than any nave designed or built during the Middle Ages, though it seems like blasphemy to say so. Such men designed according to a conscious theory of Gothic or Renaissance or Enlightenment architecture; they built according to a construct that attempted to formulize the essence of the Gothic or Renaissance architectural spirit. To deny the exquisite perfection of the Morgan Library is aesthetic pedantry. Free manipulation and conscious perfecting of immanent principles, then, are the forms of the spirit of Romantic architecture; and its sources are highly similar to those of the Virtuoso and the Dandy. On the one hand it is a studied reference to the superiority of the past. It is a nostalgia which symbolizes alienation. On the other hand, it is a completely personal manipulation of a social tradition. The Romantic architect, at least for a long time, could not create a Romantic nonhistorical style, for to do so would have been to serve his society, which his alienation prevented. He could serve it only by providing for its bourgeois, Enlightenment, adaptational functions a completely inappropriate setting, cathedrals for railroad stations, aristocratic palaces for the new rich, classic temples for Christian services.

But historicism pervaded all aspects of Romantic culture. The great period of literary history, as opposed to modern scholarly history, was the nineteenth century, and the histories of Michelet, of Ranke, of Carlyle, of Froude, are still the best historical reading in the world. What the Historian symbolized was, in fact, the Romantic historical consciousness. For this consciousness there were two sources. Anyone who had gone through the profoundly disorienting transition of experiencing the failure of the great hopes of the Enlightenment, of experiencing also the consequent total loss of meaning and value and identity, and then of arriving at the new Romantic vision, saw his own life as history. Psychology became history; personality became history; the manifestation of the Self became history. But there was another way of arriving at the same result, a way of which Hegel is the great exemplar. Once the Subject and the Object, the mind and nature, have been sundered, once an unbridgeable gap has been placed between them, once the *strangeness* of human existence has been experienced without any falling back on Original Sin, then one concludes that the only way the Subject can know itself is through what it does to the Object, and the only way the Object can be known is through what it does with the Subject. What can we talk about? The interaction between the two, the interpretational tension between mind and world. For mind cannot know reality, it can only interpret it, dictated by its profoundest interests, which are in fact unknowable. Neither the Self nor the world can be known, that is, talked about; they can only be experienced, the one in terms of the other. Reality, then, is what mind has done to world and what world has done to mind. Reality is history, the history of how, in its dealings with the phenomenal world, the interests of the mind, the Will, as Schopenhauer called it, has been revealed; that is, the Will to creation, to order, to meaning, to value, to identity. Just as the early Romantic could understand himself only in terms of what had happened to him, so man can be understood only in terms of his history, and reality can be understood only in terms of the history of man's dealings with the world. "Spirit" is the term many Romantics used for the interpretational tension from Subject to Object, and reality, therefore, is the history of Spirit. Thus, in understanding Picasso, it is the history of his style which provides the clue for the individual painting. The Enlightenment placed perceptions by putting them into the frame of unchanging nature; Romanticism places them by putting them into the frame of historical process. Reality is neither space nor time; it is the process of history.

These, then: Byronic Hero, Visionary Artist, Bohemian, Virtuoso, Dandy, Historian, are the novel roles that mark the emergence of Romanticism, and are sufficient proof that Romanticism is the profoundest cultural transformation in human history since the invention of the city. I do not insist that it is an exhaustive list, but these are the only novel roles which I have been able to discover. And they are roles, in Romantic culture, but to non-Romantic culture they were and still are anti-roles. Existentialism centers upon the problem of alienation, which is the necessary preliminary to the act of commitment, the creation and realization and symbolization of the self. But this modern position could not have been arrived at without intermediate stages. It is post-Nietzschean, for it depends upon and derives from Nietzsche's solution to the problem of the ground of value, its authority, its metaphysical meaningfulness.

To the discovery of that ground there can be discerned, I believe, four stages.

The first of these is Analogism. This was the initial stage of positive Romanticism, the first result of the attempt to find a ground for value. Its essence we have already seen in examining the Visionary Artist, the Romantic Mystic. It depended upon a particular mode of perceiving, or more properly, of interpreting, the world, particularly the natural world. Nature worship, which is often identified as the hallmark of Romanticism, is actually in origin an Enlightenment idea. Its source lay in the great Enlightenment notion of adaptation; psychological or emotional adaptation to the natural world was felt to be a necessary preliminary, a kind of rehearsal, for the adaptation of the total organism and of society to the structure of nature. It had two aspects, the sentimental and the sublime. The first Romantics made use of this idea, but deprived it of its metaphysical assumptions, or rather, changed them. Instead of being the model for all other experience, it became a unique, superior, transcendent mode of experience, to be achieved only after long preparation, great difficulty, and profound introspection. Instead of leading to successful role-playing, Romantic nature worship was designed to lead away from any role-playing at all. And in fact, it was not, strictly speaking, nature worship; rather it was the use of the natural world — free from human social enterprise — as a screen against which to project that sense of value which is also the sense of the Self. Yet at the same time, because the experience was not yet fully understood, it was interpreted as both projective and revelatory. In such heightened moods one became aware, it was thought, of the immanent in the natural world. One saw *through* the phenomenon of nature into the divine noumenon (or ultimate reality) that lay behind it. And at the same time, one released the noumenal Self from the bondage of the phenomenal Self, the personality and the world of social roles. Both the natural noumenon and the noumenon of personality derived from God. This mode of perception, then, was like the closing of an electrical circuit. The ultimate union in the divine of the thing-in-itself of nature, and of the Self of the human being, gave a ground of value both to nature and to the purely human. This was the vision of which Wordsworth in poetry and Caspar David Friedrich in painting are the purest examples. Goethe, however, felt the difficulties, and in *Faust* proposed a solution: the eternal postponement of value, the acceptance of the inadequacy of human beings to meet the demands of experience.

For Analogism had real difficulties. One was that nothing could be done with such an experience. No morality could be derived from it; no metaphysic which could be used as a guide to action could be deduced from it. It was pure contentless experience. So a second difficulty was that it failed to solve the problem of reality, that is, of the relation of Subject to Object. It deprived the Object of all substance, turning it into a mere transparency. This was unsatisfactory, for one of the basic determinations of Romanticism was to meet reality head-on, that determination arising from the realization that all metaphysical systems were derivations from the needs of the individual, and that those needs could be met only by the encounter with experience itself. To the Romantic, nothing is sweeter than the white bone of a pure fact. Since Analogism offered no basis for action, it was reduced to the status of a mere psychological experience, of a value-state, not of a value-ground, which was what was needed. Hence its third difficulty; it was static. The Negative Romantic, finding no ground for value, found no imperative to action. The best that Kant could do was to prate about conscience and duty; but he could give no reason for action, no imperative to act. Even Goethe, asserting that the act was the essential character of man, shows Faust surrendering over and over again to the illusion of a final action. Analogism offered a ground for value, but no imperative to act. And without action, reality could not be encountered and the Self could not be realized. Finally, by its staticism it denied history; and to the Romantic, history — at least his own history — was reality.

Schopenhauer was the first to see that the way out lay through the denial of the Analogistic symmetry between Self and thing-in-itself, which threatened to abolish or reduce to meaninglessness everything in between. Or, as with Hegel, to return to a conservative Enlightenment position which asserted that whatever is, is right; for Hegel attempted to solve the difficulty by converting history into the noumenal, into the divine. He attempted to fill up the gap between Subject and Object and to preserve both by erecting "Spirit," as defined above, into value. But this threatened to deny freedom of choice, and therefore the basis for action, which comes into existence only when choice is offered. It was obvious that an asymmetrical position was the only solution. To Analogism succeeded Transcendentalism. This deprived the world wholly of value, turned it once again into a meaningless chaos, but preserved the Self and gave the Self's drive for meaning, order, value, and identity a divine authority. This is the heroic, world-redemptive stage of Romanticism. It has survived in numerous forms: German Fascism was one; Marxist Communism is another. It is evident that Transcendentalism was filled with numerous dangers. Its success at the highest cultural levels for several decades lay in its solution to the problem of action. The Transcendental hero was to redeem the Self in the act of redeeming the world. The Visionary Artist and the Bohemian, both products of Analogism, denied the value of society, but the Transcendental Virtuoso, as we have seen, adopted a social role and pushed it beyond the point that existent society could achieve. He imagined himself, then, as creating a model, or paradigm, for the future action of mankind. The literature of the time is filled with schemes to save the world, schemes so powerful that the mind of Western man is still haunted by them. Marx was a Virtuoso of economics. Taking the assumptions of the English political economists, Ricardo, Bentham, and the elder Mill, he developed them by a Transcendental, Virtuoso manipulation into a breath-taking vision of world-redemption, just as Liszt took piano technique and developed it into something nobody would have thought possible.

But Transcendentalism also ran into difficulties. It had placed value in the human being; it had found authority for that value in the divine or in the material (Marx's metaphysic) or in history (the other post-Hegelians); and it had provided an imperative for action. But it also placed the Transcendental hero in the position of imposing his will upon other human beings. Contemporary accounts of responses to Paganini and Liszt and Carlyle and Turner and Chopin emphasize the sense of being swept away, of being dominated, of being violated. This is what people meant when they gossiped that Paganini had sold his soul to the devil. But the Romantic cannot violate another person. If he does so, he violates himself. This is the morality of Wagner's *The Ring of the Nibelung*. The basis of Romantic morality is, and must be, empathy. If one consists of Self and personality and role, then so do other human beings. Schopenhauer saw this very clearly, as did all the really perceptive Romantics. One can assert the existence of the Self only by affirming the Self of others through empathy. One can assert one's own value only by asserting and affirming and recognizing the value of others. Therefore, to impose one's will upon others, even for the sake of redeeming them

and the world, even for the sake of revealing value to them, is to treat
them as mere instruments for realizing the will, to treat them as objects,
to treat them, in short, as society treats the alienated Romantic. It means
that either their humanity is denied or that the humanity of the Transcendental hero is denied. It cries out against the fact of the situation,
which is that all human beings belong to the same category. Each has a
Self to be revealed; to insist that one way and one way only is proper
for the revealing of that Self is to deny the ultimate conviction of Romanticism, that a metaphysic with its derived value-system cannot be an
absolute, that the only absolute, at best, is the *drive* to a metaphysic,
the *drive* to order and value, never to a particular order or a particular
set of values. Morality is something in and of this world, of the world
between Subject and Object, which is the only reality we can know with
the understanding. If the Transcendental hero sets up a morality and
imposes it upon others for the sake of revealing and realizing the Self,
it makes no difference, really, what that morality is; it can perfectly well
be an evil and tyrannous morality, if it does the job for him. This is
what Browning's hero Sordello realizes, and the realization kills him:
Browning's way of stating the impossibility of the morality of the Transcendental hero.

The solution to this difficulty lay in withdrawing any suprahuman or
supra-individual authority for the ground of value. There followed the
Objectist stage of Romantic development. It is a new symmetry, like
Analogism, but it differs from Analogism in that the noumenal is denied
both to the Self and to the thing-in-itself. There is left only the phenomenal. The theme of this stage is "illusion." All metaphysics, all moral
systems, are not even human instruments for realizing value; they are at
best human instruments for dealing with the world, for staying alive, but
in themselves they provide no imperative to action, no imperative to
duty, no imperative to morality, no imperative to world-redemption, for
the world cannot be redeemed: any scheme for redemption is but another
illusion. The result was a new wave of alienation, an alienation that was
profounder than anything that had occurred before. The conclusion to
The Ring revealed all action as an illusion. The drive to create order
creates society, freedom, and love; but it also destroys what it creates,
for each of these insists on its total adequacy; each creates the illusion
that it alone is the ground of value; each fancies that the world is redeemable. The full terror of human behavior always justifies itself by

an appeal to society or freedom or love. Each fancies that the world is redeemable, can be penetrated in its entirety with value. Each can offer only an illusion, for the world is unredeemable. Yet *The Ring,* which appears to be tragic, is really triumphant. It is the realization of what Goethe had adumbrated: man's inadequacy lies in his illusion that he can be adequate, in the illusion that the drive to order and value can be finally gratified. No, the Objectist says, the only perfect order is death. Life, and value, then, lie in the pure encounter of Self and Object, of Subject and reality, without illusions. Society and personality are seen to be natural products, and therefore unredeemable, because inaccessible to man. Alienation has now extended to everything man can understand, including his personality, including eventually, as Freud was to show (but as many Romantics knew long before Freud made it scientifically acceptable), his unconscious mind, which hitherto had been identified with the divine.

But what of the Self? If it can no longer be identified with the unconscious, as Wordsworth, for example, had identified it, how can it be experienced? The answer to that question was that the Self, and therefore value, can be experienced only by facing, unflinchingly, the unredeemable character of experience, in saying only what is, in talking only about the phenomenal world. Nature and society and personality are meaningless; therefore, they are hell. Value flowed from the confrontation of that hell. It was an antiheroic heroism; such as Baudelaire's. It was a scientific heroism; such as Zola's and Manet's. It was the exaltation of the nakedly human, without the traditional consolations of religion, or metaphysics, or idealisms. The peculiar exaltation of the objective scientist of today derives from this stage of Romanticism. Its Bible was Darwin's *On the Origin of Species,* published in 1859, just when it was badly needed by the cultural pioneers of Objectism.

But Objectism also had its difficulties. One was that like Analogism, it deprived the individual of any imperative to action. The only action possible was description, and that was done in heroic despair. Further, there was no way to symbolize the experience of value which flowed from the naked encounter with unredeemable reality. For this reason, there was no defense against the hell of existence. It required a tough-mindedness which even the tough-minded could not endure, for it provided no mode of existence, of getting from day to day. The next, and in the nineteenth century the final, stage of Romanticism solved all but the first of these

problems. It was the stage traditionally called Aestheticism, but which
I prefer to call Stylism. It was successful in that it symbolized the experience of value and offered a defense against the hell of existence. And,
in a peculiar way, it even provided an imperative to action, though not
to political or social moral action. But it at least provided an imperative
to live without illusion, the problem Ibsen exposed in *The Wild Duck,*
though he did not there solve it.

Style, which is so often identified with art, partly because of the success of Stylism, is in fact a universal quality of human behavior. For every
situation which a society recognizes and categorizes and institutionalizes
either in language or in behavior, there is a culturally transmitted pattern of action. But the rules or pattern of action are applicable only to
categories of situations. Each actual situation requires the individual to
improvise, to innovate, in order to fill in the gap between the learned
pattern and the actual unique situation. In each category of situation,
then, each individual creates for himself a special set of rules or a special
pattern of behavior which is unique to himself. It is an energy-conserving
device, which saves him from having to innovate in every situation. This
individually created pattern of behavior is style. It is his unique mode
of arming himself against the surprises every actual situation offers; it
keeps him going when the social pattern does not work. It maintains his
sense of identity while he summons his resources to meet the contingent.
It narrows the gap between behavioral pattern and situational demand.
This universal characteristic of human behavior, then, the Stylist seized
upon. It permitted him, first of all, to symbolize the continuity of identity
from situation to situation, from hell to hell. But it also provided him a
defense against that hell, because style precisely was pattern, an individual's unique pattern; it was, therefore, the perfect way of symbolizing the
sense of order and value and meaning without tempting him to impose
that pattern upon reality. It even to a certain extent permitted him to
solve the problem of the imperative to action, for it gave him an imperative, if not to act upon the world, at least to create a unique style
which, as it was perfected, offered him a new and richer gratification of
the drive to order and value, and therefore a promise of greater gratification. Further, it was at once a universal human characteristic, not only
possible to everyone but even required of everyone, and one that required
no authority for its existence other than the necessities of the human
condition. It could do without authority derived from metaphysics, or

religion, or history, or science. It was the most complete and satisfactory solution to the problem of freedom humanity had yet found. Nor was it morally irresponsible, because with an alienation even deeper than that of the Objectist, the Stylist could look at the world and face its heaven as well as its hell. So defended, he could say things about human behavior with an objectivity that even the Objectist could not summon, because the Stylist was free from pain, while the Objectist was necessarily involved in suffering. It was not heroic but it was debonair. The Dandy had been created before, but Stylism is the fullest possible realization of the possibilities of Dandyism.

The writing and the life — and the death — of Ernest Hemingway provide a perfect twentieth-century example of Stylism, though culturally belated and old-fashioned even in the 1920's. Hemingway and his friends lived by a code, not because it was a code of right and wrong but simply because it was a code, that is, a style. And the older he got, the more he was involved with the style of everything; of hunting, of fishing, of writing. The Old Fisherman in *The Old Man and the Sea* is a redemptive or Christ figure simply because he knows how to fish, and in knowing how to·fish, he knows how to endure, and how to die. Hemingway's suicide was not a betrayal of his life but a fulfillment of it. And in that lies the weakness of Stylism.

For Stylism ultimately revealed that it too had a weakness; it too, though it solved problems, created new ones. For one thing, it had not solved the problem of the imperative to action, only to living. It provided no basis for moral responsibility, except its freedom from moral commitment and suffering. But most of all, it degenerated, with all the great Stylists, into mannerism, from Swinburne to Hemingway himself. For mannerism, in this sense, is the consequence of devoting oneself to the creation of a unique personal style. And the more successful one is at this task, the more that style becomes a role, so that Swinburne and Debussy ended up playing the roles of "Swinburne" and "Debussy," which they had invented, and Hemingway ended up playing the role of "Hemingway." He *had* to commit suicide, in order to play the role of facing the ultimate horror, death, with style, just as in the Second World War he was more interested in playing Hemingway-as-War-Correspondent than in being a war correspondent. In short, the great Romantic problem of re-entry, of commitment, of solving the paradox of entering into social action without betraying one's own selfhood or the selfhood of others

— this central problem of Romanticism remained unsolved, for the problem of the ground of value remained unsolved. Stylism had found its ground in one aspect of human behavior, but it left the rest of human behavior unaccounted for. It could symbolize the Self. But how was one to *be* the Self? It had separated itself from history, for it had separated itself from all but one aspect of human life, but to the Romantic, sooner or later, history must be encountered, for history is reality.

It was Friedrich Nietzsche, whose achievement is only now being understood, who solved the problem and returned the Stylist to history. Each of the stages of Romanticism had been threatened by the static. It was Nietzsche who saw that the answer lay in the various metamorphoses of Romanticism. The fault was in the very search for a ground of value, a resting place from which the rest of the world might be moved. It was that primitive desire for a ground, a finality, an answer, that led to the debacle of Analogism, Transcendentalism, Objectism, and Stylism, though Nietzsche also saw that Stylism, with its dandyism, its insouciance, its armor, had made an astounding contribution. The answer, therefore, lay in reversing this system, in the transvaluation of all values, and in the continuous transvaluation. The sorrow of the nineteenth century rose from its continuous failure to find a ground for value that would not give beneath the pressures put upon it. Nietzsche saw that to search for such a ground was to involve mankind in an infinite regress, a regress that took it farther and farther from the world, the only reality there is. If, therefore, one accepted the fact that there was no ground, that there was no justification for the search for order and meaning and value, that the world was quite meaningless, quite without value, in both Subject and Object — for Subject and Object are one — then sorrow could be converted to joy. Eternal recurrence was the answer, continuous renewal of identity by continuous transformation and transvaluation of style in art, in thought, and in individuality. Nietzsche realized that this is neither a world which once held value nor a world which holds value now or a world which ever will hold it. It is without value, without order, without meaning. The world is nothing. Value and identity are the ultimate illusions. We emerge from nothingness and encounter the nothingness of the world, and in so doing, we create being. But being can be renewed only if we recognize that being is illusion. With that recognition as our ultimate weapon we can re-create it, not from sorrow but from joy. From the desire for value we create ourselves, but to renew that value, we must destroy ourselves. The profoundest satisfaction of the human mind is the creation of the world — out of nothingness. From that act of creation emerges the *sense* of value, the *sense* of identity, which are sources of joy only if we recognize them as illusions. The sense of order, the sense of meaning, and the sense of identity are but instruments for the act of creation. Thus the Romantic once more enters into history and human life, for to create is to choose, without ever knowing whether or not the choice is the right choice, for the act of choice changes the world. And so we can never know, even by hindsight, whether or not we chose rightly, for the situation in which we performed the act of creation and choice no longer exists. And this solves the problem of re-entry, for it is clear that alienation is the illusion of the Romantic.

And so Nietzsche's work is the triumph of Romanticism, for he solved its problem of value and returned the Romantic to history, by showing that there is no ground to value and that there is no escape from history. As the Romantic had always known but had never, until Nietzsche, been able to believe, reality is history, and only the experience of reality has value, an experience to be achieved by creating illusions so that we may live and by destroying them so that we may recover our freedom. Value is process, a perpetual weaving and unweaving of our own identities. Sorrow is a sentimental lust for finality; joy is the penetration beyond that sentimentality into the valuelessness of reality, into its freedom, the achievement of which is inevitably its loss. Joy is the eternal recurrence of the same problem, forever solved and forever unsolvable. Nietzsche found what the Romantic had sought for a hundred years, a way of encompassing, without loss of tension, the contraries and paradoxes of human experience. The *feel* of reality, in the Subject, is tension and the sense of contradiction. As for violating others, that is the ultimate moral responsibility, for to maintain the tension of human experience, which is to achieve and destroy and re-achieve value, we must violate others — as we must violate ourselves.

PART

I

Analogism

At the end of the eighteenth century, the Enlightenment, which had seemed to promise a perfect life for mankind, collapsed—for a few Europeans of great insight and awareness. They were left in a world without value: neither Nature nor Society could be perceived as a source of value. This was the stage of Negative Romanticism, from which the problem of Romanticism emerged: How was value to be introduced into the world, and from what source? The first step was to separate the personality into two antithetical aspects: the Self and the Role. Value could be gained by going around the Role, that is, Society, and perceiving Nature as an analogy of the Self. Thus value was located in a peculiar and unique mode of experiencing reality.

The Sufferings
of Young Werther

JOHANN WOLFGANG VON GOETHE

(1749–1832)

Goethe's short epistolary novel was first published in 1774 and reissued in a revised edition in 1787. Superficially, it is a typical sentimental love story of the Enlightenment, but important novelties mark it as the first truly modern discovery of the Waste Land. Werther, who shows the usual Enlightenment distaste for traditional feudal society, discovers that the loss of Lotte means the loss of all value, for she is, for him, the symbol of his capacity to feel identity and meaning. Thus the source of value is revealed to be independent of Nature, located within the personality and mysteriously unreliable. The following excerpts illustrate a strain of feeling which leads to Werther's suicide.

August 4.

I am not alone in this. All people are deceived in their hopes, duped in their expectations. I called on my good young woman under the linden. The oldest boy ran to meet me, and his cry of joy brought out his mother, who looked very depressed. Her first word was, "Good sir, alas, my Hans has died!" That was her youngest boy. I was silent. "And my husband," said she, "came back from Switzerland and brought nothing with him, and without the help of good people he would have

37

had to beg his way out, for he had caught a fever on the way." I could say nothing to her, but gave something to the youngster; she begged me to accept some apples, which I did, and then forsook the place of sad recollection.

August 21.

.   .   .

If I go out of the gate along the road on which I drove for the first time to fetch Lotte for the dance, how very different that was! Everything, everything has gone by! No hint of that former world, not one pulse-beat of the feeling I knew then. I feel as a spirit must, if it returned to the fire-gutted, ruined castle which as a thriving prince he had once built and furnished with all the attributes of splendour, and which at death he had hopefully bequeathed to his beloved son.

.   .   .

September 15.

It is infuriating, Wilhelm, that there are human beings without feeling or appreciation for the few things on earth that still have some value. You know the walnut trees under which I sat with Lotte at the house of the honest pastor of St. ***, those magnificent trees which, God knows, filled my soul with the greatest joy! How familiar they made the parsonage, how cool! and how splendid the branches were! and recollection extending back to the honest pastor-couple that planted them so many years ago. The schoolmaster often told us one of their names, which he had heard from his grandfather; and he is said to have been such a good man, and his memory was always sacred to me under those trees. I tell you, the schoolmaster had tears in his eyes as we spoke yesterday of their having been cut down — Cut down! I could go mad, I could murder the cur that struck the first blow. I, who could grieve myself to death if such a pair of trees stood in my yard and one of them died of old age, I have to see this done. My dear fellow, there is one compensation all the same! What a thing is human feeling! The whole village is murmuring, and I hope the pastor's wife will be made to feel, by a lack of butter and eggs and of other marks of confidence, the wound she has dealt her village. For it is *she*, the wife of the new pastor (our old one has died too), a lean, sickly creature, who has every reason to take no interest in the world, for no one takes an interest in her. A silly fool she is, who makes pretensions to being learned, who meddles with the problem of which books of the Bible are genuine, works a great deal at the new-fashioned moral and critical re-evaluation of Christian ethics, and shrugs her shoulders at Lavater's enthusiasms, and whose health is thoroughly broken down, for which reason she has no joy on God's earth. Nor would it have been possible for any other creature to cut down my walnut trees. See, I can't get over it! Just imagine, the falling leaves make her yard disorderly and dank, the trees rob her of daylight, and when the nuts are ripe the boys throw stones at them: that gets on her nerves, that disturbs her deep meditations when she is weighing Kennikot, Semler, and Michaelis one against the other. When I saw that the people in the village, especially the old ones, were so discontented, I said, "Why did you permit it?" They said, "If the mayor is willing, here in the country, what can be done?" But one thing was rightly done. The mayor and the pastor, who was hoping to get some advantage from the silly notions of his wife — which don't make his soup any more savoury — thought they would divide the profit; but the treasury got wind of it and said, "Hand it over!" For it still had old claims to that part of the parsonage where the trees stood, and it sold them to the highest bidder. They are down! O, if I were the prince! I would see to it that the pastor's wife, the mayor, and the treasury — Prince! — Well, if I were the prince, what would I care about the trees in my land?

.   .   .

October 19.

Oh, this void! this fearful void which I feel here in my breast! — I often think to myself: if you could press her just once to this heart, just once, then this entire void would be filled.

October 26.

Yes, it is becoming certain to me, friend, certain and ever more certain, that little importance attaches to the existence of any being, very little. A woman friend came to see Lotte, and I went into the adjoining room to get a book, but could not read, and then I took a pen to do some writing. I heard them speaking quietly; they were telling each other unimportant matters, town gossip: this girl is getting married, that one is sick, very sick. "She has a hacking cough, her face is only skin and bones, and she has fainting spells; I wouldn't give a penny for her life," said the one. "And Mr. N. N. is in a bad way too," said Lotte. "He is already bloated," said the other. And my vivid imagination took me to the bedside of these poor people; I saw with what reluctance they were turning their backs upon life, how they — Wilhelm! and my little ladies were talking about it as people do talk about the fact that a stranger is dying. — And when I look about me and survey the room, and around me are Lotte's dresses and Albert's writings and these furnishings, with which I am on such friendly terms, including this inkwell, and I think, "See what you mean to this household! All in all. Your friends honour you! You are often a joy to them, and to your heart it seems as if that joy were indispensable, and yet — if you were to go, if you parted from their circle? Would they, and how long would they feel the void that the loss of you would inflict upon their destiny? how long?" — O, man is so transitory that even where he finds the only evidence for his existence, even where his presence makes its only true impression, namely, in the memory, in the souls of his loved ones, even there he must be extinguished and disappear, and how quickly!

October 27.

Often I would like to rend my breast and knock in my brain, seeing that people can be so little to each other. Ah, the love, joy, warmth, and rapture which I cannot bestow will not be given to me by the other, and even with a whole heart full of bliss I shall not delight one who stands before me cold and sapless.

Evening.

I have so much, and my feeling for her engulfs it all; I have so much, and without her I find everything turned into nothing.

.   .   .

November 3.

God knows, I often get into bed with the desire, indeed at times with the hope, of not awaking again; and in the morning I open my eyes, see the sun again, and am wretched. O that I could be capricious, could put the blame on the weather, on a third party, on a frustrated undertaking, then I would only have to bear half the unendurable burden of ill-humour. But woe is me! I feel too plainly that all the guilt is mine alone, — no, not guilt! Bad enough that in me the source of all my misery lies concealed, as formerly the source of all my joys. Am I not still the very one who formerly revelled in all the fullness of his feeling, whose every step was followed by paradise, who had a heart that could lovingly embrace an entire world? And that heart is dead now, no raptures issue from it any more, my eyes are dried up, and my thoughts, no longer regaled with refreshing tears, draw my brow into anxious folds. I suffer much, for I have lost what was the sole rapture of my life, that holy, animating force with which I created worlds all about me; it is gone! — When I gaze out of my window toward the distant height, seeing how the morning sun breaks through the mist above it and lights up the quiet valley meadow, and the gentle stream meanders toward me between its leafless willows, — O, when that glorious natural scene stands before me as lifeless as a chromo, and all this rapture cannot pump one drop of bliss from my heart up into my brain, and this whole fellow stands before the countenance of God like a dried-up well or a leaky bucket, I have often flung myself on the ground and begged God for tears, as a ploughman prays for rain when the sky is brazen above him and around him the earth is parching.

But alas, I feel that God does not give rain and sunshine in response to our impetuous requests, and those former days whose memory torments me, why were they so blissful? why else than because I awaited his spirit with patience, and welcomed the rapture which he poured over me with undivided, deeply grateful heart.

. . .

November 15.
I thank you, Wilhelm, for your heartfelt sympathy, for your well-meant advice, and beg you to be calm. Let me endure to the end: for all my wearisomeness I still have force enough to hold out. I honour religion, as you know, and I realize that it is a staff to many a weary wanderer, re-

freshment to the languishing. Only — can it, must it be so to every one? If you behold the great world, you will see thousands who did not find it so, thousands who will never find it so, whether preached to them or not — and must it be so to me? Does not even the Son of God say that those would be around him whom the Father has given to him? What if I am not given to him? what if the Father wants to keep me for Himself, as my heart tells me? — I beg you not to misinterpret this; do not see a mockery in these innocent words; it is my whole soul that I am laying before you: else I should wish I had held my peace: just as I am reluctant to say anything about all those matters of which everyone knows as little as I do. What is human destiny other than to endure his measure of suffering, drink his cup to the dregs? — And if the God from heaven found the cup too bitter for his human lips, why should I exalt myself and act as if it tasted sweet to me? And why should I be ashamed, in the terrible moment when my whole existence is trembling between being and not-being, when the past shines like a flash of lightning over the dark abyss of the future, and everything about me is sinking, and the world going to destruction with me — Isn't it then the voice of the creature which is being driven back into itself, fails to find a self, and irresistibly tumbles to its fall, that groans from the inner depths of its vainly aspiring powers, "My God! my God! why hast thou forsaken me?" And should I be ashamed of that saying, should I be afraid of that moment, seeing that he who rolls up the heavens like a robe did not escape it?

·　　·　　·

November 30.

It is, it *is* my fate not to come to my senses! Where-ever I go, I encounter some apparition which robs me of all composure. Today! O fate! O humanity!

I was strolling along the stream in the noon hour, having no desire to eat. All was desolate, a moist, chill west wind blew down from the mountain, and the grey rain clouds were drifting into the valley. From afar I saw a man in a worn green coat, who was crawling about among the rocks and seemed to be seeking herbs. When I came closer, and he turned around at the noise I made, I saw a most interesting face, in which a quiet sorrow was the main feature, but which otherwise expressed nothing but a good, straightforward mind; his black locks were put up in two rolls with hairpins, the rest being braided into a heavy plait that hung down his back. As his clothing seemed to me to indicate a man of lowly station, I thought he would not take it amiss if I paid attention to his occupation, and so I asked him what he was seeking. "I am seeking flowers," he answered with a deep sigh, "and I find none." "Nor is this the season," I said with a smile. "There are so many flowers," he said, coming down to me. "In my garden there are roses and two kinds of honeysuckle, one of which my father gave me, and they grow like weeds; I have been looking for them for two days, and I can't find them. Out yonder, too, there are always flowers, yellow and blue and red ones, and the centaury has a pretty little flower. I can't find any of them." I saw that something was wrong, and so I asked a roundabout question: "What do you want to do with the flowers?" A strange, twitching smile puckered his face. "If you will not give me away," he said, putting a finger on his lips, "I have promised my sweetheart a bouquet." "That is nice," I said. "O," said he, "she has lots of other things, she is rich." "And yet she loves your bouquet," I responded. "O!" he continued, "she has jewels and a crown." "Why, what is her name?" "If the States-General would pay me," he replied, "I'd be a different person! Yes, there once was a time when I was so happy! Now it's all over with me. I am now — " A moist glance toward the sky expressed everything. "So you were happy?" I asked. "Oh, I wish I were again like that!" said he. "At that time I was as happy, as merry, as unburdened as a fish in water!" "Heinrich!" called an old woman who came along the path, "Heinrich, where are you hiding? we have been looking for you everywhere, come to lunch!" "Is that your son?" I asked, approaching her. "Indeed, my poor son," she replied. "God has given me a heavy cross to bear." "How long has he been so?" I asked. "In this calm state," she said, "he has been for half a year now. Thank God that it is no worse than this; before that he was raving for a whole year and lay chained up in the mad house. Now he harms nobody, only he is always having to do with kings and emperors. He was such a good, quiet person, wrote a fine hand, and helped to support me; all at once he grew melancholy, fell into a high fever, which turned into madness, and now he is as you see him. If I were to tell you, sir — " I broke in upon the stream of her words by asking, "What kind of a time was it that he praises so, saying that he was so happy then, so well off?" "The foolish fellow!" she cried with a compassionate smile, "he means the time when he was out of his mind, he is always praising that; that is the time when he was in the mad house, when he knew nothing about himself — " This struck me like a thunderclap, and I put a coin in her hand and left her in haste.

"When you were happy!" I exclaimed, walking rapidly toward the town, "when you felt as cheerful as a fish in water!" — God in heaven! have you made that to be the fate of men, that they are not happy until they have acquired some sense and then lose it again? — Poor wretch! and yet how I envy your clouded mind, the confusion of thought in which you are languishing! You go out in the hope of picking flowers for your queen — in the winter — and mourn because you find none, and fail to understand why you can find none. And I — and I go out without hope, without purpose, and return home the same as when I went. — You dream of what a man you would be if the States-General paid you. Happy creature! able as you are to ascribe your lack of happiness to an earthly obstacle. You do not feel! you do not feel that in your ravaged heart, in your deranged brain, your misery lies, from which you cannot be freed by all the kings of the earth.

That man should die disconsolate who scoffs at a sufferer journeying toward the remotest well-spring, which will augment his illness, make his death more painful! or who looks down upon the hard-pressed heart which, in order to rid itself of pangs of conscience, and to lay aside the sufferings of his soul, makes a pilgrimage to the Holy Sepulchre. Every step which cuts through his shoes on his pathless way is a drop of balm for the terrified soul, and with every completed day's journey his heart is relieved of many distresses as it lays itself down. — Have you a right to call that a delusion, you phrasemongers on your beds of ease? — Delusion! — O God, you see my tears! Having created man with poverty enough, must you also endow him with brothers who would rob him of even the little he had, of his bit of trust in you, in you, you all-loving one? For man's trust in a healing root, in the tears of the grapevine, what is that but trust in you, trust that you have put into all that surrounds us the curative and alleviating force of which we have an hourly need? Father whom I do not know! Father who once filled my whole soul, and who has now turned his countenance away from me! call me to you! keep silence no longer! your silence will not sustain this thirsting soul — And would a man, a father, be able to show anger, if his unexpectedly returning son should fall upon his neck and cry, "I am here again, my father! Be not angry that I am cutting short the journey which it was

your will that I should endure still longer. The world is everywhere
the same, reward and joy following upon effort and toil; but what does
that mean to me? I only feel content where you are, and in your presence
I wish to suffer and to enjoy." — And you, dear heavenly Father, should
you thrust him from you?

.   .   .

December 6.

How that figure pursues me! Waking and dreaming it fills my whole
soul! Here, when I close my eyes, here in my brow, where the power of
inner vision unites, are her black eyes. Here! I cannot put it into words
for you. If I close my eyes, there they are; like an ocean, like an abyss they
lie still before me, in me, filling all the thoughts within my brow.

What is man, the eulogized demigod? Does he not lack force at the
very point where he needs it most? And when he soars upward in joy,
or sinks down in suffering, is he not checked in both, is he not returned
again to the dull, cold sphere of awareness, just when he was longing to
lose himself in the fullness of the infinite?

.   .   .

[TRANSLATED BY BAYARD QUINCY TAYLOR]

Manfred

LORD BYRON
(1788–1824)

*The impact of Byron on the imagination of all Europe and
America is incalculable. For decades poetry and novels were
populated with figures derived from Manfred, Childe Harold,
the Giaour, and all the other Byronic heroes, the symbols of
that initial alienation and isolation which is the first or negative stage of Romanticism. Byron completed what Werther had
started. The following passage from Act III, Scene I, illustrates
most of the Negative Romantic themes and reveals dramati-
cally the failure of traditional Christianity. The two speakers
are Manfred and the Abbot of St. Maurice. The scene is
Manfred's castle in the wildest Alps.*

ABBOT.   Peace be with Count Manfred:

MANFRED.   Thanks, holy father! welcome to these walls;
   Thy presence honours them, and blesseth those
   Who dwell within them.

ABBOT.   Would it were so, Count! —
   But I would fain confer with thee alone.

MANFRED.   Herman, retire. — What would my reverend guest?

ABBOT. Thus, without prelude: — Age and zeal — my office —
    And good intent must plead my privilege;
    Our near, though not acquainted neighbourhood,
    May also be my herald. Rumours strange,
    And of unholy nature, are abroad,
    And busy with thy name — a noble name
    For centuries: may he who bears it now
    Transmit it unimpaired!

MANFRED.   Proceed, — I listen.

ABBOT. 'Tis said thou holdest converse with the things
    Which are forbidden to the search of man;
    That with the dwellers of the dark abodes,
    The many evil and unheavenly spirits
    Which walk the valley of the Shade of Death,
    Thou communest. I know that with mankind,
    Thy fellows in creation, thou dost rarely
    Exchange thy thoughts, and that thy solitude
    Is as an Anchorite's — were it but holy.

MANFRED. And what are they who do avouch these things?

ABBOT. My pious brethren — the scarèd peasantry —
    Even thy own vassals — who do look on thee
    With most unquiet eyes. Thy life's in peril!

MANFRED. Take it.

ABBOT. I come to save, and not destroy:
    I would not pry into thy secret soul;
    But if these things be sooth, there still is time
    For penitence and pity: reconcile thee
    With the true church, and through the church to Heaven.

MANFRED. I hear thee. This is my reply — whate'er
    I may have been, or am, doth rest between
    Heaven and myself — I shall not choose a mortal
    To be my mediator — Have I sinned
    Against your ordinances? prove and punish!

ABBOT. My son! I did not speak of punishment,
    But penitence and pardon; — with thyself

The choice of such remains — and for the last,
Our institutions and our strong belief
Have given me power to smooth the path from sin
To higher hope and better thoughts; the first
I leave to Heaven, — "Vengeance is mine alone!"
So saith the Lord, and with all humbleness
His servant echoes back the awful word.

MANFRED. Old man! there is no power in holy men,
Nor charm in prayer, nor purifying form
Of penitence, nor outward look, nor fast,
Nor agony — nor, greater than all these,
The innate tortures of that deep Despair,
Which is Remorse without the fear of Hell,
But all in all sufficient to itself
Would make a hell of Heaven — can exorcise
From out the unbounded spirit the quick sense
Of its own sins — wrongs — sufferance — and revenge
Upon itself; there is no future pang
Can deal that justice on the self-condemned
He deals on his own soul.

ABBOT.   All this is well;
For this will pass away, and be succeeded
By an auspicious hope, which shall look up
With calm assurance to that blessed place,
Which all who seek may win, whatever be
Their earthly errors, so they be atoned:
And the commencement of atonement is
The sense of its necessity.   Say on —
And all our church can teach thee shall be taught;
And all we can absolve thee shall be pardoned.

MANFRED. When Rome's sixth Emperor was near his last,
The victim of a self-inflicted wound,
To shun the torments of a public death
From senates once his slaves, a certain soldier,
With show of loyal pity, would have stanched
The gushing throat with his officious robe;
The dying Roman thrust him·back, and said —

Some empire still in his expiring glance —
"It is too late — is this fidelity?"

ABBOT.   And what of this?

MANFRED.   I answer with the Roman —
"It is too late!"

ABBOT.   It never can be so,
To reconcile thyself with thy own soul,
And thy own soul with Heaven.   Hast thou no hope?
'Tis strange — even those who do despair above,
Yet shape themselves some fantasy on earth,
To which frail twig they cling, like drowning men.

MANFRED.   Aye — father! I have had those early visions,
And noble aspirations in my youth,
To make my own the mind of other men,
The enlightener of nations; and to rise
I knew not whither — it might be to fall;
But fall, even as the mountain-cataract,
Which having leapt from its more dazzling height,
Even in the foaming strength of its abyss,
(Which casts up misty columns that become
Clouds raining from the re-ascended skies,)
Lies low but mighty still. — But this is past,
My thoughts mistook themselves.

ABBOT.   And wherefore so?

MANFRED.   I could not tame my nature down; for he
Must serve who fain would sway; and soothe, and sue,
And watch all time, and pry into all place,
And be a living Lie, who would become
A mighty thing amongst the mean — and such
The mass are; I disdained to mingle with
A herd, though to be leader — and of wolves.
The lion is alone, and so am I.

ABBOT.   And why not live and act with other men?

MANFRED.   Because my nature was averse from life;
And yet not cruel; for I would not make,

But find a desolation.   Like the Wind,
The red-hot breath of the most lone Simoom,
Which dwells but in the desert, and sweeps o'er
The barren sands which bear no shrubs to blast,
And revels o'er their wild and arid waves,
And seeketh not, so that it is not sought,
But being met is deadly, — such hath been
The course of my existence; but there came
Things in my path which are no more.

ABBOT.   Alas!
    I 'gin to fear that thou art past all aid
    From me and from my calling; yet so young,
    I still would ——

MANFRED.   Look on me! there is an order
    Of mortals on the earth, who do become
    Old in their youth, and die ere middle age,
    Without the violence of warlike death;
    Some perishing of pleasure — some of study —
    Some worn with toil, some of mere weariness, —
    Some of disease — and some insanity —
    And some of withered, or of broken hearts;
    For this last is a malady which slays
    More than are numbered in the lists of Fate,
    Taking all shapes, and bearing many names.
    Look upon me! for even of all these things
    Have I partaken; and of all these things,
    One were enough; then wonder not that I
    Am what I am, but that I ever was,
    Or having been, that I am still on earth.

ABBOT.   Yet, hear me still ——

MANFRED.   Old man! I do respect
    Thine order, and revere thine years; I deem
    Thy purpose pious, but it is in vain:
    Think me not churlish; I would spare thyself,
    Far more than me, in shunning at this time
    All further colloquy — and so — farewell.

The Rime of the Ancient Mariner

SAMUEL TAYLOR COLERIDGE

(1772–1834)

Coleridge first published this poem in 1798 anonymously in Lyrical Ballads, which also included a number of poems by William Wordsworth. He revised it extensively and added the marginal glosses when he reissued it under his own name in Sibylline Leaves, 1817. For a century and a quarter it was taken to be a poem of pure fantasy, with a moral tacked on. It is now generally agreed that Coleridge here created a new language to talk about the subjective aspects of experience, separated from particular situations. The clue to the poem's meaning comes from certain repetitive patterns — or syndromes — which appear in the Mariner's interruption of the Wedding Feast, his shooting of the albatross, the sinking of the ship at the end of the voyage, the saddened Wedding Guest, and the Mariner's compulsive repetition of his story. All of these are instances of the violation of community, that is, alienation. But the poem also recounts the discovery of value in the Self in the blessing of the water snakes, the releasing energy of the Spirit of the Pole (which is at the maximum distance from England, or community), and the marvelous activities of wind and angels, all of which are best interpreted as aspects of the nonsocial resources of the Self.

THE RIME OF THE ANCIENT MARINER
IN SEVEN PARTS

Argument

How a Ship having passed the Line was driven by storms to the cold
Country towards the South Pole; and how from thence she made her
course to the tropical Latitude of the Great Pacific Ocean; and of the
strange things that befell; and in what manner the Ancyent Marinere
came back to his own Country.

PART I

An ancient
Mariner meet-
eth three Gal-
lants bidden
to a wedding-
feast, and
detaineth one.

It is an ancient Mariner,
And he stoppeth one of three.
"By thy long grey beard and glittering eye,
Now wherefore stopp'st thou me?

The Bridegroom's doors are opened wide,
And I am next of kin;
The guests are met, the feast is set:
May'st hear the merry din."

He holds him with his skinny hand,
"There was a ship," quoth he.
"Hold off! unhand me, grey-beard loon!"
Eftsoons his hand dropt he.

The Wedding-
Guest is spell-
bound by the
eye of the old
seafaring man,
and con-
strained to
hear his tale.

He holds him with his glittering eye —
The Wedding-Guest stood still,
And listens like a three years' child:
The Mariner hath his will.

The Wedding-Guest sat on a stone:
He cannot choose but hear;
And thus spake on that ancient man,
The bright-eyed Mariner.

The Mariner
tells how the
ship sailed

"The ship was cheered, the harbour cleared,
Merrily did we drop

southward
with a good
wind and fair
weather, till it
reached the line.

Below the kirk, below the hill,
Belów the lighthouse top,

The Sun came up upon the left,
Out of the sea came he!
And he shone bright, and on the right
Went down into the sea.

Higher and higher every day,
Till over the mast at noon — "
The Wedding-Guest here beat his breast,
For he heard the loud bassoon.

The Wedding-
Guest heareth
the bridal
music; but
the Mariner
continueth
his tale.

The bride hath paced into the hall,
Red as a rose is she;
Nodding their heads before her goes
The merry minstrelsy.

The Wedding-Guest he beat his breast,
Yet he cannot choose but hear;
And thus spake on that ancient man,
The bright-eyed Mariner.

The ship
driven by a
storm toward
the south pole.

"And now the STORM-BLAST came, and he
Was tyrannous and strong:
He struck with his o'ertaking wings,
And chased us south along.

With sloping masts and dipping prow,
As who pursued with yell and blow
Still treads the shadow of his foe,
And forward bends his head,
The ship drove fast, loud roared the blast,
And southward aye we fled.

And now there came both mist and snow,
And it grew wondrous cold:
And ice, mast-high, came floating by,
As green as emerald.

The land of
ice, and of
fearful sounds

And through the drifts the snowy clifts
Did send a dismal sheen:

where no
living thing
was to be seen.

Nor shapes of men nor beasts we ken —
The ice was all between.

The ice was here, the ice was there,
The ice was all around:
It cracked and growled, and roared and howled,
Like noises in a swound!

Till a great
sea-bird,
called the
Albatross,
came through
the snow-fog,
and was
received with
great joy and
hospitality.

At length did cross an Albatross,
Through the fog it came;
As if it had been a Christian soul,
We hailed it in God's name.

It ate the food it ne'er had eat,
And round and round it flew.
The ice did split with a thunder-fit;
The helmsman steered us through!

And lo! the
Albatross
proveth a bird
of good omen,
and followeth
the ship as it
returned
northward
through fog
and floating ice

And a good south wind sprung up behind;
The Albatross did follow,
And every day, for food or play,
Came to the mariner's hollo!

In mist or cloud, on mast or shroud,
It perched for vespers nine;
Whiles all the night, through fog-smoke white,
Glimmered the white Moon-shine."

The ancient
Mariner
inhospitably
killeth the
pious bird of
good omen.

"God save thee, ancient Mariner!
From the fiends, that plague thee thus! —
Why look'st thou so?" — With my cross-bow
I shot the ALBATROSS.

PART II

The Sun now rose upon the right:
Out of the sea came he,
Still hid in mist, and on the left
Went down into the sea.

And the good south wind still blew behind,
But no sweet bird did follow,

Nor any day for food or play
Came to the mariners' hollo!

His shipmates cry out against the ancient Mariner, for killing the bird of good luck.

And I had done a hellish thing,
And it would work 'em woe:
For all averred, I had killed the bird
That made the breeze to blow.
Ah wretch! said they, the bird to slay,
That made the breeze to blow!

But when the fog cleared off, they justify the same, and thus make themselves accomplices in the crime.

Nor dim nor red, like God's own head,
The glorious Sun uprist:
Then all averred, I had killed the bird
That brought the fog and mist.
'Twas right, said they, such birds to slay,
That bring the fog and mist.

The fair breeze continues; the ship enters the Pacific Ocean, and sails northward, even till it reaches the Line.

The fair breeze blew, the white foam flew,
The furrow followed free;
We were the first that ever burst
Into that silent sea.

The ship hath been suddenly becalmed.

Down dropt the breeze, the sails dropt down,
'Twas sad as sad could be;
And we did speak only to break
The silence of the sea!

All in a hot and copper sky,
The bloody Sun, at noon,
Right up above the mast did stand,
No bigger than the Moon.

Day after day, day after day,
We stuck, nor breath nor motion;
As idle as a painted ship
Upon a painted ocean.

And the Albatross begins to be avenged.

Water, water, every where,
And all the boards did shrink;
Water, water, every where,
Nor any drop to drink.

The very deep did rot: O Christ!
That ever this should be!
Yea, slimy things did crawl with legs
Upon the slimy sea.

About, about, in reel and rout
The death-fires danced at night;
The water, like a witch's oils,
Burnt green, and blue and white.

A Spirit had followed them; one of the invisible inhabitants of this planet, neither departed souls nor angels; concerning whom the learned Jew, Josephus, and the Platonic Constantinopolitan, Michael Psellus, may be consulted. They are very numerous, and there is no climate or element without one or more.

And some in dreams assuréd were
Of the Spirit that plagued us so;
Nine fathom deep he had followed us
From the land of mist and snow.

And every tongue, through utter drought,
Was withered at the root;
We could not speak, no more than if
We had been choked with soot.

The shipmates, in their sore distress, would fain throw the whole guilt on the ancient Mariner; in sign whereof they hang the dead sea-bird round his neck.

Ah! well a-day! what evil looks
Had I from old and young!
Instead of the cross, the Albatross
About my neck was hung.

PART III

There passed a weary time. Each throat
Was parched, and glazed each eye.
A weary time! a weary time!
How glazed each weary eye,
When looking westward, I beheld
A something in the sky.

The ancient Mariner beholdeth a sign in the element afar off.

At first it seemed a little speck,
And then it seemed a mist;
It moved and moved, and took at last
A certain shape, I wist.

A speck, a mist, a shape, I wist!
And still it neared and neared:
As if it dodged a water-sprite,
It plunged and tacked and veered.

At its nearer approach, it seemeth him to be a ship; and at a dear ransom he freeth his speech from the bonds of thirst.

With throats unslaked, with black lips baked,
We could nor laugh nor wail;
Through utter drought all dumb we stood!
I bit my arm, I sucked the blood,
And cried, A sail! a sail!

A flash of joy;

With throats unslaked, with black lips baked,
Agape they heard me call:
Gramercy! they for joy did grin,
And all at once their breath drew in,
As they were drinking all.

And horror follows. For can it be a ship that comes onward without wind or tide?

See! see! (I cried) she tacks no more!
Hither to work us weal;
Without a breeze, without a tide,
She steadies with upright keel!

The western wave was all a-flame.
The day was well nigh done!
Almost upon the western wave
Rested the broad bright Sun;
When that strange shape drove suddenly
Betwixt us and the Sun.

It seemeth him but the skeleton of a ship.

And straight the Sun was flecked with bars,
(Heaven's Mother send us grace!)
As if through a dungeon-grate he peered
With broad and burning face.

And its ribs are seen as bars on the face of the setting Sun. The Spectre-Woman and her Death-mate, and no

Alas! (thought I, and my heart beat loud)
How fast she nears and nears!
Are those *her* sails that glance in the Sun,
Like restless gossameres?

Are those *her* ribs through which the Sun
Did peer, as through a grate?
And is that Woman all her crew?

other on
board the
skeleton ship.

Is that a DEATH? and are there two?
Is DEATH that woman's mate?

Like vessel,
like crew!
Death and
Life-in-Death
have diced for
the ship's
crew, and she
(the latter)
winneth the
ancient
Mariner.

Her lips were red, *her* looks were free,
Her locks were yellow as gold:
Her skin was as white as leprosy,
The Night-mare LIFE-IN-DEATH was she,
Who thicks man's blood with cold.

The naked hulk alongside came,
And the twain were casting dice;
"The game is done! I've won! I've won!"
Quoth she, and whistles thrice.

No twilight
within the courts
of the Sun.

The Sun's rim dips; the stars rush out:
At one stride comes the dark;
With far-heard whisper, o'er the sea,
Off shot the spectre-bark.

At the rising
of the Moon,

We listened and looked sideways up!
Fear at my heart, as at a cup,
My life-blood seemed to sip!
The stars were dim, and thick the night,
The steersman's face by his lamp gleamed white;
From the sails the dew did drip —
Till clomb above the eastern bar
The hornéd Moon, with one bright star
Within the nether tip.

One after
another,

One after one, by the star-dogged Moon,
Too quick for groan or sigh,
Each turned his face with a ghastly pang,
And cursed me with his eye.

His shipmates
drop down
dead.

Four times fifty living men,
(And I heard nor sigh nor groan)
With heavy thump, a lifeless lump,
They dropped down one by one.

But Life-in-
Death begins
her work on

The souls did from their bodies fly, —
They fled to bliss or woe!

And every soul, it passed me by,
Like the whizz of my cross-bow!

PART IV

The Wedding-
Guest feareth
that a Spirit
is talking to him;

"I fear thee, ancient Mariner!
I fear thy skinny hand!
And thou art long, and lank, and brown,
As is the ribbed sea-sand.

I fear thee and thy glittering eye,
And thy skinny hand, so brown." —
Fear not, fear not, thou Wedding-Guest!
This body dropt not down.

But the
ancient Mari-
ner assureth
him of his
bodily life, and
proceedeth to
relate his hor-
rible penance.

Alone, alone, all, all alone,
Alone on a wide wide sea!
And never a saint took pity on
My soul in agony.

The many men, so beautiful!
And they all dead did lie:
And a thousand thousand slimy things
Lived on; and so did I.

I looked upon the rotting sea,
And drew my eyes away;
I looked upon the rotting deck,
And there the dead men lay.

I looked to heaven, and tried to pray;
But or ever a prayer had gusht,
A wicked whisper came, and made
My heart as dry as dust.

I closed my lids, and kept them close,
And the balls like pulses beat;
For the sky and the sea, and the sea and the sky
Lay like a load on my weary eye,
And the dead were at my feet.

But the curse
liveth for him
in the eye of
the dead men.

The cold sweat melted from their limbs,
Nor rot nor reek did they:
The look with which they looked on me
Had never passed away.

An orphan's curse would drag to hell
A spirit from on high;
But oh! more horrible than that
Is the curse in a dead man's eye!
Seven days, seven nights, I saw that curse,
And yet I could not die.

In his loneliness and
fixedness he yearneth
towards the
journeying Moon,
and the stars that
still sojourn, yet
still move onward;
and every where
the blue sky belongs
to them, and is
their appointed rest,
and their native
country and their
own natural homes,
which they enter
unannounced, as lords
that are certainly
expected and yet there
is a silent joy at
their arrival.

The moving Moon went up the sky,
And no where did abide:
Softly she was going up,
And a star or two beside —

Her beams bemocked the sultry main,
Like April hoar-frost spread;
But where the ship's huge shadow lay,
The charmèd water burnt alway
A still and awful red.

By the light
of the Moon he
beholdeth
God's crea-
tures of the
great calm.

Beyond the shadow of the ship,
I watched the water-snakes:
They moved in tracks of shining white,
And when they reared, the elfish light
Fell off in hoary flakes.

Within the shadow of the ship
I watched their rich attire:
Blue, glossy green, and velvet black,
They coiled and swam; and every track
Was a flash of golden fire.

Their beauty
and their
happiness.

O happy living things! no tongue
Their beauty might declare:

A spring of love gushed from my heart,
And I blessed them unaware:
Sure my kind saint took pity on me,
And I blessed them unaware.

*He blesseth
them in his
heart.*

The self-same moment I could pray;
And from my neck so free
The Albatross fell off, and sank
Like lead into the sea.

*The spell begins
to break.*

PART V

Oh sleep! it is a gentle thing,
Beloved from pole to pole!
To Mary Queen the praise be given!
She sent the gentle sleep from Heaven,
That slid into my soul.

The silly buckets on the deck,
That had so long remained,
I dreamt that they were filled with dew;
And when I awoke, it rained.

*By grace of
the holy
Mother, the
ancient
Mariner is
refreshed with
rain.*

My lips were wet, my throat was cold,
My garments all were dank;
Sure I had drunken in my dreams,
And still my body drank.

I moved, and could not feel my limbs:
I was so light — almost
I thought that I had died in sleep,
And was a blesséd ghost.

And soon I heard a roaring wind:
It did not come anear;
But with its sound it shook the sails,
That were so thin and sere.

*He heareth
sounds and
seeth strange
sights and
commotions in
the sky and
the element.*

The upper air burst into life!
And a hundred fire-flags sheen,
To and fro they were hurried about!

And to and fro, and in and out,
The wan stars danced between.

And the coming wind did roar more loud,
And the sails did sigh like sedge;
And the rain poured down from one black cloud;
The Moon was at its edge.

The thick black cloud was cleft, and still
The Moon was at its side:
Like waters shot from some high crag,
The lightning fell with never a jag,
A river steep and wide.

The bodies of
the ship's crew
are inspired
and the
ship moves on;

The loud wind never reached the ship,
Yet now the ship moved on!
Beneath the lightning and the Moon
The dead men gave a groan.

They groaned, they stirred, they all uprose,
Nor spake, nor moved their eyes;
It had been strange, even in a dream,
To have seen those dead men rise.

The helmsman steered, the ship moved on;
Yet never a breeze up-blew;
The mariners all 'gan work the ropes,
Where they were wont to do;
They raised their limbs like lifeless tools —
We were a ghastly crew.

The body of my brother's son
Stood by me, knee to knee:
The body and I pulled at one rope,
But he said nought to me.

But not by the
souls of the
men, nor by
dæmons of
earth or
middle air, but
by a blessed

"I fear thee, ancient Mariner!"
Be calm, thou Wedding-Guest!
'Twas not those souls that fled in pain,
Which to their corses came again,
But a troop of spirits blest:

troop of
angelic spirits,
sent down by
the invocation
of the guard-
ian saint.

For when it dawned — they dropped their arms,
And clustered round the mast;
Sweet sounds rose slowly through their mouths,
And from their bodies passed.

Around, around, flew each sweet sound,
Then darted to the Sun;
Slowly the sounds came back again,
Now mixed, now one by one.

Sometimes a-dropping from the sky
I heard the sky-lark sing;
Sometimes all little birds that are,
How they seemed to fill the sea and air
With their sweet jargoning!

And now 'twas like all instruments,
Now like a lonely flute;
And now it is an angel's song,
That makes the heavens be mute.

It ceased; yet still the sails made on
A pleasant noise till noon,
A noise like of a hidden brook
In the leafy month of June,
That to the sleeping woods all night
Singeth a quiet tune.

Till noon we quietly sailed on,
Yet never a breeze did breathe:
Slowly and smoothly went the ship,
Moved onward from beneath.

The lonesome
Spirit from
the south-pole
carries on the
ship as far as
the Line, in
obedience to
the angelic
troop, but still
requireth
vengeance.

Under the keel nine fathom deep,
From the land of mist and snow,
The spirit slid: and it was he
That made the ship to go.
The sails at noon left off their tune,
And the ship stood still also.

The Sun, right up above the mast,
Had fixed her to the ocean:

But in a minute she 'gan stir,
With a short uneasy motion —
Backwards and forwards half her length
With a short uneasy motion.

Then like a pawing horse let go,
She made a sudden bound:
It flung the blood into my head,
And I fell down in a swound.

How long in that same fit I lay,
I have not to declare;
But ere my living life returned,
I heard and in my soul discerned
Two voices in the air.

"Is it he?" quoth one, "Is this the man?
By him who died on cross,
With his cruel bow he laid full low
The harmless Albatross.

The spirit who bideth by himself
In the land of mist and snow,
He loved the bird that loved the man
Who shot him with his bow."

The other was a softer voice,
As soft as honey-dew:
Quoth he, "The man hath penance done,
And penance more will do."

PART VI

First Voice

"But tell me, tell me! speak again,
Thy soft response renewing —
What makes that ship drive on so fast?
What is the ocean doing?"

Second Voice

"Still as a slave before his lord,
The ocean hath no blast;
His great bright eye most silently
Up to the Moon is cast —

If he may know which way to go;
For she guides him smooth or grim.
See, brother, see! how graciously
She looketh down on him."

First Voice

The Mariner
hath been
cast into a
trance; for the
angelic power
causeth the
vessel to drive
northward
faster than
human life
could endure.

"But why drives on that ship so fast,
Without or wave or wind?"

Second Voice

"The air is cut away before,
And closes from behind.

Fly, brother, fly! more high, more high!
Or we shall be belated:
For slow and slow that ship will go,
When the Mariner's trance is abated."

The super-
natural motion
is retarded;
the Mariner
awakes, and
his penance
begins anew.

I woke, and we were sailing on
As in a gentle weather:
'Twas night, calm night, the moon was high;
The dead men stood together.

All stood together on the deck,
For a charnel-dungeon fitter:
All fixed on me their stony eyes,
That in the Moon did glitter.

The pang, the curse, with which they died,
Had never passed away:
I could not draw my eyes from theirs,
Nor turn them up to pray.

The curse is
finally ex-
piated.

And now this spell was snapt: once more
I viewed the ocean green,
And looked far forth, yet little saw
Of what had else been seen —

Like one, that on a lonesome road
Doth walk in fear and dread,
And having once turned round walks on,
And turns no more his head;
Because he knows, a frightful fiend
Doth close behind him tread.

But soon there breathed a wind on me,
Nor sound nor motion made:
Its path was not upon the sea,
In ripple or in shade.

It raised my hair, it fanned my cheek
Like a meadow-gale of spring —
It mingled strangely with my fears,
Yet it felt like a welcoming.

Swiftly, swiftly flew the ship,
Yet she sailed softly too:
Sweetly, sweetly blew the breeze —
On me alone it blew.

And the
ancient
Mariner be-
holdeth his
native
country.

Oh! dream of joy! is this indeed
The light-house top I see?
Is this the hill? is this the kirk?
Is this mine own countree?

We drifted o'er the harbour-bar,
And I with sobs did pray —
O let me be awake, my God!
Or let me sleep alway.

The harbour-bay was clear as glass,
So smoothly it was strewn!
And on the bay the moonlight lay,
And the shadow of the Moon.

The rock shone bright, the kirk no less,
That stands above the rock:
The moonlight steeped in silentness
The steady weathercock.

And the bay was white with silent light,
Till rising from the same,
Full many shapes, that shadows were,
In crimson colours came.

A little distance from the prow
Those crimson shadows were:
I turned my eyes upon the deck —
Oh, Christ! what saw I there!

Each corse lay flat, lifeless and flat,
And, by the holy rood!
A man all light, a seraph-man,
On every corse there stood.

This seraph-band, each waved his hand:
It was a heavenly sight!
They stood as signals to the land,
Each one a lovely light;

This seraph-band, each waved his hand,
No voice did they impart —
No voice; but oh! the silence sank
Like music on my heart.

But soon I heard the dash of oars,
I heard the Pilot's cheer;
My head was turned perforce away,
And I saw a boat appear.

The Pilot and the Pilot's boy,
I heard them coming fast:
Dear Lord in Heaven! it was a joy
The dead men could not blast.

I saw a third — I heard his voice:
It is the Hermit good!

He singeth loud his godly hymns
That he makes in the wood.
He'll shrieve my soul, he'll wash away
The Albatross's blood.

Part VII

The Hermit of
the Wood,

This Hermit good lives in that wood
Which slopes down to the sea.
How loudly his sweet voice he rears!
He loves to talk with marineres
That come from a far countree.

He kneels at morn, and noon, and eve —
He hath a cushion plump:
It is the moss that wholly hides
The rotted old oak-stump.

The skiff-boat neared: I head them talk,
"Why, this is strange, I trow!
Where are those lights so many and fair,
That signal made but now?"

Approacheth
the ship with
wonder.

"Strange, by my faith!" the Hermit said —
"And they answered not our cheer!
The planks looked warped! and see those sails,
How thin they are and sere!
I never saw aught like to them,
Unless perchance it were

Brown skeletons of leaves that lag
My forest-brook along;
When the ivy-tod is heavy with snow,
And the owlet whoops to the wolf below,
That eats the she-wolf's young."

"Dear Lord! it hath a fiendish look —
(The Pilot made reply)
I am a-feared" — "Push on, push on!"
Said the Hermit cheerily.

The boat came closer to the ship,
But I nor spake nor stirred;
The boat came close beneath the ship,
And straight a sound was heard.

The ship
suddenly
sinketh.

Under the water it rumbled on,
Still louder and more dread:
It reached the ship, it split the bay;
The ship went down like lead.

The ancient
Mariner is
saved in the
Pilot's boat.

Stunned by that loud and dreadful sound,
Which sky and ocean smote,
Like one that hath been seven days drowned
My body lay afloat;
But swift as dreams, myself I found
Within the Pilot's boat.

Upon the whirl, where sank the ship,
The boat spun round and round;
And all was still, save that the hill
Was telling of the sound.

I moved my lips—the Pilot shrieked
And fell down in a fit;
The holy Hermit raised his eyes,
And prayed where he did sit.

I took the oars: the Pilot's boy,
Who now doth crazy go,
Laughed loud and long, and all the while
His eyes went to and fro.
"Ha! ha!" quoth he, "full plain I see,
The Devil knows how to row."

And now, all in my own countree,
I stood on the firm land!
The Hermit stepped forth from the boat,
And scarcely he could stand.

The ancient
Mariner
earnestly en-

"O shrieve me, shrieve me, holy man!"
The Hermit crossed his brow.

treateth the
Hermit to
shrieve him;
and the
penance of
life falls on
him.

"Say quick," quoth he, "I bid thee say —
What manner of man art thou?"

Forthwith this frame of mine was wrenched
With a woful agony,
Which forced me to begin my tale;
And then it left me free.

And ever and
anon through-
out his future
life an agony
constraineth
him to travel
from land to
land;

Since then, at an uncertain hour,
That agony returns:
And till my ghastly tale is told,
This heart within me burns.

I pass, like night, from land to land;
I have strange power of speech;
That moment that his face I see,
I know the man that must hear me:
To him my tale I teach.

What loud uproar bursts from that door!
The wedding-guests are there:
But in the garden-bower the bride
And bride-maids singing are:
And hark the little vesper bell,
Which biddeth me to prayer!

O Wedding-Guest! this soul hath been
Alone on a wide wide sea:
So lonely 'twas, that God himself
Scarce seeméd there to be.

O sweeter than the marriage-feast,
'Tis sweeter far to me,
To walk together to the kirk
With a goodly company! —

To walk together to the kirk,
And all together pray,
While each to his great Father bends,
Old men, and babes, and loving friends
And youths and maidens gay!

And to teach,
by his own
example, love
and reverence
to all things
that God made
and loveth.

Farewell, farewell! but this I tell
To thee, thou Wedding-Guest!
He prayeth well, who loveth well
Both man and bird and beast.

He prayeth best, who loveth best
All things both great and small;
For the dear God who loveth us,
He made and loveth all.

The Mariner, whose eye is bright,
Whose beard with age is hoar,
Is gone: and now the Wedding-Guest
Turned from the bridegroom's door.

He went like one that hath been stunned,
And is of sense forlorn:
A sadder and a wiser man,
He rose the morrow morn.

Faust, Part II

JOHANN WOLFGANG VON GOETHE

(1749–1832)

*Goethe worked on his huge dramatic poem all of his life.
Part I appeared in 1808, Part II in 1832, after his death. Faust
is the Romantic Subject, passionately seeking the Object. The
central theme of the poem is the Romantic drive toward
reality; hence, the essence of humanity is the Act. Mephistopheles is the spirit in man that denies the validity of such a
search, denies the value of reality, which can never be grasped
but only reached for, and offers the consolations of magic, that
is, metaphysics, final explanations, the illusions of adequacy
and mastery. Faust is saved because he never makes the ultimate surrender to the illusions of satisfaction. The world, then,
is only a symbol to man of his drive toward the world; its
otherness is symbolized by the Eternal Womanhead, or Femi-
nine. The following are the last three scenes of the drama.*

GREAT FORECOURT OF THE PALACE
(*Torches*)

MEPHISTOPHELES (*leading the way, as foreman*):
>Come on, come on! Come in, come in!
>You gangling gang of Lemurs,
>You half-alives patched up with thin
>Sinews and skulls and femurs.

LEMURS (*in chorus*):
>You call us, here we are at hand;
>And, as we understand it,
>We stand to win a stretch of land
>Intended as our mandate.

>Our pointed staves we have them here,
>Our chain to measure sections,
>But why you called on us, we fear,
>Has slipped our recollections.

MEPHISTOPHELES:
>Artistic efforts we can spare;
>And just let each one's nature guide him!
>Let now the longest lie his length down there,
>You others prise away the turf beside him;
>As for your forebears long asleep,
>Dig you an oblong, long and deep.
>To narrow house from palace hall
>Is such a stupid way to end it all.

(*The Lemurs begin to dig, with mocking gestures*)

LEMURS:
>When I was young and lived and loved,
>Methought it was passing sweet;
>In the merry rout and roundabout
>There would I twirl my feet.

>But sneaking Age has upped his crutch
>And downed me unaware;
>I stumbled over the door of the grave —
>Why was it open *there*?

FAUST (*groping his way from the palace*):
    Oh how this clink of spades rejoices me!
    For that is my conscripted labour,
    The earth is now her own good neighbour
    And sets the waves a boundary —
    Confinement strict and strenuous.

MEPHISTOPHELES (*aside*):
    And yet you've only toiled for *us*
    With all your damming, all your dyking —
    Spreading a feast to Neptune's liking
    To glut that water-demon's maw.
    In all respects you're lost and stranded,
    The elements with us have banded —
    Annihilation is the law.

FAUST:
    Foreman!

MEPHISTOPHELES:
        Here!

FAUST:
              Use every means you can;
    Bring all your gangs up and exhort them —
    Threaten them if you like or court them —
    But pay or woo or force each man!
    And day by day send word to me, assessing
    How my intended earthworks are progressing.

MEPHISTOPHELES (*half aloud*):
    The word to-day, from what I've heard,
    Is not "intended" but "interred."

FAUST:
    A swamp along the mountains' flank
    Makes all my previous gains contaminate;
    My deeds, if I could drain this sink,
    Would culminate as well as terminate:
    To open to the millions living space,
    Not danger-proof but free to run their race.
    Green fields and fruitful; men and cattle hiving

Upon this newest earth at once and thriving,
Settled at once beneath this sheltering hill
Heaped by the masses' brave and busy skill.
With such a heavenly land behind this hedge,
The sea beyond may bluster to its edge
And, as it gnaws to swamp the work of masons,
To stop the gap one common impulse hastens.
Aye! Wedded to this concept like a wife,
I find this wisdom's final form:
He only earns his freedom and his life
Who takes them every day by storm.
And so a man, beset by dangers here,
As child, man, old man, spends his manly year.
Oh to see such activity,
Treading free ground with people that are free!
Then could I bid the passing moment:
"Linger a while, thou art so fair!"
The traces of my earthly days can never
Sink in the aeons unaware.
And I, who feel ahead such heights of bliss,
At last enjoy my highest moment — this.

(*Faust sinks back; the Lemurs seize him and lay him on the ground*)

MEPHISTOPHELES:
By no joy sated, filled by no success,
Still whoring after shapes that flutter past,
This last ill moment of sheer emptiness —
The poor man yearns to hold it fast.
He who withstood me with such strength,
Time masters him and here he lies his length.
The clock stands still —

CHORUS:
                              Stands still! Like
                                    midnight . . . silent . . . stilled.
Its hand drops down.

MEPHISTOPHELES:
                              Drops down; it is fulfilled.

LEMURS:
   It is gone by.

MEPHISTOPHELES:
           Gone by! A stupid phrase.
   Why say gone by?
   Gone by — pure naught — complete monotony.
   What use these cycles of creation!
   Or snatching off the creatures to negation!
   "It is gone by!" — and we can draw the inference:
   If it had *not* been, it would make no difference;
   The wheel revolves the same, no more, no less.
   I should prefer eternal emptiness.

INTERMENT

LEMUR SOLO:
   Oh who has built the house so ill
   With spade and shovel rough?

LEMUR CHORUS:
   For you, dull guest in hempen garb,
   Yon house is fine enough.

LEMUR SOLO:
   No chair or table in the hall —
   Who's furnished it so meagre?

LEMUR CHORUS:
   The loan was only for a time;
   The creditors are eager.

MEPHISTOPHELES:
   Here lies the corpse and if the soul would flee
   At once I show the bond, the blood-signed scroll;
   Though now, alas, they have so many means
   To cheat the devil of a soul.
   Our old procedure gives offence,
   Our new has not yet found endorsement;
   Once I'd have managed it alone,
   Now I must look for reinforcement.

Come up, you devils! Make it double quick!
You straight-horned peers and crooked-horned as well,
You old and sterling devil-stock,
Come up — and bring with you the jaws of Hell!

(*The Jaws of Hell open upon the left*)

The eye-teeth gape; the throat's enormous vault
Spews forth a raging fiery flow
And through the smoking cyclone of the gullet
I see the infernal city's eternal glow.
You do right well to make the sinner quake;
And yet they think it all a dream, a fake.
Now, devils, watch this body! How does it seem?
See if you see a phosphorescent gleam.
That is the little soul, Psyche with wings —
Pull out her wings and it's a noisome worm;
With my own seal I'll set my stamp upon her,
Then forth with her into the fiery storm!
Come, claw and comb the air, strain every nerve
To catch her though she flutter, though she swerve.
To stay in her old lodging gives her pain;
The genius is about to leave the brain.

(*Glory, from above, on the right*)

THE HOST OF HEAVEN:
 Fly, as directed,
 Heaven's elected,
 Serenely whereby
 Sin shall have pardon,
 Dust become garden;
 Stay your progression,
 Make intercession,
 Trace for all natures
 A path to the sky.

MEPHISTOPHELES:
 Discords I hear, a filthy strumming tumbling
 Down from the sky with the unwelcome day;
 That is the angels' boyish-girlish fumbling,

Their canting taste *likes* it to sound that way.
You know how we, in hours of deep damnation,
Have schemed annihilation for mankind;
Those angels use for adoration
The greatest stigma we could find.
They come so fawningly, the milksops!
They've kidnapped many souls before our eyes,
They fight us back with our own weapons;
They too are devils — in disguise.
Defeat to-day would mean disgrace eternal;
So stand around the grave and stand infernal!

CHORUS OF ANGELS (*scattering roses*):
Roses, you glowing ones,
Balsam-bestowing ones!
Fluttering peaceably,
Healing invisibly,
Spraylets to glide upon,
Budlets unspied upon,
Hasten to bloom!

Green and empurpled,
Spring must have room;
Carry your heaven
Into the tomb!

MEPHISTOPHELES (*to the Satans*):
Why duck and squirm? Is that our wont in hell?
Stand fast and let them strew their roses!
Each gawk to his post and guard it well!
With such small flowers the enemy proposes
To snow up overheated devils;
Why, at your breath it melts and shrivels.
Now puff, you blow-fiends!

. . . Here! Stop! Stop!
Your reek is bleaching the whole flight and crop.
Don't blow so hard! Muzzle your chops and noses!
I'll swear you've *over*blown those roses!
You never know when you have passed the turn!

They're more than shrunk — they're browned, they're
   dry, they *burn*!
Bright flames of poison pelt on us already;
In close formation, devils! Steady! Steady!
What! All your valour gone! Your strength burns low!
The devils sense a strange insidious glow.

CHORUS OF ANGELS:

   Blooms of pure blessedness,
   Flames of pure joyfulness,
   Love is their ministry,
   Rapture their legacy,
   All we could pray.
   Hosts of eternity
   Find in such verity
   Heavens of clarity,
   Aeons of day!

MEPHISTOPHELES:

   A curse upon these louts! How scurvy!
   My Satans are all topsy-turvy
   And turning cartwheels in their path
   And tumbling arse-up into Hell.
   I hope you like your well-earned sulphur bath!
   I stand my ground and wish you well.

(He beats off the roses falling around him)

CHORUS OF ANGELS:

   What is not right for you
   You must beware it,
   What does despite to you
   You may not bear it.
   Lightnings may dart on us,
   We must have heart in us.
   Lovers can only be
   Rescued by love.

MEPHISTOPHELES:

   My head's aflame! Liver and heart aflame!
   A super-devilish element!

Hell's fires to this are damped and tame.
That's why you make such wild lament,
You luckless folk in love, despised alas,
Who sprain your necks to watch your sweethearts pass.

Me too! What draws my head in that direction?
I, their sworn enemy! Is this defection?
To see them once was agony or worse.
Has something alien entered me completely?
To see their flower of youth affects me now so sweetly;
I want to curse them — but what chokes the curse?
And, if I let them now befool me,
Whom can the future call a fool?
These dashing fellows, though I hate them,
Inspire a longing that I cannot rule.
Beautiful children, must I not infer
That you like me are kin to Lucifer?
With every look you seem more fair, more fair.
Oh come near, angels, glance on me! Come near!

ANGEL:
See, we approach — why do you shrink away?
We come; if you can face us — why, then, stay!

(*The Angels, closing in, occupy all the space*)

CHOIR OF ANGELS:
Flames of dear feeling,
Rise beyond seeing!
Self-condemned being —
Truth be its healing!
Blessed transition
Forth from perdition,
Into Eternity,
Into the One!

MEPHISTOPHELES (*collecting himself*):
Look! The damned flames are out that caused my fall.
Now I become myself and curse you one and all!

CHOIR OF ANGELS:
Light of Creation!

Whom it embraces
Finds all the graces
Found in salvation.
Praising in unison
Rise to your goal!
Purged is the air now —
Breathe now the soul!

(*They soar up, carrying away the immortal part of Faust*)

MEPHISTOPHELES (*looking around him*):
But how is this? Where have they moved away to?
You juveniles, to take me by surprise!
Flying off heavenwards — and with my prey too;
They nibbled at this grave to win this prize.
Wresting from me a great and matchless treasure,
That noble soul which gave me right of seizure
They've filched by throwing rose-dust in my eyes.
Who is there now to lend an ear to
My wrong, restore my hard-earned right?
You have been hoaxed — so late in your career too —
It's your own fault, you're in a lurid plight.
Such gross mismanagement — outrageous!
Such a great outlay squandered! Oh the shame!
Erotic folly, vulgar lust, contagious
To an old devil at the game!
Experience has indulged its appetite
On such a childish-foolish level;
When all is said, the folly is not slight
Which in the end has seized the devil.

MOUNTAIN GORGES

(*Forest, Rock, Wilderness. Holy anchorites, disposed here and there,
at different heights among the chasms*)

CHORUS AND ECHO:
Woods clamber tremblingly,
Crags bear down weightily,
Roots cling tenaciously,

Trunks make a density;
Spurting of wave on wave —
Deep lies our hermits' cave.
Lions around in dumb
Friendliness gently come,
Honour our sanctuary,
Love's holy privacy.

PATER ECSTATICUS (*floating up and down*):
Rapture which yearns ever,
Love-bond which burns ever,
Pain in me seething up,
Love of God foaming up.
Arrows, pierce through me and,
Lances, subdue me and,
Clubs, leave no form in me,
Thunderstorms, storm in me!
That now the Nothingness
Drown all in emptiness,
One constant star must shine,
Kernel of love divine.

PATER PROFUNDUS (*from the depths*):
As at my feet a craggy chasm
Weighs on a deeper chasm's prop,
As streams in thousands flow and sparkle
Towards the dread rapids' foaming drop,
As with its own strong urge the tree-trunk
Climbs up the air, erect and tall,
Even so is that almighty love
Which all things forms and fosters all.

Around me here a frantic rushing
Makes wood and cleft a stormy sea,
Yet full of love the water's fullness
Roars as it plumbs the cavity,
Ordained to straightway feed the valley;
The thunderbolt which crashed in flame
To cleanse the air which bore within it
Poison and evil mists, these same

Are messengers of love, announcing
What round us ever moves and makes.
May that light kindle too within me
Where the cold spirit gropes and quakes,
Self-racked in body's bonds of dullness,
Riveted fast in chains that smart.
O God, have mercy on my thoughts,
Give light to my impoverished heart!

PATER SERAPHICUS (*at a middle height*):
What a morning cloudlet hovers
Through the pine-trees' waving hair!
I divine what lives within it —
Newborn souls are gathered there.

CHORUS OF BLESSED BOYS:
Tell us, Father, where we wander,
Tell us, good one, who we are!
All of us are happy, living
In a state that naught can mar.

PATER SERAPHICUS:
Innocents — who, born at midnight
With half-opened soul and brain,
Were at once your parents' loss,
Were at once the angels' gain.
That a living man is present,
That you feel, so draw you near!
Though earth's rugged ways are barred you,
Alien to your happy sphere.
Climb up then into my eyes —
Organ matching world and earth;
See this region, using mine
For the eyes you lost at birth.

(*He takes them into himself*)

Those are trees — and those are crags —
See that river plunging deep,
Which with its enormous welter
Delves a passage, short though deep.

BLESSED BOYS (*from inside him*):
    Yes, that is a mighty prospect —
    But too sad this world below,
    Shaking us with fear and horror.
    Reverend father, let us go!

PATER SERAPHICUS:
    Aye. Ascend to higher circles,
    Ever grow invisibly
    As God's presence makes you stronger
    Through eternal purity.
    It is this which feeds the spirit,
    Rules the heights of revelation:
    Window into love eternal
    Opening upon salvation.

BLESSED BOYS (*circling round the highest peak*):
    Joyfully gyring
    Dance ye in union,
    Hands linked and choiring
    Blessed communion!
    Pattern before you,
    Godly, to cheer you,
    Whom you adore, you
    Soon shall see near you.

ANGELS (*floating in the higher air, carrying the immortal part of Faust*):
    Saved, saved now is that precious part
    Of our spirit world from evil:
    "Should a man strive with all his heart,
    Heaven can foil the devil."
    And if love also from on high
    Has helped him through his sorrow,
    The hallowed legions of the sky
    Will give him glad good morrow.

THE YOUNGER ANGELS:
    Ah those roses, *their* donation —
    Loving-holy penitent women —
    Helped us to defeat Apollyon,

Brought our work to consummation,
To this priceless spirit's capture.
Devils, as we scattered rapture,
Struck by roses, fled in panic,
Feeling not their pains Satanic
But the pains of love's disaster;
Even that old Satan-master
Felt a torment arrowed, marrowed.
Alleluia! Hell is harrowed.

THE MORE PERFECT ANGELS:
This scrap of earth, alas,
We must convoy it;
Were it asbestos, yet
Earth would alloy it.
When soul's dynamic force
Has drawn up matter
Into itself, then no
Angel could shatter
The bonds of that twoness —
The oneness that tied it;
Eternal love alone
Knows to divide it.

THE YOUNGER ANGELS:
Close, round the mountain top,
To my perceiving
Moves like a mist a
Spiritual living.
Those clouds are turning bright,
I see a sainted flight:
Children unmeshed from
Meshes of earth, they
Fly in a ring,
Being refreshed from
Heaven's rebirth they
Bask in its spring.
Faust, to begin to rise
Towards highest Paradise,

With them must wing.

THE BLESSED BOYS:
>Gladly receiving this
>Chrysalid entity,
>Now we achieve, in this,
>Angels' identity.
>Let the cocoon which is
>Round him be broken!
>Great! Fair! How soon he is
>Heaven-awoken!

DOCTOR MARIANUS (*in the highest, purest cell*):
>Here is the prospect free,
>Spirit-uplifting.
>Yonder go women's shapes
>Over me drifting;
>And, wreathed in her seven
>Bright stars, they attend her —
>The high queen of Heaven;
>I gaze on her splendour.

>(*Entranced*)

>Highest empress of the world,
>Let these blue and sacred
>Tents of heaven here unfurled
>Show me now thy secret!
>Sanction that which in man's breast
>Soft and strong prepares him —
>Love which joyful, love which blest
>Towards thy presence bears him.

>Thine august commands are such,
>Nothing can subdue us —
>Fires burn gentler at thy touch
>Should thy peace imbue us.
>Virgin, pure as none are pure,
>Mother, pearl of honour,
>Chosen as our queen, the sure
>Godhead stamped upon her!

>Light clouds enlacing

Circle her splendour —
These are the penitent
Women, a tender
Race. At thy knee,
Sipping the air, they
Call upon thee.

Thou, albeit immaculate,
It is of thy fashion
That the easily seduced
Sue to thy compassion.

Such whom frailty reft, are hard,
Hard to save, if ever;
Who can burst the bonds of lust
Through his own endeavour?
Do not sliding gradients cause
Sudden slips? What maiden
Is not fooled by flattering glance,
Tokens flattery-laden?

(*The Mater Gloriosa floats into vision*)

CHORUS OF PENITENT WOMEN:

Mary, in soaring
To kingdoms eternal,
Hear our imploring
Thou beyond rival!
Fount of survival!

MAGNA PECCATRIX:

By my love which mingled tears with
Balm to bathe His feet, revering
Him thy son, now God-transfigured,
When the Pharisees were jeering;
By that vessel which so sweetly
Spilt its perfumed wealth profusely,
By my hair which dried those holy
Limbs, around them falling loosely —

MULIER SAMARITANA:

By the well where Father Abram
Watered once his flocks when marching,

By the bucket once allowed to
Touch and cool Christ's lips when parching;
By that pure and generous source which
Now extends its irrigation,
Overbrimming, ever-crystal,
Flowing through the whole creation —

MARIA AEGYPTIACA:
By that more than sacred garden
Where they laid the Lord to rest,
By the arm which from the portal
Thrust me back with stern behest;
By my forty years' repentance
Served out in a desert land,
By the blessed word of parting
Which I copied in the sand —

THE THREE:
Thou who to most sinning women
Thy dear presence ne'er deniest,
Raising us repentant women
To eternities the highest,
Make to *this* good soul concession —
Only once misled by pleasure
To a never-dreamt transgression;
Grant her pardon in her measure.

ONE OF THE PENITENTS (*formerly named Gretchen*):
Uniquely tender,
Thou queen of splendour,
Thy visage render
Benign towards my felicity!
My love of old, he
Is now consoled, he
Comes back to me.

BLESSED BOYS (*approaching, flying in circles*):
Passing beyond us
So soon in resplendence,
He will make ample
Return for our tendance;

    Early we left the
    Terrestrial chorus;
    He will instruct us,
    Instructed before us.

THE SINGLE PENITENT (*formerly named Gretchen*):
    By choirs of noble souls surrounded
    This new one scarcely feels his soul,
    Can scarcely sense this life unbounded,
    Yet fills at once his heavenly role.
    See how he sheds the earthly leaven,
    Tears off each shroud of old untruth,
    And from apparel woven in heaven
    Shines forth his pristine power of youth!
    Mary, grant me to instruct him,
    Dazzled as yet by this new day.

MATER GLORIOSA:
    Come then! To higher spheres conduct him!
    Divining *you,* he knows the way.

DOCTOR MARIANUS (*bowing in adoration*):
    All you tender penitents,
    Gaze on her who saves you —
    Thus you change your lineaments
    And salvation laves you.
    To her feet each virtue crawl,
    Let her will transcend us;
    Virgin, Mother, Queen of All,
    Goddess, still befriend us!

CHORUS MYSTICUS:
    All that is past of us
    Was but reflected;
    All that was lost in us
    Here is corrected;
    All indescribables
    Here we descry;
    Eternal Womanhead
    Leads us on high.

[TRANSLATED BY LOUIS MACNEICE]

The Recluse

WILLIAM WORDSWORTH

(1770–1850)

Wordsworth planned a long poem in three parts. Of Part I, he wrote only Book I, which appears in part below; Part II was published in 1814 as The Excursion; *of Part III nothing was written. Instead he wrote a long poem prefatory to the planned* Excursion, The Prelude, *published posthumously in 1850. The poem presented here was not published until 1888. It is concerned with the turning away from ordinary society to a half-secret paradise in order to find the proper setting for the Visionary Artist-Poet, whose anti-role it is to unite Subject and Object in the Romantic mode of "mystic" experience. At the end of the poem Wordsworth makes clear what is often ignored, that he is not a poet of nature but a poet of the mind, a psychological poet.*

Bleak season was it, turbulent and bleak,
When hitherward we journeyed, side by side,
Through bursts of sunshine and through flying showers,
Paced the long Vales, how long they were, and yet
How fast that length of way was left behind,
Wensley's rich Vale and Sedbergh's naked heights.

The frosty wind, as if to make amends
For its keen breath, was aiding to our steps,
And drove us onward like two ships at sea,
Or like two Birds, companions in mid air,
Parted and re-united by the blast.
Stern was the face of Nature; we rejoiced
In that stern countenance, for our Souls thence drew
A feeling of their strength. The naked Trees,
The icy brooks, as on we passed, appeared
To question us. "Whence come ye? to what end?"
They seemed to say; "What would ye," said the shower,
"Wild Wanderers, whither through my dark domain?"
The sunbeam said, "be happy." When this Vale
We entered, bright and solemn was the sky
That faced us with a passionate welcoming,
And led us to our threshold. Daylight failed
Insensibly, and round us gently fell
Composing darkness, with a quiet load
Of full contentment, in a little Shed
Disturbed, uneasy in itself as seemed,
And wondering at its new inhabitants.
It loves us now, this Vale so beautiful
Begins to love us! By a sullen storm,
Two months unwearied of severest storm,
It put the temper of our minds to proof,
And found us faithful through the gloom, and heard
The Poet mutter his prelusive songs
With chearful heart, an unknown voice of joy,
Among the silence of the woods and hills;
Silent to any gladsomeness of sound
With all their Shepherds.
                              But the gates of Spring
Are opened; churlish Winter hath given leave
That she should entertain for this one day,
Perhaps for many genial days to come,
His guests, and make them jocund. They are pleased,
But most of all the Birds that haunt the flood,
With the mild summons; inmates though they be

Of Winter's household, they keep festival
This day, who drooped, or seemed to droop, so long;
They shew their pleasure, and shall I do less?
Happier of happy though I be, like them
I cannot take possession of the sky,
Mount with a thoughtless impulse, and wheel there,
One of a mighty multitude, whose way
Is a perpetual harmony, and dance
Magnificent. Behold, how with a grace
Of ceaseless motion, that might scarcely seem
Inferior to angelical, they prolong
Their curious pastime, shaping in mid air,
And sometimes with ambitious wing that soars
High as the level of the mountain tops,
A circuit ampler than the lake beneath,
Their own domain; — but ever, while intent
On tracing and retracing that large round,
Their jubilant activity evolves
Hundreds of curves and circlets, to and fro,
Upwards and downwards, progress intricate
Yet unperplexed, as if one spirit swayed
Their indefatigable flight. 'Tis done —
Ten times and more, I fancied it had ceased;
But lo! the vanished company again
Ascending, they approach — I hear their wings
Faint, faint at first; and then an eager sound
Passed in a moment — and as faint again!
They tempt the sun to sport among their plumes;
Tempt the smooth water, or the gleaming ice,
To shew them a fair image, — 'tis themselves,
Their own fair forms, upon the glimmering plain,
Painted more soft and fair as they descend,
Almost to touch; — then up again aloft,
Up with a sally, and a flash of speed,
As if they scorned both resting-place and rest!

This day is a thanksgiving, 'tis a day
Of glad emotion and deep quietness;

Not upon me alone hath been bestowed,
Me rich in many onward-looking thoughts,
The penetrating bliss; oh surely these
Have felt it, not the happy Quires of Spring,
Her own peculiar family of love
That sport among green leaves, a blither train.
   But two are missing — two, a lonely pair
Of milk-white Swans, wherefore are they not seen
Partaking this day's pleasure? From afar
They came, to sojourn here in solitude,
Chusing this Valley, they who had the choice
Of the whole world. We saw them day by day,
Through those two months of unrelenting storm,
Conspicuous at the centre of the Lake,
Their safe retreat; we knew them well, I guess
That the whole Valley knew them; but to us
They were more dear than may be well believed,
Not only for their beauty, and their still
And placid way of life, and constant love
Inseparable, not for these alone,
But that their state so much resembled ours,
They having also chosen this abode;
They strangers, and we strangers; they a pair,
And we a solitary pair like them.
They should not have departed; many days
Did I look forth in vain, nor on the wing
Could see them, nor in that small open space
Of blue unfrozen water, where they lodged,
And lived so long in quiet, side by side.
Shall we behold them, consecrated friends,
Faithful Companions, yet another year
Surviving, they for us, and we for them,
And neither pair be broken? Nay perchance
It is too late already for such hope,
The Dalesmen may have aimed the deadly tube,
And parted them; or haply both are gone
One death, and that were mercy given to both.
Recal my song the ungenerous thought; forgive,

Thrice favoured Region, the conjecture harsh
Of such inhospitable penalty,
Inflicted upon confidence so pure.
Ah, if I wished to follow where the sight
Of all that is before my eyes, the voice
Which speaks from a presiding Spirit here,
Would lead me, I should whisper to myself;
They who are dwellers in this holy place
Must needs themselves be hallowed, they require
No benediction from the Stranger's lips,
For they are blest already. None would give
The greeting "peace be with you" unto them,
For peace they have, it cannot but be theirs,
And mercy, and forbearance. Nay — not these,
Their healing offices a pure good-will
Precludes, and charity beyond the bounds
Of charity — an overflowing love,
Not for the Creature only, but for all
That is around them, love for every thing
Which in this happy Region they behold!

Thus do we soothe ourselves, and when the thought
Is pass'd we blame it not for having come.
What, if I floated down a pleasant Stream
And now am landed, and the motion gone,
Shall I reprove myself? Ah no, the Stream
Is flowing, and will never cease to flow,
And I shall float upon that Stream again.
By such forgetfulness the Soul becomes,
Words cannot say, how beautiful; then hail,
Hail to the visible Presence, hail to thee,
Delightful Valley, habitation fair!
And to whatever else of outward form
Can give us inward help, can purify,
And elevate, and harmonise, and soothe,
And steal away, and for a while deceive
And lap in pleasing rest, and bear us on
Without desire in full complacency,

Contemplating perfection absolute
And entertained as in a placid sleep.

   But not betrayed by tenderness of mind
That feared, or wholly overlook'd the truth,
Did we come hither, with romantic hope
To find, in midst of so much loveliness,
Love, perfect love; of so much majesty
A like majestic frame of mind in those
Who here abide, the persons like the place.
Not from such hope, or aught of such belief
Hath issued any portion of the joy
Which I have felt this day. An awful voice,
'Tis true, hath in my walks been often heard,
Sent from the mountains or the sheltered fields,
Shout after shout — reiterated whoop
In manner of a bird that takes delight
In answering to itself; or like a hound
Single at chase among the lonely woods,
His yell repeating; yet it was in truth
A human voice — a Spirit of coming night,
How solemn when the sky is dark, and earth
Not dark, nor yet enlightened, but by snow
Made visible, amid a noise of winds
And bleatings manifold of mountain sheep,
Which in that iteration recognize
Their summons, and are gathering round for food,
Devoured with keenness ere to grove or bank
Or rocky *bield* with patience they retire.

   That very voice, which, in some timid mood
Of superstitious fancy, might have seemed
Awful as ever stray Demoniac uttered,
His steps to govern in the Wilderness;
Or as the Norman Curfew's regular beat,
To hearths when first they darkened at the knell:
That Shepherd's voice, it may have reached mine ear
Debased and under profanation, made
The ready Organ of articulate sounds

From ribaldry, impiety, or wrath
Issuing when shame hath ceased to check the brawls
Of some abused Festivity — so be it.
I came not dreaming of unruffled life,
Untainted manners; born among the hills,
Bred also there, I wanted not a scale
To regulate my hopes. Pleased with the good,
I shrink not from the evil with disgust,
Or with immoderate pain. I look for Man,
The common Creature of the brotherhood,
Differing but little from the Man elsewhere,
For selfishness, and envy, and revenge,
Ill neighbourhood — pity that this should be —
Flattery and double-dealing, strife and wrong.

Yet is it something gained, it is in truth
A mighty gain, that Labour here preserves
His rosy face, a Servant only here
Of the fire-side, or of the open field,
A Freeman, therefore, sound and unimpaired;
That extreme penury is here unknown,
And cold and hunger's abject wretchedness,
Mortal to body, and the heaven-born mind;
That they who want, are not too great a weight
For those who can relieve. Here may the heart
Breathe in the air of fellow-suffering
Dreadless, as in a kind of fresher breeze
Of her own native element, the hand
Be ready and unwearied without plea
From tasks too frequent, or beyond its power
For languor, or indifference, or despair.
And as these lofty barriers break the force
Of winds, this deep Vale, — as it doth in part
Conceal us from the Storm, — so here abides
A Power and a protection for the mind,
Dispensed indeed to other solitudes,
Favoured by noble privilege like this,
Where kindred independence of estate

Is prevalent, where he who tills the field,
He, happy Man! is Master of the field,
And treads the mountains which his Fathers trod.

.   .   .

No, we are not alone, we do not stand,
My Sister, here misplaced and desolate,
Loving what no one cares for but ourselves;
We shall not scatter through the plains and rocks
Of this fair Vale, and o'er its spacious heights
Unprofitable kindliness, bestowed
On objects unaccustomed to the gifts
Of feeling, which were chearless and forlorn
But few weeks past, and would be so again
Were we not here; we do not tend a lamp
Whose lustre we alone participate,
Which shines dependent upon us alone,
Mortal though bright, a dying, dying flame.
Look where we will, some human heart has been
Before us with its offering; not a tree
Sprinkles these little pastures but the same
Hath furnished matter for a thought; perchance,
For some one serves as a familiar friend.
Joy spreads, and sorrow spreads; and this whole Vale,
Home of untutored Shepherds as it is,
Swarms with sensation, as with gleams of sunshine,
Shadows or breezes, scents or sounds. Nor deem
These feelings, though subservient more than ours
To every day's demand for daily bread,
And borrowing more their spirit, and their shape
From self-respecting interests, deem them not
Unworthy therefore, and unhallowed: no,
They lift the animal being, do themselves
By Nature's kind and ever-present aid
Refine the selfishness from which they spring,
Redeem by love the individual sense
Of anxiousness with which they are combined.
And thus it is that fitly they become

Associates in the joy of purest minds,
They blend therewith congenially: meanwhile,
Calmly they breathe their own undying life
Through this their mountain sanctuary; long,
Oh long may it remain inviolate,
Diffusing health and sober chearfulness,
And giving to the moments as they pass
Their little boons of animating thought
That sweeten labour, make it seen and felt
To be no arbitrary weight imposed,
But a glad function natural to Man.

Fair proof of this, Newcomer though I be,
Already have I gained. The inward frame
Though slowly opening, opens every day
With process not unlike to that which chears
A pensive Stranger, journeying at his leisure
Through some Helvetian dell, when low-hung mists
Break up, and are beginning to recede;
How pleased he is where thin and thinner grows
The veil, or where it parts at once, to spy
The dark pines thrusting forth their spiky heads;
To watch the spreading lawns with cattle grazed,
Then to be greeted by the scattered huts,
As they shine out; and *see* the streams whose murmur
Had soothed his ear while they were hidden: how pleased
To have about him, which way e'er he goes,
Something on every side concealed from view,
In every quarter something visible,
Half-seen or wholly, lost and found again,
Alternate progress and impediment,
And yet a growing prospect in the main.

Such pleasure now is mine, albeit forced,
Herein less happy than the Traveller
To cast from time to time a painful look
Upon unwelcome things, which unawares
Reveal themselves; not therefore is my heart
Depressed, nor does it fear what is to come,

But confident, enriched at every glance.
The more I see the more delight my mind
Receives, or by reflexion can create.
Truth justifies herself, and as she dwells
With Hope, who would not follow where she leads?

Nor let me pass unheeded other loves
Where no fear is, and humbler sympathies.
Already hath sprung up within my heart
A liking for the small grey horse that bears
The paralytic Man, and for the brute —
In Scripture sanctified — the patient brute,
On which the cripple, in the Quarry maim'd,
Rides to and fro: I know them and their ways.
The famous Sheep-dog, first in all the Vale,
Though yet to me a Stranger, will not be
A Stranger long; nor will the blind man's guide,
Meek and neglected thing, of no renown!
Soon will peep forth the primrose; ere it fades
Friends shall I have at dawn, blackbird and thrush
To rouse me, and a hundred Warblers more;
And if those Eagles to their ancient Hold
Return, Helvellyn's Eagles! with the Pair
From my own door I shall be free to claim
Acquaintance as they sweep from cloud to cloud.
The Owl that gives the name to Owlet-Crag
Have I heard whooping, and he soon will be
A chosen one of my regards. See there
The Heifer in yon little croft belongs
To one who holds it dear; with duteous care
She reared it, and in speaking of her charge
I heard her scatter some endearing words
Domestic, and in spirit motherly
She being herself a Mother, happy Beast
If the caresses of a human voice
Can make it so, and care of human hands.

And ye as happy under Nature's care,
Strangers to me, and all men, or at least

Strangers to all particular amity,
All intercourse of knowledge or of love
That parts the individual from his kind,
Whether in large communities ye keep
From year to year, not shunning Man's abode,
A settled residence, or be from far,
Wild creatures, and of many homes, that come
The gift of winds, and whom the winds again
Take from us at your pleasure — yet shall ye
Not want, for this, your own subordinate place
In my affections. Witness the delight
With which erewhile I saw that multitude
Wheel through the sky, and see them now at rest,
Yet not at rest, upon the glassy lake.
They *cannot* rest, they gambol like young whelps;
Active as lambs, and overcome with joy,
They try all frolic motions; flutter, plunge,
And beat the passive water with their wings.
Too distant are they for plain view, but lo!
Those little fountains, sparkling in the sun,
Betray their occupation, rising up,
First one and then another silver spout,
As one or other takes the fit of glee,
Fountains and spouts, yet somewhat in the guise
Of play-thing fire-works, that on festal nights
Sparkle about the feet of wanton boys.
— How vast the compass of this theatre,
Yet nothing to be seen but lovely pomp
And silent majesty; the birch-tree woods
Are hung with thousand thousand diamond drops
Of melted hoar-frost, every tiny knot
In the bare twigs, each little budding-place
Cased with its several bead, what myriads there
Upon one tree, while all the distant grove
That rises to the summit of the steep
Shows like a mountain built of silver light.
See yonder the same pageant, and again
Behold the universal imagery

Inverted, all its sun-bright features touched
As with the varnish, and the gloss of dreams;
Dreamlike the blending also of the whole
Harmonious landscape; all along the shore
The boundary lost, the line invisible
That parts the image from reality;
And the clear hills, as high as they ascend
Heavenward, so piercing deep the lake below.
Admonished of the days of love to come
The raven croaks, and fills the upper air
With a strange sound of genial harmony;
And in and all about that playful band,
Incapable although they be of rest,
And in their fashion very rioters,
There is a stillness, and they seem to make
Calm revelry in that their calm abode.
Them leaving to their joyous hours I pass,
Pass with a thought the life of the whole year
That is to come, the throng of woodland flowers,
And lillies that will dance upon the waves.

．　　　．　　　．

Dismissing therefore, all Arcadian dreams,
All golden fancies of the golden Age,
The bright array of shadowy thoughts from times
That were before all time, or are to be
Ere time expire, the pageantry that stirs
And will be stirring when our eyes are fixed
On lovely objects, and we wish to part
With all remembrance of a jarring world,
— Take we at once this one sufficient hope,
What need of more? that we shall neither droop,
Nor pine for want of pleasure in the life
Scattered about us, nor through dearth of aught
That keeps in health the insatiable mind;
That we shall have for knowledge and for love
Abundance; and that, feeling as we do
How goodly, how exceeding fair, how pure

From all reproach is yon ethereal vault,
And this deep Vale its earthly counterpart,
By which, and under which, we are enclosed
To breathe in peace, we shall moreover find
(If sound, and what we ought to be ourselves,
If rightly we observe and justly weigh)
The Inmates not unworthy of their home
The Dwellers of their Dwelling.
                                  And if this
Were otherwise, we have within ourselves
Enough to fill the present day with joy,
And overspread the future years with hope,
Our beautiful and quiet home, enriched
Already with a Stranger whom we love
Deeply, a Stranger of our Father's House,
A never-resting Pilgrim of the Sea,
Who finds at last an hour to his content
Beneath our roof. And others whom we love
Will seek us also, Sisters of our hearts,
And One, like them, a Brother of our hearts,
Philosopher and Poet, in whose sight
These Mountains will rejoice with open joy.
— Such is our wealth; O Vale of Peace, we are
And must be, with God's will, a happy Band.

    Yet 'tis not to enjoy that we exist,
For that end only; something must be done.
I must not walk in unreproved delight
These narrow bounds, and think of nothing more,
No duty that looks further, and no care.
Each Being has his office, lowly some
And common, yet all worthy if fulfilled
With zeal, acknowledgment that with the gift
Keeps pace a harvest answering to the seed —
Of ill-advised Ambition and of Pride
I would stand clear, but yet to me I feel
That an internal brightness is vouchsafed
That must not die, that must not pass away.

Why does this inward lustre fondly seek,
And gladly blend with outward fellowship?
Why do *they* shine around me whom I love?
Why do they teach me whom I thus revere?
Strange question, yet it answers not itself.
That humble Roof embowered among the trees,
That calm fire-side, it is not even in them,
Blest as they are, to furnish a reply,
That satisfies and ends in perfect rest.
Possessions have I that are solely mine,
Something within which yet is shared by none,
Not even the nearest to me and most dear,
Something which power and effort may impart,
I would impart it, I would spread it wide,
Immortal in the world which is to come.
Forgive me if I add another claim,
And would not wholly perish even in this,
Lie down and be forgotten in the dust,
I and the modest Partners of my days
Making a silent company in death;
Love, Knowledge, all my manifold delights
All buried with me without monument
Or profit unto any but ourselves.
It must not be, if I, divinely taught,
Be privileged to speak as I have felt
Of what in man is human or divine.

    While yet an innocent Little-one, with a heart
That doubtless wanted not its tender moods,
I breathed (for this I better recollect)
Among wild appetites and blind desires,
Motions of savage instinct my delight
And exaltation. Nothing at that time
So welcome, no temptation half so dear
As that which urged me to a daring feat.
Deep pools, tall trees, black chasms, and dizzy crags,
And tottering towers; I loved to stand and read
Their looks forbidding, read and disobey,

Sometimes in act, and evermore in thought.
With impulses that scarcely were by these
Surpassed in strength, I heard of danger, met
Or sought with courage; enterprize forlorn
By one, sole keeper of his own intent,
Or by a resolute few who for the sake
Of glory, fronted multitudes in arms.
Yea to this hour I cannot read a tale
Of two brave Vessels matched in deadly fight,
And fighting to the death, but I am pleased
More than a wise man ought to be. I wish,
Fret, burn, and struggle, and in soul am there;
But me hath Nature tamed, and bade to seek
For other agitations, or be calm;
Hath dealt with me as with a turbulent Stream,
Some nursling of the mountains, whom she leads
Through quiet meadows, after he has learnt
His strength, and had his triumph and his joy,
His desperate course of tumult and of glee.
That which in stealth by Nature was performed
Hath Reason sanctioned. Her deliberate Voice
Hath said, "Be mild and cleave to gentle things,
Thy glory and thy happiness be there.
Nor fear, though thou confide in me, a want
Of aspirations that *have* been, of foes
To wrestle with, and victory to complete,
Bounds to be leapt, darkness to be explored,
All that inflamed thy infant heart, the love,
The longing, the contempt, the undaunted quest,
All shall survive — though changed their office, all
Shall live, — it is not in their power to die."

Then farewell to the Warrior's schemes, farewell
The forwardness of Soul which looks that way
Upon a less incitement than the cause
Of Liberty endangered, and farewell
That other hope, long mine, the hope to fill
The heroic trumpet with the Muse's breath!

Yet in this peaceful Vale we will not spend
Unheard-of days, though loving peaceful thoughts.
A Voice shall speak, and what will be the Theme?
On Man on Nature and on human life
Musing in solitude, from time to time
I feel sweet passions traversing my soul
Like Music, unto these, where'er I may
I would give utterance in numerous verse:
Of truth, of grandeur, beauty love and hope
Hope for this earth and hope beyond the grave
Of virtue and of intellectual power
Of blessed consolations in distress
Of joy in widest commonalty spread
Of the individual mind that keeps its own
Inviolate retirement, and consists
With being limitless, the one great Life
I sing, fit audience let me find though few —
Fit audience find tho' few, thus pray'd the Bard
Holiest of Men. Urania I shall need
Thy guidance or a greater Muse if such
Descend to earth or dwell in highest heaven
For I must tread on shadowy ground must sink
Deep, and aloft ascending breathe in worlds
To which the Heaven of Heavens is but a veil.
All strength, all terror, single or in bands
That ever was put forth in personal forms,
Jehovah with his thunder and the quire
Of shouting Angels and the empyreal thrones
I pass them unalarmed. The darkest Pit
Of the profoundest Hell and chaos, night,
Nor aught of blinder vacancy scoop'd out
By help of dreams can breed such fear and awe
As fall upon us often when we look
Into our minds, into the Mind of Man,
My haunt and the main region of my song.
Beauty whose living home is the green earth
Surpassing the most fair ideal Forms
Which craft of delicate spirits hath compos'd

From earth's materials waits upon my steps
Pitches her tents before me where I move
An hourly Neighbour. Paradise and groves
Elysian, fortunate (islands) fields like those
In the deep ocean wherefore should they be
A History or but a dream, when minds
Once wedded to this outward frame of things
In love find these the growth of common day.
I, long before the blessed hour arrives,
Would sing in solitude the spousal verse
Of this great consummation, would proclaim
Speaking of nothing more than what we are
How exquisitely the individual Mind,
And the progressive powers perhaps no less
Of the whole species to the external world
Is fitted, and how exquisitely too,
Theme this but little heard of among men,
The external world is fitted to the mind
And the creation, (by no lower name
Can it be call'd), which they with blended might
Accomplish: this is my great argument
Such grateful foregoing if I oft
Must turn elsewhere and travel near the tribes
And fellowships of men and see ill sights
Of passions ravenous from each other's rage
Must hear humanity in fields and groves
Pipe solitary anguish or must hang
Brooding above the fierce confederate storm
Of Sorrow barricadoed evermore
Within the walls of Cities, may these sounds
Have their authentic comment that even these
Hearing, I be not heartless or forlorn.
Come thou prophetic Spirit, Soul of Man
Thou human Soul of the wide earth that hast
Thy metropolitan Temple in the hearts
Of mighty Poets, unto me vouchsafe
Thy guidance, teach me to discern and part
Inherent things from casual, what is fixed

From fleeting, that my verse may live and be
Even as a light hung up in heaven to chear
Mankind in times to come. And if with this
I blend more lowly matter with the thing
Contemplated describe the mind and man
Contemplating and who and what he was
The transitory Being that beheld
This vision when and where and how he lived
With all his little realties of life
Be not the labour useless: if such theme
With highest things may mingle, then, great God,
Thou who art breath and being, way and guide
And power and understanding, may my life
Express the image of a better time
More wise desires and simple manners; nurse
My heart in genuine freedom; all pure thoughts
Be with me and uphold me to the end.

Ode to a Nightingale

JOHN KEATS

(1795–1821)

This poem, written in 1819 and first published in the famous 1820 volume of Keats's poems, dramatizes the weakness of the Romantic Visionary Artist-Poet. The Vision is reduced to the status of illusory dream by the poet's discovery that the attempt to realize the vision and to fixate it results only in the desire for death.

1.

My heart aches, and a drowsy numbness pains
   My sense, as though of hemlock I had drunk,
Or emptied some dull opiate to the drains
   One minute past, and Lethe-wards had sunk:
'Tis not through envy of thy happy lot,
   But being too happy in thine happiness, —
     That thou, light-winged Dryad of the trees,
     In some melodious plot
Of beechen green, and shadows numberless,
   Singest of summer in full-throated ease,

2.

O, for a draught of vintage! that hath been
  Cool'd a long age in the deep-delved earth,
Tasting of Flora and the country green,
  Dance, and Provençal song, and sunburnt mirth!
O for a beaker full of the warm South,
  Full of the true, the blushful Hippocrene,
    With beaded bubbles winking at the brim,
      And purple-stained mouth;
  That I might drink, and leave the world unseen,
  And with thee fade away into the forest dim:

3.

Fade far away, dissolve, and quite forget
  What thou among the leaves hast never known,
The weariness, the fever, and the fret
  Here, where men sit and hear each other groan;
Where palsy shakes a few, sad, last gray hairs,
  Where youth grows pale, and spectre-thin, and dies;
    Where but to think is to be full of sorrow
      And leaden-eyed despairs,
  Where Beauty cannot keep her lustrous eyes,
  Or new Love pine at them beyond to-morrow.

4.

Away! away! for I will fly to thee,
  Not charioted by Bacchus and his pards,
But on the viewless wings of Poesy,
  Though the dull brain perplexes and retards:
Already with thee! tender is the night,
  And haply the Queen-Moon is on her throne,
    Cluster'd around by all her starry Fays;
      But here there is no light,
  Save what from heaven is with the breezes blown
  Through verdurous glooms and winding mossy ways.

5.

I cannot see what flowers are at my feet,
  Nor what soft incense hangs upon the boughs,

But, in embalmed darkness, guess each sweet
    Wherewith the seasonable month endows
The grass, the thicket, and the fruit-tree wild;
    White hawthorn, and the pastoral eglantine;
        Fast fading violets cover'd up in leaves;
            And mid-May's eldest child,
    The coming musk-rose, full of dewy wine,
        The murmurous haunt of flies on summer eves.

6.

Darkling I listen; and, for many a time
    I have been half in love with easeful Death,
Call'd him soft names in many a mused rhyme,
    To take into the air my quiet breath;
Now more than ever seems it rich to die,
    To cease upon the midnight with no pain,
        While thou art pouring forth thy soul abroad
            In such an ecstasy!
    Still wouldst thou sing, and I have ears in vain —
        To thy high requiem become a sod.

7.

Thou wast not born for death, immortal Bird!
    No hungry generations tread thee down;
The voice I hear this passing night was heard
    In ancient days by emperor and clown:
Perhaps the self-same song that found a path
    Through the sad heart of Ruth, when, sick for home,
        She stood in tears amid the alien corn;
            The same that oft-times hath
    Charm'd magic casements, opening on the foam
        Of perilous seas, in faery lands forlorn.

8.

Forlorn! the very word is like a bell
    To toll me back from thee to my sole self!
Adieu! the fancy cannot cheat so well
    As she is fam'd to do, deceiving elf.
Adieu! adieu! thy plaintive anthem fades

Past the near meadows, over the still stream,
Up the hill-side; and now 'tis buried deep
In the next valley-glades:
Was it a vision, or a waking dream?
Fled is that music: — Do I wake or sleep?

NOTE ON ILLUSTRATIONS: GROUP I
Numbers 1 to 16

The first two pictures in this group are emblems of the problem posed by the entry into the first stage of Romanticism, which in the Introduction I have called Analogism. Friedrich is little known in this country, but in Germany he is recognized as one of the great Romantic painters, a judgment accepted by a number of English critics at the time of the Council of Europe Romanticism exhibition held in London in 1959. According to the artist's own account, The Cross in the Mountains signifies the sunset of Christianity, while the second picture illustrates both the Romantic isolation from society and the Analogistic confrontation with a mysterious and incomprehensible natural world. The Ingres of the same year displays the Romantic's intense concern with the appearance of the phenomenal world. The Constable and Corot show the same interest, but combined with a symbolization, through the loose "impressionistic" technique, of the perceiving Self. This is further brought out in the extreme symmetry of Runge's Morning, while Number 7 shows, as with Ingres, a self-conscious reference to and use of early sixteenth-century idioms. Again, Runge symbolizes the Self by employing in both paintings a highly personal mythology. Géricault, on the other hand, is a Byron among painters, who, like so many Analogistic poets and artists, revived Baroque formal concepts to revivify the flaccid forms of the late Enlightenment.

Numbers 9 to 12 show ·various uses of the Classical idiom, for it is a great, though common, error to think of Romantic architects as exclusively Gothic revivalists. Soane had designed in the very late Enlightenment mode of absolutely pure and scarcely articulated geo-

metric forms, but with his design for the Bank of England he began to develop an extraordinary personal idiom, so violently expressive of a unique mode of architectural imagination and so entirely without followers that one is half tempted to think of him as a kind of Byronic architect, utterly isolated and alienated in his vision. The equivalent of realism in literature and painting was achieved by the historicizing architect in his extreme correctness of the detail of past idioms, whether Classic or Gothic; at the same time, however, these details were manipulated in such a way as to continue the theme of Soane, the symbolization of a unique Self. Schinkel could design equally well in either idiom (Numbers 10 and 14 through 16), but he typically combines archaeological correctness with a subtle manipulation of the dominating forms; and in this he is like the later Soane, Nash, and Smirke (Numbers 9, 11 and 12). Nash's "Muslim" Brighton pavilion, the ancestor of all amusement parks, presents another Romantic architectural theme, a formal layout from one tradition (here, the Renaissance) and a derivation of ornamental details from another. The Mausoleum by Schinkel is included to indicate that the manipulation of traditional idioms was not a consequence of ineptitude or ignorance, but a means of solving a cultural problem, the symbolization of the Self. It is similar in intention to the effort Keats made to revivify classical mythology.

1. Caspar David Friedrich, *The Cross in the Mountains* (Tetschen Altar-Piece), 1808.

2. Caspar David Friedrich, *Monk on the Shore,* 1808.

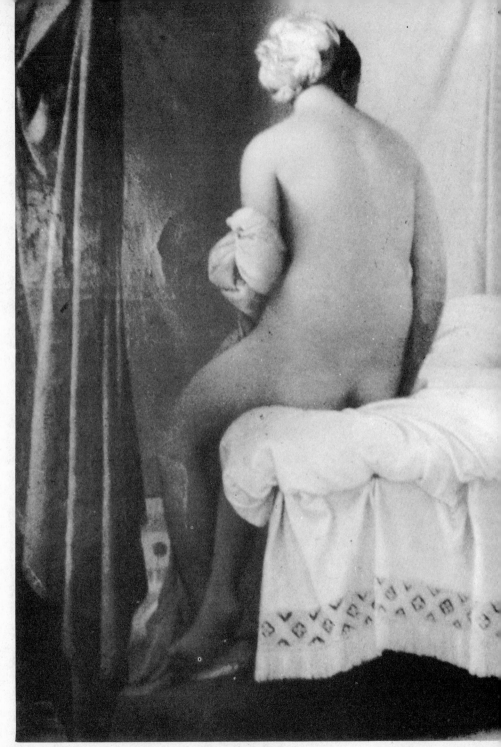

3. Jean Auguste Dominique Ingres, *Woman Bathing*, 1808.

4. John Constable,
Weymouth Bay, 1825(?).

5. Philip Otto Runge,
Morning, 1809.

6. Jean Baptiste Camille Corot, *The Bridge at Narni*, 1826.

7. Philip Otto Runge, *Rest on the Flight to Egypt*, 1805–1806.

8. Théodore Géricault, *Riderless Race at Rome*, 1817.

9. Sir John Soane, *The Bank of England*, 1788–1808.

10. Karl Friedrich Schinkel, *Sketch for a Hall for Orianda Castle.*

11. John Nash, *Carlton House Terrace,* London, 1827.

12. Robert Smirke and Sir John Soane, *British Museum*, London, 1823–1847.

13. John Nash, *Royal Pavilion*, Brighton, 1815–1823.

14. Karl Friedrich Schinkel, *Project for a Gothic Cathedral*.

15. Karl Friedrich Schinkel,
Project for a Mausoleum.

16. Karl Friedrich Schinkel,
Project for a Mausoleum,
interior.

The weakness of Analogism as a solution to the problem of the value of existence arose from its quietism: it offered a mode of experiencing value, but no way of introducing value into the world. The full valuelessness of the world now became inescapably apparent. Since Analogism had revealed value as a mode of experience, it was apparent that the source of value lay in the Self. Analogism had made its mode of experiencing value into evidence of the Divine Ground of the universe. It seemed to follow, therefore, that the Self was grounded in the Divine. And with that authority, the Self had a basis for action; its task was to introduce value into the world by heroic world-redemption.

The World as Will and Representation

ARTHUR SCHOPENHAUER

(1788–1860)

This philosophical masterpiece, published in 1819, is one of the most bracing and invigorating discourses ever written. Schopenhauer's hatred for Hegel was a hatred for the illusions and dangers and moral uselessness of Analogism, which Keats was discovering at the same time. Schopenhauer drained the Object of all value; its only value lay in its potentiality to serve as material for the Will, the Unconscious, to wreak itself on. But since the Will was also valueless, being but an aspect of the world, one would think that all value had been excluded from existence. Surprisingly, and perhaps illegitimately, Schopenhauer does not come to this conclusion. The Will can be denied — that is, its value and its reality can be denied — by the human being freed from illusions about the value of Will and World; that is, by the Self. Schopenhauer solves much, but leaves an infinitude of new problems to be faced by Nietzsche.

.   .   .   .

The will, which, considered purely in itself, is without knowledge, and is merely a blind incessant impulse, as we see it appear in unorganised and vegetable nature and their laws, and also in the vegetative part of our own life, receives through the addition of the world as idea, which is developed in subjection to it, the knowledge of its own willing and of what it is that it wills. And this is nothing else than the world as idea, life, precisely as it exists. Therefore we called the phenomenal world the mirror of the will, its objectivity. And since what the will wills is always life, just because life is nothing but the representation of that willing for the idea, it is all one and a mere pleonism if, instead of simply saying "the will," we say, "the will to live."

Will is the thing-in-itself, the inner content, the essence of the world. Life, the visible world, the phenomenon, is only the mirror of the will. Therefore life accompanies the will as inseparably as the shadow accompanies the body; and if will exists, so will life, the world, exist. Life is, therefore, assured to the will to live; and so long as we are filled with the will to live we need have no fear for our existence, even in the presence of death. It is true we see the individual come into being and pass away; but the individual is only phenomenal, exists only for the knowledge which is bound to the principle of sufficient reason, to the *principium individuationis*. Certainly, for this kind of knowledge, the individual receives his life as a gift, rises out of nothing, then suffers the loss of this gift through death, and returns again to nothing. But we desire to consider life philosophically, *i.e.,* according to its Ideas, and in this sphere we shall find that neither the will, the thing-in-itself in all phenomena, nor the subject of knowing, that which perceives all phenomena, is affected at all by birth or by death. Birth and death belong merely to the phenomenon of will, thus to life; and it is essential to this to exhibit itself in individuals which come into being and pass away, as fleeting phenomena appearing in the form of time — phenomena of that which in itself knows no time, but must exhibit itself precisely in the way we have said, in order to objectify its peculiar nature. Birth and death belong in like manner to life, and hold the balance as reciprocal conditions of each other, or, if one likes the expression, as poles of the whole phenomenon of life. The wisest of all mythologies, the Indian, expresses this by giving to the very god that symbolises destruction, death (as Brahma, the most sinful and the lowest god of the Trimurti, symbolises generation, coming into being, and Vishnu maintaining or preserving), by giving, I say, to Siva as an attribute not only the necklace of skulls, but also the lingam, the symbol of generation, which appears here as the counterpart of death, thus signifying that generation and death are essentially correlatives, which reciprocally neutralise and annul each other. It was precisely the same sentiment that led the Greeks and Romans to adorn their costly sarcophagi, just as we see them now, with feasts, dances, marriages, the chase, fights of wild beasts, bacchanalians, &c.; thus with representations of the full ardour of life, which they place before us not only in such revels and sports, but also in sensual groups, and even go so far as to represent the sexual intercourse of satyrs and goats. Clearly the aim was to point in the most impressive manner away from the death of the mourned individual to the immortal life of nature, and thus to indicate, though without abstract knowledge, that the whole of nature is the phenomenon and also the fulfilment of the will to live. The form of this phenomenon is time, space, and causality, and by means of these individuation, which carries with it that the individual must come into being and pass away. But this no more affects the will to live, of whose manifestation the individual is, as it were, only a particular example or specimen, than the death of an individual injures the whole of nature. For it is not the individual, but only the species that Nature cares for, and for the preservation of which she so earnestly strives, providing for it with the utmost prodigality through the vast surplus of the seed and the great strength of the fructifying impulse. The individual, on the contrary, neither has nor can have any value for Nature, for her kingdom is infinite time and infinite space, and in these infinite multiplicity of possible individuals. Therefore she is always ready to let the individual fall, and hence it is not only exposed to destruction in a thousand ways by the most insignificant accident, but originally destined for it, and conducted towards it by Nature herself from the moment it has served its end of maintaining the species. Thus Nature naïvely expresses the great truth that only the Ideas, not the individuals, have, properly speaking, reality, *i.e.*, are complete objectivity of the will. Now, since man is Nature itself, and indeed Nature at the highest grade of its self-consciousness, but Nature is only the objectified will to live, the man who has comprehended and retained this point of view may well console himself, when contemplating his own death and that of his friends, by turning his eyes to the immortal life of Nature, which he himself is. This is the significance of Siva with the lingam, and of those ancient sarcophagi with their pictures of glowing life, which say to the mourning beholder, *Natura non contristatur*.

.   .   .

Apart from the fact that the will as the true thing-in-itself is actually original and independent, and that the feeling of its originality and absoluteness must accompany its acts in self-consciousness, though here they are already determined, there arises the illusion of an empirical freedom of the will (instead of the transcendental freedom which alone is to be attributed to it), and thus a freedom of its particular actions, from the attitude of the intellect towards the will. The intellect knows the conclusions of the will only *a posteriori* and empirically; therefore when a choice is presented, it has no data as to how the will is to decide. For the intelligible character, by virtue of which, when motives are given, only *one* decision is possible and is therefore necessary, does not come within the knowledge of the intellect, but merely the empirical character is known to it through the succession of its particular acts. Therefore it seems to the intellect that in a given case two opposite decisions are possible for the will. But this is just the same thing as if we were to say of a perpendicular beam that has lost its balance, and is hesitating which way to fall, "It can fall either to the right hand or the left." This *can* has merely a subjective significance, and really means "as far as the data known to us are concerned." Objectively, the direction of the fall is necessarily determined as soon as the equilibrium is lost. Accordingly, the decision of one's own will is undetermined only to the beholder, one's own intellect, and thus merely relatively and subjectively for the subject of knowing. In itself and objectively, on the other hand, in every choice presented to it, its decision is at once determined and necessary. But this determination only comes into consciousness through the decision that follows upon it. Indeed, we receive an empirical proof of this when any difficult and important choice lies before us, but only under a condition which is not yet present, but merely hoped for, so that in the meanwhile we can do nothing, but must remain passive. Now we consider how we shall decide when the circumstances occur that will give us a free activity and choice. Generally the foresight of rational deliberation recommends one decision, while direct inclination leans rather to the other. So long as we are compelled to remain passive, the side of reason seems to wish to keep the upper-hand; but we see before-hand how strongly the other side will influence us when the opportunity for action arises. Till then we are eagerly concerned to place the motives on both sides in the clearest light, by calm meditation on the *pro et contra,* so that every motive may exert its full influence upon the will when the time arrives, and it may not be misled by a mistake on the part of the intellect to decide otherwise than it would have done if all the motives had their due influence upon it. But this distinct unfolding of the motives on both sides is all that the intellect can do to assist the choice. It awaits the real decision just as passively and with the same intense curiosity as if it were that of a foreign will. Therefore from its point of view both decisions must seem to it equally possible; and this is just the illusion of the empirical freedom of the will. Certainly the decision enters the sphere of the intellect altogether empirically, as the final conclusion of the matter; but yet it proceeded from the inner nature, the intelligible character, of the individual will in its conflict with given motives, and therefore with complete necessity. The intellect can do nothing more than bring out clearly and fully the nature of the motives; it cannot determine the will itself; for the will is quite inaccessible to it, and, as we have seen, cannot be investigated.

.　　　.　　　.

As the result of the whole of this discussion of the freedom of the will and what relates to it, we find that although the will may, in itself and apart from the phenomenon, be called free and even omnipotent, yet in its particular phenomena enlightened by knowledge, as in men and brutes, it is determined by motives to which the special character regularly and necessarily responds, and always in the same way. We see that because of the possession on his part of abstract or rational knowledge, man, as distinguished from the brutes, has a *choice,* which only makes him the scene of the conflict of his motives, without withdrawing him from their control. This choice is therefore certainly the condition of the possibility of the complete expression of the individual character, but is by no means to be regarded as freedom of the particular volition, *i.e.,* independence of the law of causality, the necessity of which extends to man as to every other phenomenon. Thus the difference between human volition and that of the brutes, which is introduced by reason or knowledge through concepts, extends to the point we have

indicated, and no farther. But, what is quite a different thing, there may
arise a phenomenon of the human will which is quite impossible in
the brute creation, if man altogether lays aside the knowledge of particular things as such which is subordinate to the principle of sufficient
reason, and by means of his knowledge of the Ideas sees through the
principium individuationis. Then an actual appearance of the real
freedom of the will as a thing-in-itself is possible, by which the
phenomenon comes into a sort of contradiction with itself, as is indicated by the word self-renunciation; and, finally, the "in-itself" of its
nature suppresses itself. But this, the one, real, and direct expression of
the freedom of the will in itself in the phenomenon, cannot be distinctly
explained here, but will form the subject of the concluding part of our
work.

.   .   .

First of all, I wish the reader to recall the passage with which we
closed the Second Book, — a passage occasioned by the question, which
met us then, as to the end and aim of the will. Instead of the answer to
this question, it appeared clearly before us how, in all the grades of
its manifestation, from the lowest to the highest, the will dispenses
altogether with a final goal and aim. It always strives, for striving is
its sole nature, which no attained goal can put an end to. Therefore it
is not susceptible of any final satisfaction, but can only be restrained by
hindrances, while in itself it goes on for ever. We see this in the simplest
of all natural phenomena, gravity, which does not cease to strive and
press towards a mathematical centre to reach which would be the annihilation both of itself and matter, and would not cease even if the whole
universe were already rolled into one ball. We see it in the other simple
natural phenomena. A solid tends towards fluidity either by melting or
dissolving, for only so will its chemical forces be free; rigidity is the
imprisonment in which it is held by cold. The fluid tends towards the
gaseous state, into which it passes at once as soon as all pressure is
removed from it. No body is without relationship, *i.e.,* without tendency
or without desire and longing, as Jakob Böhm would say. Electricity
transmits its inner self-repulsion to infinity, though the mass of the earth
absorbs the effect. Galvanism is certainly, so long as the pile is working,
an aimless, unceasingly repeated act of repulsion and attraction. The
existence of the plant is just such a restless, never satisfied striving, a

ceaseless tendency through ever-ascending forms, till the end, the seed, becomes a new starting-point; and this repeated *ad infinitum* — nowhere an end, nowhere a final satisfaction, nowhere a resting-place. It will also be remembered, from the Second Book, that the multitude of natural forces and organised forms everywhere strive with each other for the matter in which they desire to appear, for each of them only possesses what it has wrested from the others; and thus a constant internecine war is waged, from which, for the most part, arises the resistance through which that striving, which constitutes the inner nature of everything, is at all points hindered; struggles in vain, yet, from its nature, cannot leave off; toils on laboriously till this phenomenon dies, when others eagerly seize its place and its matter.

We have long since recognised this striving, which constitutes the kernel and in-itself of everything, as identical with that which in us, where it manifests itself most distinctly in the light of the fullest consciousness, is called *will*. Its hindrance through an obstacle which places itself between it and its temporary aim we call *suffering*, and, on the other hand, its attainment of the end satisfaction, well-being, happiness. We may also transfer this terminology to the phenomena of the unconscious world, for though weaker in degree, they are identical in nature. Then we see them involved in constant suffering, and without any continuing happiness. For all effort springs from defect — from discontent with one's estate — is thus suffering so long as it is not satisfied; but no satisfaction is lasting, rather it is always merely the starting-point of a new effort. The striving we see everywhere hindered in many ways, everywhere in conflict, and therefore always under the form of suffering. Thus, if there is no final end of striving, there is no measure and end of suffering.

But what we only discover in unconscious Nature by sharpened observation, and with an effort, presents itself distinctly to us in the intelligent world in the life of animals, whose constant suffering is easily proved. But without lingering over these intermediate grades, we shall turn to the life of man, in which all this appears with the greatest distinctness, illuminated by the clearest knowledge; for as the phenomenon of will becomes more complete, the suffering also becomes more and more apparent. In the plant there is as yet no sensibility, and therefore no pain. A certain very small degree of suffering is experienced by the lowest species of animal life — infusoria and radiata; even in insects the capacity to feel and suffer is still limited. It first appears in a high degree

with the complete nervous system of vertebrate animals, and always in a
higher degree the more intelligence develops. Thus, in proportion as
knowledge attains to distinctness, as consciousness ascends, pain also
increases, and therefore reaches its highest degree in man. And then,
again, the more distinctly a man knows, the more intelligent he is, the
more pain he has; the man who is gifted with genius suffers most of all.
In this sense, that is, with reference to the degree of knowledge in general, not mere abstract rational knowledge, I understand and use here
that saying of the Preacher: *Qui auget scientiam, auget et dolorem.*
That philosophical painter or painting philosopher, Tischbein, has
very beautifully expressed the accurate relation between the degree of
consciousness and that of suffering by exhibiting it in a visible and clear
form in a drawing. The upper half of his drawing represents women
whose children have been stolen, and who in different groups and attitudes, express in many ways deep maternal pain, anguish, and despair.
The lower half of the drawing represents sheep whose lambs have been
taken away. They are arranged and grouped in precisely the same way;
so that every human head, every human attitude of the upper half, has
below a brute head and attitude corresponding to it. Thus we see distinctly how the pain which is possible in the dull brute consciousness is
related to the violent grief, which only becomes possible through
distinctness of knowledge and clearness of consciousness.

We desire to consider in this way, in *human existence,* the inner and
essential destiny of will. Every one will easily recognise that same destiny
expressed in various degrees in the life of the brutes, only more weakly,
and may also convince himself to his own satisfaction, from the suffering
animal world, *how essential to all life is suffering.*

·   ·   ·

For the most part, however, we close our minds against the knowledge,
which may be compared to a bitter medicine, that suffering is essential
to life, and therefore does not flow in upon us from without, but that
every one carries about with him its perennial source in his own heart.
We rather seek constantly for an external particular cause, as it were,
a pretext for the pain which never leaves us, just as the free man makes
himself an idol, in order to have a master. For we unweariedly strive from
wish to wish; and although every satisfaction, however much it promised,
when attained fails to satisfy us, but for the most part comes presently

to be an error of which we are ashamed, yet we do not see that we draw water with the sieve of the Danaides, but ever hasten to new desires. Thus it either goes on for ever, or, what is more rare and presupposes a certain strength of character, till we reach a wish which is not satisfied and yet cannot be given up. In that case we have, as it were, found what we sought, something that we can always blame, instead of our own nature, as the source of our suffering. And thus, although we are now at variance with our fate, we are reconciled to our existence, for the knowledge is again put far from us that suffering is essential to this existence itself, and true satisfaction impossible. The result of this form of development is a somewhat melancholy disposition, the constant endurance of a single great pain, and the contempt for all lesser sorrows or joys that proceeds from it; consequently an already nobler phenomenon than that constant seizing upon ever-new forms of illusion, which is much more common.

All satisfaction, or what is commonly called happiness, is always really and essentially only *negative,* and never positive. It is not an original gratification coming to us of itself, but must always be the satisfaction of a wish. The wish, *i.e.,* some want, is the condition which precedes every pleasure. But with the satisfaction the wish and therefore the pleasure cease. Thus the satisfaction or the pleasing can never be more than the deliverance from a pain, from a want; for such is not only every actual, open sorrow, but every desire, the importunity of which disturbs our peace, and, indeed, the deadening ennui also that makes life a burden to us. It is, however, so hard to attain or achieve anything; difficulties and troubles without end are opposed to every purpose, and at every step hindrances accumulate. But when finally everything is overcome and attained, nothing can ever be gained but deliverance from some sorrow or desire, so that we find ourselves just in the same position as we occupied before this sorrow or desire appeared. All that is even directly given us is merely the want, *i.e.,* the pain. The satisfaction and the pleasure we can only know indirectly through the remembrance of the preceding suffering and want, which ceases with its appearance. Hence it arises that we are not properly conscious of the blessings and advantages we actually possess, nor do we prize them, but think of them merely as a matter of course, for they gratify us only negatively by restraining suffering. Only when we have lost them do we become sensible of their value; for the want, the privation, the sorrow, is the positive, communicating itself directly to us. Thus also we are pleased by the remembrance of past need, sickness, want, and such like, because this is the only means of enjoying the present blessings. And, further, it cannot be denied that in this respect, and from this standpoint of egoism, which is the form of the will to live, the sight or the description of the sufferings of others affords us satisfaction and pleasure. . . .

That all happiness is only of a negative not a positive nature, that just on this account it cannot be lasting satisfaction and gratification, but merely delivers us from some pain or want which must be followed either by a new pain, or by languor, empty longing, and ennui; this finds support in art, that true mirror of the world and life, and especially in poetry. Every epic and dramatic poem can only represent a struggle, an effort, and fight for happiness, never enduring and complete happiness itself. It conducts its heroes through a thousand difficulties and dangers to the goal; as soon as this is reached, it hastens to let the curtain fall; for now there would remain nothing for it to do but to show that the glittering goal in which the hero expected to find happiness had only disappointed him, and that after its attainment he was no better off than before. Because a genuine enduring happiness is not possible, it cannot be the subject of art. Certainly the aim of the idyll is the description of such a happiness, but one also sees that the idyll as such cannot continue. The poet always finds that it either becomes epical in his hands, and in this case it is a very insignificant epic, made up of trifling sorrows, trifling delights, and trifling efforts — this is the commonest case — or else it becomes a merely descriptive poem, describing the beauty of nature, i.e., pure knowing free from will, which certainly, as a matter of fact, is the only pure happiness, which is neither preceded by suffering or want, nor necessarily followed by repentance, sorrow, emptiness, or satiety; but this happiness cannot fill the whole life, but is only possible at moments. What we see in poetry we find again in music; in the melodies of which we have recognised the universal expression of the inmost history of the self-conscious will, the most secret life, longing, suffering, and delight; the ebb and flow of the human heart. Melody is always a deviation from the keynote through a thousand capricious wanderings, even to the most painful discord, and then a final return to the keynote which expresses the satisfaction and appeasing of the will, but with which nothing more can then be done, and the continuance of which any longer would only be a wearisome and unmeaning monotony corresponding to ennui.

All that we intend to bring out clearly through these investigations, the impossibility of attaining lasting satisfaction and the negative nature of all happiness, finds its explanation in what is shown at the conclusion of the Second Book: that the will, of which human life, like every phenomenon, is the objectification, is a striving without aim or end. We find the stamp of this endlessness imprinted upon all the parts of its whole manifestation, from its most universal form, endless time and space, up to the most perfect of all phenomena, the life and efforts of man. We may theoretically assume three extremes of human life, and treat them as elements of actual human life. First, the powerful will, the strong passions (Radscha-Guna). It appears in great historical characters; it is described in the epic and the drama. But it can also show itself in the little world, for the size of the objects is measured here by the degree in which they influence the will, not according to their external relations. Secondly, pure knowing, the comprehension of the Ideas, conditioned by the freeing of knowledge from the service of will: the life of genius (Satwa-Guna). Thirdly and lastly, the greatest lethargy of the will, and also of the knowledge attaching to it, empty longing, life-benumbing languor (Tama-Guna). The life of the individual, far from becoming permanently fixed in one of these extremes, seldom touches any of them, and is for the most part only a weak and wavering approach to one or the other side, a needy desiring of trifling objects, constantly recurring, and so escaping ennui. It is really incredible how meaningless and void of significance when looked at from without, how dull and unenlightened by intellect when felt from within, is the course of the life of the great majority of men. It is a weary longing and complaining, a dreamlike staggering through the four ages of life to death, accompanied by a series of trivial thoughts. Such men are like clockwork, which is wound up, and goes it knows not why; and every time a man is begotten and born, the clock of human life is wound up anew, to repeat the same old piece it has played innumerable times before, passage after passage, measure after measure, with insignificant variations. Every individual, every human being and his course of life, is but another short dream of the endless spirit of nature, of the persistent will to live; is only another fleeting form, which it carelessly sketches on its infinite page, space and time; allows to remain for a time so short that it vanishes into nothing in comparison with these, and then obliterates to make new room. And yet, and here lies the serious side of life, every one of these fleeting forms, these empty fancies, must be paid for by the whole will to live, in all its activity, with many and deep sufferings, and finally with a bitter death, long feared and coming at last. This is why the sight of a corpse makes us suddenly so serious.

The life of every individual, if we survey it as a whole and in general, and only lay stress upon its most significant features, is really always a tragedy, but gone through in detail, it has the character of a comedy. For the deeds and vexations of the day, the restless irritation of the moment, the desires and fears of the week, the mishaps of every hour, are all through chance, which is ever bent upon some jest, scenes of a comedy. But the never-satisfied wishes, the frustrated efforts, the hopes unmercifully crushed by fate, the unfortunate errors of the whole life, with increasing suffering and death at the end, are always a tragedy. Thus, as if fate would add derision to the misery of our existence, our life must contain all the woes of tragedy, and yet we cannot even assert the dignity of tragic characters, but in the broad detail of life must inevitably be the foolish characters of a comedy.

If we have so far convinced ourselves *a priori*, by the most general consideration, by investigation of the primary and elemental features of human life, that in its whole plan it is capable of no true blessedness, but is in its very nature suffering in various forms, and throughout a state of misery, we might now awaken this conviction much more vividly within us if, proceeding more *a posteriori*, we were to turn to more definite instances, call up pictures to the fancy, and illustrate by examples the unspeakable misery which experience and history present, wherever one may look and in whatever direction one may seek. But the chapter would have no end, and would carry us far from the standpoint of the universal, which is essential to philosophy; and, moreover, such a description might easily be taken for a mere declamation on human misery, such as has often been given, and, as such, might be charged with one-sidedness, because it started from particular facts. From such a reproach and suspicion our perfectly cold and philosophical investigation of the inevitable suffering which is founded in the nature of life is free, for it starts from the universal and is conducted *a priori*. But confirmation *a posteriori* is everywhere easily obtained. Every one who has awakened from the first dream of youth, who has considered his own experience and that of others, who has studied himself in life, in the history of the past and of his own time, and finally in the works of the great poets, will, if his judgment is not paralysed by some indelibly imprinted prejudice, certainly arrive at the conclusion that this human world is the kingdom of chance and error, which rule without mercy in great things and in small, and along with which folly and wickedness also wield the scourge. Hence it arises that everything better only struggles through with difficulty; what is noble and wise seldom attains to expression, becomes effective and claims attention, but the absurd and the perverse in the sphere of thought, the dull and tasteless in the sphere of art, the wicked and deceitful in the sphere of action, really assert a supremacy, only disturbed by short interruptions. On the other hand, everything that is excellent is always a mere exception, one case in millions, and therefore, if it presents itself in a lasting work, this, when it has outlived the enmity of its contemporaries, exists in isolation, is preserved like a meteoric stone, sprung from an order of things different from that which prevails here. But as far as the life of the individual is concerned, every biography is the history of suffering, for every life is, as a rule, a continual series of great and small misfortunes, which each one conceals as much as possible, because he knows that others can seldom feel sympathy or compassion, but almost always satisfaction at the sight of the woes from which they are themselves for the moment exempt. But perhaps at the end of life, if a man is sincere and in full possession of his faculties, he will never wish to have it to live over again, but rather than this, he will much prefer absolute annihilation. The essential content of the famous soliloquy in "Hamlet" is briefly this: Our state is so wretched that absolute annihilation would be decidedly preferable. If suicide really offered us this, so that the alternative "to be or not to be," in the full sense of the word, was placed before us, then it would be unconditionally to be chosen as "a consummation devoutly to be wished." But there is something in us which tells us that this is not the case: suicide is not the end; death is not absolute annihilation. In like manner, what was said by the father of history has not since him been contradicted, that no man has ever lived who has not wished more than once that he had not to live the following day. According to this, the brevity of life, which is so constantly lamented, may be the best quality it possesses. If, finally, we should bring clearly to a man's sight the terrible sufferings and miseries to which his life is constantly exposed, he would be seized with horror; and if we were to conduct the confirmed optimist through the hospitals, infirmaries, and surgical operating-rooms, through the prisons, torture-chambers, and slave-kennels, over battle-fields and places of execution; if we were to open to him all the dark abodes of misery, where it hides itself from the glance

of cold curiosity, and, finally, allow him to glance into the starving dungeon of Ugolino, he, too, would understand at last the nature of this "best
of possible worlds." For whence did Dante take the materials for his hell
but from this our actual world? And yet he made a very proper hell of
it. And when, on the other hand, he came to the task of describing heaven
and its delights, he had an insurmountable difficulty before him, for our
world affords no materials at all for this. Therefore there remained nothing for him to do but, instead of describing the joys of paradise, to repeat to us the instruction given him there by his ancestor, by Beatrice,
and by various saints. But from this it is sufficiently clear what manner
of world it is. Certainly human life, like all bad ware, is covered over
with a false lustre: what suffers always conceals itself; on the other hand,
whatever pomp or splendour any one can get, he makes a show of openly,
and the more inner contentment deserts him, the more he desires to exist
as fortunate in the opinion of others: to such an extent does folly go,
and the opinion of others is a chief aim of the efforts of every one, although the utter nothingness of it is expressed in the fact that in almost
all languages vanity, *vanitas,* originally signifies emptiness and nothingness. But under all this false show, the miseries of life can so increase —
and this happens every day — that the death which hitherto has been
feared above all things is eagerly seized upon. Indeed, if fate will show
its whole malice, even this refuge is denied to the sufferer, and, in the
hands of enraged enemies, he may remain exposed to terrible and slow
tortures without remedy. In vain the sufferer then calls on his gods for
help; he remains exposed to his fate without grace. But this irremediable-
ness is only the mirror of the invincible nature of his will, of which his
person is the objectivity. As little as an external power can change or
suppress this will, so little can a foreign power deliver it from the miseries which proceed from the life which is the phenomenal appearance of
that will. In the principal matter, as in everything else, a man is always
thrown back upon himself. In vain does he make to himself gods in
order to get from them by prayers and flattery what can only be accomplished by his own will-power. The Old Testament made the world and
man the work of a god, but the New Testament saw that, in order to
teach that holiness and salvation from the sorrows of this world can only
come from the world itself, it was necessary that this god should become
man. It is and remains the will of man upon which everything depends
for him. Fanatics, martyrs, saints of every faith and name, have volun-

tarily and gladly endured every torture, because in them the will to live had suppressed itself; and then even the slow destruction of its phenomenon was welcome to them. But I do not wish to anticipate the later exposition. For the rest, I cannot here avoid the statement that, to me, *optimism*, when it is not merely the thoughtless talk of such as harbour nothing but words under their low foreheads, appears not merely as an absurd, but also as a really *wicked* way of thinking, as a bitter mockery of the unspeakable suffering of humanity. Let no one think that Christianity is favourable to optimism; for, on the contrary, in the Gospels world and evil are used as almost synonymous.

.   .   .

The genital organs are, far more than any other external member of the body, subject merely to the will, and not at all to knowledge. Indeed, the will shows itself here almost as independent of knowledge, as in those parts which, acting merely in consequence of stimuli, are subservient to vegetative life and reproduction, in which the will works blindly as in unconscious Nature. For generation is only reproduction passing over to a new individual, as it were reproduction at the second power, as death is only excretion at the second power. According to all this, the genitals are properly the *focus* of will, and consequently the opposite pole of the brain, the representative of knowledge, *i.e.*, the other side of the world, the world as idea. The former are the life-sustaining principle ensuring endless life to time. In this respect they were worshipped by the Greeks in the *phallus,* and by the Hindus in the *lingam,* which are thus the symbol of the assertion of the will. Knowledge, on the other hand, affords the possibility of the suppression of willing, of salvation through freedom, of conquest and annihilation of the world.

.   .   .

The world, in all the multiplicity of its parts and forms, is the manifestation, the objectivity, of the one will to live. Existence itself, and the kind of existence, both as a collective whole and in every part, proceeds from the will alone. The will is free, the will is almighty. The will appears in everything, just as it determines itself in itself and outside time. The world is only the mirror of this willing; and all finitude, all suffering, all miseries, which it contains, belong to the expression of that which the will wills, are as they are because the will so wills. Accordingly with perfect right every being supports existence in general, and also the existence of its species and its peculiar individuality, entirely as it is and in circumstances as they are, in a world such as it is, swayed by chance and error, transient, ephemeral, and constantly suffering; and in all that it experiences, or indeed can experience, it always gets its due. For the will belongs to it; and as the will is, so is the world. Only this world itself can bear the responsibility of its own existence and nature — no other; for by what means could another have assumed it? Do we desire to know what men, morally considered, are worth as a whole and in general, we have only to consider their fate as a whole and in general. This is want, wretchedness, affliction, misery, and death. Eternal justice reigns; if they were not, as a whole, worthless, their fate, as a whole, would not be so sad. In this sense we may say, the world itself is the judgment of the world. If we could lay all the misery of the world in one scale of the balance, and all the guilt of the world in the other, the needle would certainly point to the centre.

.   .   .

The explanation of the concept *true* has already been given in the essay on the principle of sufficient reason. The content of the concept *beautiful* found for the first time its proper explanation through the whole of the Third Book of the present work. We now wish to discover the significance of the concept *good,* which can be done with very little trouble. This concept is essentially relative, and signifies *the conformity of an object to any definite effort of the will.* Accordingly everything that corresponds to the will in any of its expressions and fulfils its end is thought through the concept *good,* however different such things may be in other respects. Thus we speak of good eating, good roads, good weather, good weapons, good omens, and so on; in short, we call everything good that is just as we wish it to be; and therefore that may be good in the eyes of one man which is just the reverse in those of another. The conception of the good divides itself into two sub-species — that of the direct and present satisfaction of any volition, and that of its indirect satisfaction which has reference to the future, *i.e.,* the agreeable, and the useful. The conception of the opposite, so long as we are speaking of unconscious existence, is expressed by the word *bad,* more rarely and abstractly by the word *evil,* which thus denotes everything that does not correspond to any effort of the will. Like all other things that can come into relation to the will, men who are favourable to the ends which happen to be desired, who further and befriend them, are called good in the same sense, and always with that relative limitation, which shows itself, for example, in the expression, "I find this good, but you don't." Those, however, who are naturally disposed not to hinder the endeavours of others, but rather to assist them, and who are thus consistently helpful, benevolent, friendly, and charitable, are called *good* men, on account of this relation of their conduct to the will of others in general. In the case of conscious beings (brutes and men) the contrary conception is denoted in German, and, within the last hundred years or so, in French also, by a different word from that which is used in speaking of unconscious existence; in German, *böse;* in French, *méchant;* while in almost all other languages this distinction does not exist; and κακος, *malus, cattivo, bad,* are used of men, as of lifeless things, which are opposed to the ends of a definite individual will. Thus, having started entirely from the passive element to the good, the inquiry could only proceed later to the active element, and investigate the conduct of the man who is called good, no longer with reference to others, but to himself; specially setting itself the task of explaining both the purely objective respect which such conduct produces in others, and the peculiar contentment with himself which it clearly produces in the man himself, since he purchases it with sacrifices of another kind; and also, on the other hand, the inner pain which accompanies the bad disposition, whatever outward advantages it brings to him who entertains it. It was from this source that the ethical systems, both the philosophical and those which are supported by systems of religion, took their rise. Both seek constantly in some way or other to connect happiness with virtue, the former either by means of the principle of contradiction or that of sufficient reason, and thus to make happiness either identical with or the consequence of virtue, always sophistically; the latter, by asserting the existence of other worlds than that which alone can be known to experience. In our system, on the contrary, virtue will show itself, not as a striving after happiness, that is, well-being and life, but as an effort in quite an opposite direction.

.   .   .

I now take up the thread of our discussion of the ethical significance of action, in order to show how, from the same source from which all goodness, love, virtue, and nobility of character spring, there finally arises that which I call the denial of the will to live.

We saw before that hatred and wickedness are conditioned by egoism, and egoism rests on the entanglement of knowledge in the *principium individuationis*. Thus we found that the penetration of that *principium individuationis* is the source and the nature of justice, and when it is carried further, even to its fullest extent, it is the source and nature of love and nobility of character. For this penetration alone, by abolishing the distinction between our own individuality and that of others, renders possible and explains perfect goodness of disposition, extending to disinterested love and the most generous self-sacrifice for others.

If, however, this penetration of the *principium individuationis,* this direct knowledge of the identity of will in all its manifestations, is present in a high degree of distinctness, it will at once show an influence upon the will which extends still further. If that veil of Mâyâ, the *principium individuationis,* is lifted from the eyes of a man to such an extent that he no longer makes the egotistical distinction between his person and that of others, but takes as much interest in the sufferings of other individuals as in his own, and therefore is not only benevolent in the highest degree, but even ready to sacrifice his own individuality whenever such a sacrifice will save a number of other persons, then it clearly follows that such a man, who recognises in all beings his own inmost and true self, must also regard the infinite suffering of all suffering beings as his own, and take on himself the pain of the whole world. No suffering is any longer strange to him. All the miseries of others which he sees and is so seldom able to alleviate, all the miseries he knows directly, and even those which he only knows as possible, work upon his mind like his own. It is no longer the changing joy and sorrow of his own person that he has in view, as is the case with him who is still involved in egoism; but, since he sees through the *principium individuationis,* all lies equally near him. He knows the whole, comprehends its nature, and finds that it consists in a constant passing away, vain striving, inward conflict, and continual suffering. He sees wherever he looks suffering humanity, the suffering brute creation, and a world that passes away. But all this now lies as near him as his own person lies to the egoist. Why should he now, with such knowledge of the world, assert this very life through constant acts of will, and thereby bind himself ever more closely to it, press it ever more firmly to himself? Thus he who is still involved in the *principium individuationis,* in egoism, only knows particular things and their relation to his own person, and these constantly become new *motives* of his volition. But, on the other hand, that knowledge of the whole, of the nature of the thing-in-itself which has been described, becomes a *quieter* of all and every volition. The will now turns away from life; it now shudders at the pleasures in which it recognises the assertion of life. Man now attains to the state of voluntary renunciation, resignation, true indifference, and perfect will-lessness. If at times, in the hard experience of our own suffering, or in the vivid recognition of that of others, the knowledge of the vanity and bitterness of life draws nigh to us also who are still wrapt in the veil of Mâyâ, and we would like to destroy the sting of the desires, close the entrance against all suffering, and purify and sanctify ourselves by complete and final renunciation; yet the illusion of the phenomenon soon entangles us again, and its motives influence the will anew; we cannot tear ourselves free. The allurement of hope, the flattery of the present, the sweetness of pleasure, the well-being which falls to our lot, amid the lamentations of a suffering world governed by chance and error, draws us back to it and rivets our bonds anew. Therefore Jesus says: "It is easier for a camel to go through the eye of a needle, than for a rich man to enter into the kingdom of God."

.   .   .

I now end the general account of ethics, and with it the whole development of that one thought which it has been my object to impart; and I by no means desire to conceal here an objection which concerns this last part of my exposition, but rather to point out that it lies in the nature of the question, and that it is quite impossible to remove it. It is this, that after our investigation has brought us to the point at which we have before our eyes perfect holiness, the denial and surrender of all volition, and thus the deliverance from a world whose whole existence we have found to be suffering, this appears to us as a passing away into empty nothingness.

That which is generally received as positive, which we call the real, and the negation of which the concept nothing in its most general significance expresses, is just the world as idea, which I have shown to be the objectivity and mirror of the will. Moreover, we ourselves are just this will and this world, and to them belongs the idea in general, as one aspect of them. The form of the idea is space and time, therefore for this point of view all that is real must be in some place and at some time. Denial, abolition, conversion of the will, is also the abolition and the vanishing of the world, its mirror. If we no longer perceive it in this mirror, we ask in vain where it has gone, and then, because it has no longer any where and when, complain that it has vanished into nothing.

A reversed point of view, if it were possible for us, would reverse the signs and show the real for us as nothing, and that nothing as the real. But as long as we ourselves are the will to live, this last — nothing as the real — can only be known and signified by us negatively, because the old saying of Empedocles, that like can only be known by like, deprives us here of all knowledge, as, conversely, upon it finally rests the possibility of all our actual knowledge, *i.e.*, the world as idea; for the world is the self-knowledge of the will.

If, however, it should be absolutely insisted upon that in some way or other a positive knowledge should be attained of that which philosophy can only express negatively as the denial of the will, there would be nothing for it but to refer to that state which all those who have attained to complete denial of the will have experienced, and which has been variously denoted by the names ecstasy, rapture, illumination, union with God, and so forth; a state, however, which cannot properly be called knowledge, because it has not the form of subject and object, and is, moreover, only attainable in one's own experience and cannot be further communicated.

We, however, who consistently occupy the standpoint of philosophy, must be satisfied here with negative knowledge, content to have reached the utmost limit of the positive. We have recognised the inmost nature of the world as will, and all its phenomena as only the objectivity of will; and we have followed this objectivity from the unconscious working of obscure forces of Nature up to the completely conscious action of man. Therefore we shall by no means evade the consequence, that with the free denial, the surrender of the will, all those phenomena are also abolished; that constant strain and effort without end and without rest at all the grades of objectivity, in which and through which the world consists; the multifarious forms succeeding each other in gradation; the whole manifestation of the will; and, finally, also the universal forms of this manifestation, time and space, and also its last fundamental form, subject and object; all are abolished. No will: no idea, no world.

Before us there is certainly only nothingness. But that which resists this passing into nothing, our nature, is indeed just the will to live, which we ourselves are as it is our world. That we abhor annihilation so greatly, is simply another expression of the fact that we so strenuously will life, and are nothing but this will, and know nothing besides it. But if we turn our glance from our own needy and embarrassed condition to those who have overcome the world, in whom the will, having attained to perfect self-knowledge, found itself again in all, and then freely denied itself, and who then merely wait to see the last trace of it vanish with the body which it animates; then, instead of the restless striving and effort, instead of the constant transition from wish to fruition, and from joy to sorrow, instead of the never-satisfied and never-dying hope which con-stitutes the life of the man who wills, we shall see that peace which is above all reason, that perfect calm of the spirit, that deep rest, that in-violable confidence and serenity, the mere reflection of which in the countenance, as Raphael and Correggio have represented it, is an entire and certain gospel; only knowledge remains, the will has vanished. We look with deep and painful longing upon this state, beside which the misery and wretchedness of our own is brought out clearly by the con-trast. Yet this is the only consideration which can afford us lasting con-solation, when, on the one hand, we have recognised incurable suffering and endless misery as essential to the manifestation of will, the world; and, on the other hand, see the world pass away with the abolition of will, and retain before us only empty nothingness. Thus, in this way, by contemplation of the life and conduct of saints, whom it is certainly rarely granted us to meet with in our own experience, but who are brought before our eyes by their written history, and, with the stamp of inner truth, by art, we must banish the dark impression of that nothing-ness which we discern behind all virtue and holiness as their final goal, and which we fear as children fear the dark; we must not even evade it like the Indians, through myths and meaningless words, such as reabsorp-tion in Brahma or the Nirvâna of the Buddhists. Rather do we freely acknowledge that what remains after the entire abolition of will is for all those who are still full of will certainly nothing; but, conversely, to those in whom the will has turned and has denied itself, this our world, which is so real, with all its suns and milky-ways — is nothing.

[TRANSLATED BY R. B. HALDANE AND J. KEMP]

Louis Lambert

HONORÉ de BALZAC

(1799–1850)

*In 1832 Balzac published in this novel his most complete ex-
position of the ideas which made it possible for him to undertake and carry to within sight of completion his fictionalized
sociology of France, including the historical aspect of its leading ideas. Balzac's monomania, which is found to some degree
in every man, is the actualization of Schopenhauer's Will. It
is the passion to impose order upon a recalcitrant and chaotic
reality, and it has three aspects: generating ideas; converting
the ideas into a desire; and imposing those ideas upon reality.
Man is all energy; the world is all resistance. In man the ultimate character of the world, which is force or motion or
energy, becomes self-conscious. Louis Lambert enters into the
Absolute, from which life flows, but dies in the process. Salvation lies in the other direction — toward man, even for the
alienated artist-sociologist.*

.   .   .

New ideas need new words, or old words in wider and better defined acceptations. To express the bases of his system, Louis Lambert had

therefore chosen certain words in common use which responded already, though vaguely, to his thought. The word WILL served to express the medium in which *thought* is evolved; or, to use a less abstract form of expression, the volume of force by which man reproduces outside of himself the actions which make up his external existence. VOLITION (a word we owe to the reflections of Locke) expressed the act by which a man makes use of Will. The word THOUGHT, to Louis the quintessential product of the Will, designated also the medium in which are born IDEAS, to which the Will serves as substance. The IDEA, not common to all creations of the brain, constitutes the act by which man makes use of *Thought*.

Thus Will and Thought are two generating agents. Volition and Idea are the two products. Will seemed to him the Idea advanced from its abstract condition to a concrete condition, from its fluid generation to a quasi-solid expression, if indeed these words can formulate perceptions so difficult to discriminate. According to Lambert, Thought and Ideas are the motion and the action of our inward organism, just as Volition and Will are those of our exterior being. He placed Will above Thought. "To think, we must needs will," he said. "Many persons live in a condition of Willing who never reach the condition of Thought. In the North we find longevity, in the South brevity of life; but also in the former a torpidity, in the latter an excitation of the Will, up to the point where, either from extreme heat or extreme cold, the organs become almost nugatory."

His expression "medium" was suggested to him by an observation made in early childhood, — the importance of which he certainly did not then suspect, though its curious singularity must have greatly struck his impressible imagination. His mother, a slender, high-strung creature, all delicacy and all love, was one of those beings predestined to represent Woman in the perfection of her attributes whom a blind fate leaves in the lower strata of the social state. All-loving, consequently all-suffering, she died young, after turning every faculty into motherly devotion. Lambert, a child of six, lying awake in a cot by his mother's bed, saw electric sparks escaping from her hair as she combed it. The man of fifteen seized upon this fact so amusing to his childhood, and fit it to the uses of science, — an undeniable fact, to be observed in almost every woman whom a certain fatality of destiny burdens with feelings misunderstood which need a vent, or with a superabundance of vigor which she needs to lose.

In support of his definitions, Lambert brought forward several problems for solution, splendid challenges offered to science, through which
he hoped to reach conclusions. He was constantly asking himself, "Does
the constituent principle of electricity enter as a basis into the particular
fluid from which Ideas and Volitions spring? Does the hair which dis-
colors, brightens, falls, and disappears from the head, according to varying
degrees of waste or of crystallization of thought, constitute a capillary
system either absorbent or exhalant, and wholly electrical? Are the fluid
phenomena of our Will (a substance procreated within us and spontaneously reactive at the bidding of conditions still unobserved) more
extraordinary than those of the invisible and intangible fluid produced
by a voltaic battery on the nervous system of a dead man? Is the formation of our ideas, and their constant emission any less incomprehensible
than the evaporation of those corpuscles, imperceptible to the eye yet
violent in action, to which a grain of musk is subjected without losing its
weight? If we leave to the cutaneous system of our outward man only
those functions that are defensive, absorbent, exudant, and tactile, does
not the circulation of the blood and its apparatus answer to the transub-
stantiation of Will, just as the circulation of the nervous fluid answers to
that of Thought? Finally, does the influence, more or less powerful, of
these two substances result from a certain perfection or imperfection of
organs, the conditions of which ought to be studied in all their manifestation?"

These principles once established, he desired to class the phenomena
of human life in two series of distinct effects, — demanding for each of
them, with the insistent ardor of conviction, a separate and special
analysis. In fact, after distinguishing in nearly all created things two
separate movements, he presented the fact and admitted it among those
of human nature, naming this vital antagonism ACTION and REACTION.

"A desire," he said, "is a fact wholly accomplished within our Will
before it reaches external accomplishment. Thus the conjunction of our
Volitions and our Ideas constitutes *Action,* and the conjunction of our
exterior acts *Reaction.*"

When, at a later day, I read the observations made by Bichat on the
dualism of our external senses, I was bewildered by recollections as I
perceived the startling identity between the ideas of the great physiologist
and those of Louis Lambert. Dying before their allotted time, the two
had walked with even steps, side by side, towards unknown truths. Na-

ture finds pleasure in giving duplicate destinies to diverse constitutional arrangements in her creatures, and the double action of our organism, a fact no longer contestable, supports, with a volume of daily proof, Lambert's deductions as to *Action* and *Reaction*. The *acting* or interior being (a term which Louis used to name the unknown *species,* the mysterious assemblage of fibrils from which proceed the different powers incompletely observed as Thought and Will, — in short, that unnamed, seeing, acting, producing being, who accomplishes all without corporeal demonstration) must, in order to conform to his own nature, be subjected to none of the physical conditions by which the *reacting,* or exterior, being, the visible man, is checked in his manifestations.

From this flowed a multitude of logical explanations on the apparently fantastic effects of our double nature, and the rectification of various theories which are equally false and true. Certain minds having perceived the phenomena of natural fire in the *acting* being are, like Swedenborg, carried beyond the world of actual things by their ardent souls, amorous of poesy, drunk with the essence of the divine. They delight, ignorant as they are of causes while admiring results, to deify this inward being and its works, and to build up a mystic universe. Hence the angels, — exquisite illusions which Lambert would not renounce. While the blade of his analysis cut off their dazzling wings, he still clasped them to his heart.

"Heaven," he said to me, "must be the survival of our perfected faculties, and hell the nothingness into which unperfected faculties return."

But how, during the ages when human understanding still retained the religious and spiritual impressions which ruled the world between the times of Christ and of Descartes, between Faith and Doubt, how could the mind avoid explaining the mysteries of our inward nature otherwise than by Divine intervention? Of whom, if not of God himself, could learned men ask an explanation of the invisible creature, so actively and so reactively sensitive; endowed with faculties so wide-reaching, so perfectible through use, so powerful under the control of certain occult conditions, that at times they saw it, by a phenomenon of sight or of locomotion, abolish space in its two aspects of Time and Distance, — the former being intellectual space, the latter physical space. Or again, they saw this being reconstruct the past, either by the power of a retrospective glance, or by the mystery of a palingenesis, like that which enables a man to trace a flower from the germ, or the teguments of a seed through all the innumerable modifications of color, fragrance, and form of its anterior bloom. And still again, and finally, they saw it divining imperfectly the future, either through a glimpse of the earlier faiths, or by a phenomenon of physical presentiments.

Other men, less poetically religious, cold reasoners, charlatans perhaps, enthusiasts, if at all, by the brain rather than by the heart, observing from time to time these isolated phenomena, have held them to be true without considering them as radiations from a common centre. Each man sought to convert a simple fact into a science. Hence, demonology, judicial astrology, sorcery; — in short, all the divining arts based on incidents that were essentially transitory because they varied according to temperaments and in accordance with circumstances still wholly unexplained. But through these errors of the learned, and from ecclesiastical trials in which so many martyrs were the victims of their own families, there came at last effulgent proof of the prodigious power of the *acting* inward being who, according to Lambert, is able to isolate himself so completely from the *reacting* external being that he can burst the shell and force the walls of flesh to open before his omnipotent mind's eye (a phenomenon called among the Hindoos the Tokeiad), and then, by virtue of another faculty, seize within the brain, in spite of its thick convolutions, ideas which are formed or forming, and all the past experience of consciousness.

"If apparitions are not impossible," said Lambert, "they must take place through some faculty of apprehending the ideas that represent man in his pure essence; the existence of which, imperishable perhaps, eludes our exterior senses, but may become perceptible to the inward being when he attains to a high degree of ecstasy, or to a rare perfection of sight."

I recall, though now somewhat vaguely, that Lambert, following step by step the effects of Thought and Will in all their manifestations, after first determining their laws, was able to account for a crowd of phenomena which till then were justly thought to be incomprehensible. Necromancers, witches, those possessed of second-sight, and demoniacs of all kinds, victims of the Middle Ages, were the objects of natural explanation whose very simplicity seemed to me to bear the stamp of truth. The marvellous gifts which the Church of Rome, jealous of mysteries, punished with the stake were, according to Louis, the result of certain affinities between the constituent principles of Matter and those of Thought, which proceed from the same source. The man with the hazel wand who found the water-springs obeyed the impulse of some sympathy, or some antipathy, to himself unknown. Such phenomena needed a certain fantasticality to give them historical preservation. Sympathies are seldom verified. They bestow pleasures which persons fortunately endowed with them seldom make known, unless through some special necessity; they are lost in the seclusion of privacy where so much is forgotten. On the other hand, antipathies, which result from reversed affinities, have been noted with great distinctness when they appear among celebrated men. Bayle was thrown into convulsions by the sound of falling water. Scaliger turned pale at the sight of cress. Erasmus took a fever from the smell of fish. These three antipathies emanated from aquatic substances. The Duc d'Épernon fainted at the sight of a hare; Tycho-Brahe at that of a fox; Henri III at that of a cat; Maréchal d'Albret at that of a wild boar, — antipathies produced by animal emanations and perceived often at long distances. The Chevalier de Guise, Marie de Medici, and many other historic personages were made ill by roses, even painted ones. Whether Francis Bacon knew or did not know of an approaching eclipse of the moon, he fell into a state of coma when it took place; life was arrested during the whole time the obscuration lasted, but recovered vigor when it was over, without any uncomfortable results. These effects of authentic antipathies, taken at random from those which history has noted, will suffice to give an idea of the effects of hidden sympathies.

This fragment of Lambert's investigations which my memory still retains will serve to show his methods in pursuing his work. I think I need not call attention to the correlation which links this theory to the collateral sciences invented by Gall and Lavater; they are its natural corollaries; and minds of even slender scientific attainments will perceive the ramifications by which the phrenological observations of the one and the physiognomical data of the other are necessarily attached to it. Mesmer's discovery, so important and so ill-understood even at the present day, would have been found entire in Lambert's treatise, though Louis knew nothing of the somewhat laconic works of the celebrated Swiss doctor. A logical and simple deduction of the principles he had observed showed him that Will could, by a movement set going solely by the inward being, accumulate itself and, by another movement, be impelled outward, and even be imparted to material objects. Thus a man's whole force had potency to react upon others and to infuse into them an essence foreign to their own, if they did not defend themselves from the aggression. The evidences of this theorem of the science of humanity are multitudinous, but nothing has yet converted them into authentic proof. The impressive disaster of Marius and his speech to the Cimbrian who was appointed to kill him, or the august command of a mother to the Lion of Florence were needed to make known historically a few of these thunderbolts of thought.

To Lambert, therefore, Will and Thought were *living forces;* and he spoke of them in a way to make me share his beliefs. To him these powers were, in a sense, visible and tangible. To him Thought was slow or quick, heavy or nimble, obscure or clear; he gave it all the qualities of active being; made it spring forth, become quiescent, re-awake, increase, grow old, shrink, wither, revive; he caught its life as he thus specified its acts through the capricious medium of language; he apprehended its spontaneity, its vigor, its capacity, by a sort of intuition which enabled him to recognize all the phenomena of the substance.

"Often," he once said to me, "in calm and silent hours, when our inward faculties are asleep, when we yield ourselves up to the sweetness of rest, when a species of shadow steals through us, and we fall into contemplation of external things, an idea suddenly springs forth and darts with the rapidity of lightning across vast spaces, a sight of which is granted to our interior perceptions. This shining thought, up-springing like a will-o'-the-wisp, goes out like a flash and returns no more, — ephemeral existence, like that of infants whose coming and whose going give boundless joy and grief to parents, — a flower still-born, as it were, in the fields of Mind. Sometimes, instead of gushing forth and dying without substance, this Idea begins to form; it stirs on the unknown confines of the organs in which it was generated; it consumes us with a long gestation; it quickens, fructifies, and develops outwardly with the grace of youth and the attributes of old age; it attracts and detains the inquiring eye, and never wearies it; the investigation it provokes commands the admiring wonder given to long-elaborated works. Sometimes ideas come to birth in swarms, — one brings forth another; they link together; they are stimulating, affluent, headlong. Or again, they rise up pallid, confused, perishing for want of nourishment or vigor; the generating substance was lacking. Then, too, on certain days, they fling themselves into the depths of the abyss, seeking to cast light into its immensity; they terrify us, they leave our souls exhausted. Ideas are a system complete within us, like any of the kingdoms of Nature, — a sort of flora whose iconography will one day be traced out by a man of genius whom the world will call a lunatic. Yes, all things, within us and without us, bear evidence to the life of Ideas, — those ravishing creations which, obeying some mysterious revelation of their nature, I compare to flowers. Their production, as the end and aim of man, is not more amazing than the emanation of perfume and color from a plant. Possibly, perfumes have ideas. When we think that the line where our flesh ends and the finger-nails begin contains the invisible and inexplicable mystery of the ceaseless transformation of our fluids into horn, we must admit that nothing is impossible in the marvellous mutations of human substance. Surely we find in the moral nature phenomena of motion and gravity similar to those of the physical nature. The emotion of *expectant attention,* to choose an example which everybody has felt, is painful through the effect of a law in virtue of which the weight of a body is multiplied by its swiftness. Does not the weight of sentiment, the moral gravity, which *waiting* produces increase by the constant addition of the past pains to present pain? To what, if not to some electric substance, can we attribute that magic by force of which the Will sits majestically enthroned in the eye to blast all obstacles at the command of genius, or breaks forth in the voice, or filters visibly, in defiance of hypocrisy, through the human cuticle? The current of this king of fluids, which, under the high pressure of Thought or Sentiment, flows forth in waves, lessens to a thread, or gathers to a volume and gushes forth in lightning jets, is the occult minister to whom we owe the efforts (be they fatal or beneficent) of the arts and the passions, — the intonations of the voice, rough, sweet, terrifying, lascivious, horrible, seductive, which vibrate in the heart, in the bowels, in the brain, at the will of our wishes; the spell of touch from which proceed the mental transfusions of artists whose creative hands, made perfect through passionate study, can evoke nature; the endless gradations of the eye, passing from sluggish atony to the discharge of lightning-flashes full of menace. God loses none of his rights in this system. Thought, material thought, tells me of new and undiscovered grandeurs in the Divine."

·   ·   ·

"No doubt Louis appears to be insane," she said, "but he is not so, if the word insanity is applied only to those whose brain, from unknown causes, becomes vitiated, and who are, therefore, unable to give a reason for their acts. The equilibrium of my husband's mind is perfect. If he does not recognize you corporeally, do not think that he has not seen you. He is able to disengage his body and to see us under another form, I know not of what nature. When he speaks, he says marvellous things. Only, in fact often, he completes in speech an idea begun in the silence of his mind, or else he begins a proposition in words and finishes it mentally. To other men he must appear insane; to me, who live in his thought, all his ideas are lucid. I follow the path of his mind; and though I cannot understand many of its turnings and digressions, I, nevertheless, reach the end with him. Does it not often happen that while thinking of some trifling matter, we are drawn into serious thought by the gradual unfolding of ideas and recollections? Often, after speaking of some frivolous thing, the accidental point of departure for rapid meditation, a thinker forgets, or neglects to mention the abstract links which have led him to his conclusions, and takes up in speech only the last rings in the chain of reflections. Common minds to whom this quickness of mental vision is unknown, and who are ignorant of the inward travail of the soul, laugh at dreamers and call them madmen if they are given to such forgetfulness of connecting thoughts. Louis is always so; he wings his way through the spaces of thought with the agility of a swallow; yet I can follow him in all his circlings. That is the history of his so-called madness. Perhaps he will one day return to this world in which we vegetate; but if now he breathes the air of heaven before the time appointed for us to live there, why should we wish him back among us? I am content to hear the beating of his heart; it is happiness enough for me to live beside him. Is he not all mine? Twice in the last two years and at separate times, I have regained him for several days, — once in Switzerland, and again in Brittany, where I took him for sea-bathing. I can live on those memories."

"But," I said, "do you not write down the thoughts he sometimes utters?"

"Why should I?" she answered.

I kept silence; human science was petty indeed beside this woman.

"At first, when he began to speak," she added, "I gathered together a few sentences, but I soon ceased to do so. I was unable then to understand him."

I asked her for that record, mutely, by a glance. She understood me; the following thoughts are those that I thus rescued from oblivion.

I.

Here below, all is the product of an ETHEREAL SUBSTANCE, the common base of several phenomena known under the vulgar names of Electricity, Heat, Light, Galvanic and Magnetic Fluid, etc. The universality of the transmutations of this Substance constitutes what is commonly called Matter.

II.

The brain is a retort, where the ANIMAL carries, according to the strength of the apparatus, all that each one of its constituent parts is able to absorb of that SUBSTANCE; and out of which it issues in the form of Will.

Will is a fluid, the attribute of every being endowed with motion. Hence the innumerable forms which the ANIMAL takes on; which are the effects of its combination with SUBSTANCE. Its instincts are the product of the necessities forced upon it by the conditions in which it develops. Hence its varieties.

III.

In man, Will becomes a force characteristic of the human species; surpassing in intensity that of all other species.

IV.

By constant nutrition Will is related to SUBSTANCE; finding it in all transmutations when penetrated by Thought, — which is a product peculiar to the human Will combined with modifications of SUBSTANCE.

V.

From the greater or the lesser perfection of the human apparatus come the innumerable forms which Thought assumes.

VI.

Will is exerted by organs vulgarly called the five senses; which are in fact but one, namely, the faculty of seeing. Touch and taste, hearing and smell, are sight, adapted to those transformations of SUBSTANCE which a man can grasp in its two conditions, modified and unmodified.

VII.

All things pertaining, through Form, to the domain of a single sense, namely, the faculty of sight, reduce themselves to a few elementary bodies whose principles are in the air, in the light, or in the principles of air and light. Sound is a modification of air; all colors are modifications of light; all perfumes are a combination of air and light; consequently, the four manifestations of matter in its relation to man, namely, sound, color, perfume, and form, have one and the same origin; the day is not far off when the affiliation of the principles of light with those of air will be recognized. Thought, allied to light, expresses itself by words, allied to sound. For it, therefore, all is derived from SUBSTANCE, the transformations of which differ only by NUMBER, by a given quantity, the proportions of which produce the individuals or the things constituting the divisions of nature called KINGDOMS.

VIII.

When SUBSTANCE is absorbed in a sufficing Number it converts man into an apparatus of enormous power, which communicates with the essence itself of Substance, and acts upon organized nature after the manner of great currents which absorb little ones. Volition sets to work this force, which is independent of thought, and, by its concentration, acquires some of the properties of SUBSTANCE, such as the rapidity of light, the interpenetrating quality of electricity, the faculty of saturating bodies; to which must be added intelligent knowledge of what it does. But there is in man a primal and controlling phenomenon which admits of no analysis. Decompose man to the utmost, and we may perhaps discover the elements of Thought and of Will, but we shall also find, without being able to solve it, the unknown quantity, that X against which I vainly flung myself in earlier days. This X is the LOGOS, whose touch burns and destroys all such as are not prepared to receive it. It ceaselessly engenders SUBSTANCE.

IX.

Anger, like all our passionate expressions, is a current of human force acting electrically; its agitation, when it is disengaged, acts upon persons present even if they are neither the object nor the cause of it. Do we not meet with men who, by a discharge of their volition, reduce and refine the sentiments of the masses?

X.

Fanaticism, and all other sentiments, are Living Forces. These forces become in certain beings rivers of Will, which gather up and carry away everything.

XI.

If space exists, certain faculties bestow the power of traversing it with such rapidity that their effects are equivalent to its abolition. From thy couch to the frontiers of the world there are but two steps: WILL — FAITH.

XII.

Facts are nought; they do not exist; Ideas alone subsist.

XIII.

The world of Ideas divides itself into three spheres, — that of Instinct; that of Abstractions; that of Specialism.

XIV.

The greater part of visible Humanity, that is, the weaker part, inhabits the sphere of Instinctivity. The Instinctives are born, work, and die, without rising to the second degree of human intelligence, namely, Abstraction.

XV.

At Abstraction Society begins. Though Abstraction as compared with Instinct is an almost divine power, it is infinitely feeble compared with the endowment of Specialism, which alone can explain God. Abstraction comprises within it a whole nature in germ, as potentially as the seed contains the system of a plant and all its products. From Abstraction are derived laws, arts, interests, social ideas. It is the glory and scourge of the world. Glorious, it creates societies; baneful, it exempts man from entering the path of Specialism which leads to the Infinite. Man judges all things by his abstractions, — good, evil, virtue, crime. His formulas of right are his scales, and his justice is blind; the justice of God sees, — in that is everything. There are, necessarily, intermediate beings who separate the Kingdom of the Instinctives from the Kingdom of the Abstractives, in whom Instinctivity mixes with Abstractivity in endless variety of proportion. Some have more of the former than of the latter, and *vice versa*. Also, there are beings in whom the action of each is neutralized because both are moved by an equal force.

XVI.

Specialism consists in seeing the things of the material world as well as those of the spiritual world in their original and consequential ramifications. The highest human genius is that which starts from the shadows of Abstraction to advance into the light of Specialism. (Specialism, *species,* sight, speculation, seeing all, and that at one glance: *Speculum,* the mirror or means of estimating a thing by seeing it in its entirety.) Jesus was a Specialist. He saw the deed in its roots and in its products; in the past which begot it, in the present where it is manifested, in the future where it develops; his sight penetrated the understanding of others. The perfection of the inward sight gives birth to the gift of Specialism. Specialism carries with it Intuition. Intuition is a faculty of the INNER MAN, of whom Specialism is an attribute. It acts by an imperceptible sensation, of which he who obeys it is ignorant — witness Napoleon instinctively changing his position before the bullet came which would have struck him.

XVII.

Between the sphere of Specialism and the sphere of Abstraction, and likewise between those spheres and that of Instinctivity, we find beings in whom the diverse attributes of the two kingdoms are mingled, producing a mixed nature, — the man of genius.

XVIII.

The Specialist is necessarily the loftiest expression of MAN, — the link which connects the visible to the superior worlds. He acts, he sees, he feels through his INNER BEING. The Abstractive thinks. The Instinctive simply acts.

XIX.

Hence three degrees for Man. As an Instinctive he is below the level; as an Abstractive he attains to it; as a Specialist he rises above it. Specialism opens to man his true career; the Infinite dawns upon him, he catches a glimpse of his destiny.

XX.

There exist three worlds — the NATURAL WORLD, the SPIRITUAL WORLD, the DIVINE WORLD. Humanity moves hither and thither in the Natural World, which is fixed neither in its essence nor in its properties. The Spiritual World is fixed in its essence and variable in its properties. The Divine World is fixed in its properties and in its essence. Consequently, there is a material worship, a spiritual worship, a divine worship; which three are manifested by Action, Word, and Prayer, or (to express it otherwise) Deed, Understanding, Love. The Instinctive desires deeds; the Abstractive turns to ideas; the Specialist sees the End, he aspires to God, whom he inwardly perceives or contemplates.

XXI.

Therefore, perhaps one day the inverse sense of ET VERBO CARO FACTUM will be the epitome of a new Gospel which will read: "AND THE FLESH SHALL BE MADE THE WORD; IT SHALL BECOME THE UTTERANCE OF GOD."

XXII.

The resurrection is brought about by the winds of heaven which sweep the worlds. The Angel borne upon the blast saith not: "Ye Dead, arise!" he saith, "Arise, ye living!"

[TRANSLATED BY KATHARINE PRESCOTT WORMELEY]

Preface to Cromwell

VICTOR HUGO

(1802–1885)

This manifesto, published as a preface to a play in 1827, is one of the best statements in the whole range of nineteenth-century literature of the radical notion of the creativity of the poet and the redemptive power of art. Hugo's insistent separation of nature from art is an excellent instance of the Romantic preference of the artificial to the natural, particularly during the Transcendental stage, when every effort was made to reveal the value of the Subject and the non-value of the Object.

The critics of the scholastic school place their poets in a strange position. On the one hand they cry incessantly: "Copy the models!" On the other hand they have a habit of declaring that "the models are inimitable"! Now, if their craftsman, by dint of hard work, succeeds in forcing through this dangerous defile some colourless tracing of the masters, these ungrateful wretches, after examining the new *refaccimiento*, exclaim sometimes: "This doesn't resemble anything!" and sometimes: "This resembles everything!" And by virtue of a logic made for the occasion each of these formulæ is a criticism.

Let us then speak boldly. The time for it has come, and it would be strange if, in this age, liberty, like the light, should penetrate everywhere except to the one place where freedom is most natural — the domain of thought. Let us take the hammer to theories and poetic systems. Let us throw down the old plastering that conceals the façade of art. There are neither rules nor models; or, rather, there are no other rules than the general laws of nature, which soar above the whold field of art, and the special rules which result from the conditions appropriate to the subject of each composition. The former are of the essence, eternal, and do not change; the latter are variable, external, and are used but once. The former are the framework that supports the house; the latter the scaffolding which is used in building it, and which is made anew for each building. In a word, the former are the flesh and bones, the latter the clothing, of the drama. But these rules are not written in the treatises on poetry. Richelet has no idea of their existence. Genius, which divines rather than learns, devises for each work the general rules from the general plan of things, the special rules from the separate *ensemble* of the subject treated; not after the manner of the chemist, who lights the fire under his furnace, heats his crucible, analyzes and destroys; but after the manner of the bee, which flies on its golden wings, lights on each flower and extracts its honey, leaving it as brilliant and fragrant as before.

The poet — let us insist on this point — should take counsel therefore only of nature, truth and inspiration which is itself both truth and nature. *"Quando he,"* says Lope de Vega:

> *Quando he de escrivir una comedia,*
> *Encierro los preceptos con seis llaves.*

> [When I have to write a comedy
> I enclose the precepts with six keys.]

To secure these precepts "six keys" are none too many, in very truth. Let the poet beware especially of copying anything whatsoever — Shakespeare no more than Molière, Schiller no more than Corneille. If genuine talent could abdicate its own nature in this matter, and thus lay aside its original personality, to transform itself into another, it would lose everything by playing this role of its own double. It is as if a god should turn valet. We must draw our inspiration from the original sources. . . .

Let there be no misunderstanding: if some of our poets have succeeded in being great, even when copying, it is because, while forming themselves on the antique model, they have often listened to the voice of nature and to their own genius — it is because they have been themselves in some one respect. Their branches became entangled in those of the

near-by tree, but their roots were buried deep in the soil of art. They
were the ivy, not the mistletoe. Then came imitators of the second rank,
who, having neither roots in the earth, nor genius in their souls, had to
confine themselves to imitation. As Charles Nodier says: "After the
school of Athens, the school of Alexandria." Then there was a deluge
of mediocrity; then there came a swarm of those treatises on poetry, so
annoying to true talent, so convenient for mediocrity. We were told that
everything was done, and God was forbidden to create more Molières or
Corneilles. Memory was put in place of imagination. Imagination itself
was subjected to hard-and-fast rules, and aphorisms were made about it:
"To imagine," says La Harpe, with his naïve assurance, "is in substance
to remember, that is all."

But nature! Nature and truth! — And here, in order to prove that, far
from demolishing art, the new ideas aim only to reconstruct it more
firmly and on a better foundation, let us try to point out the impassable
limit which in our opinion, separates reality according to art from reality
according to nature. It is careless to confuse them as some ill-informed
partisans of *romanticism* do. Truth in art cannot possibly be, as several
writers have claimed, *absolute* reality. Art cannot produce the thing itself.
Let us imagine, for example, one of those unreflecting promoters of absolute nature, of nature viewed apart from art, at the performance of a
romantic play, say *Le Cid.* "What's that?" he will ask at the first word.
"The Cid speaks in verse? It isn't *natural* to speak in verse." — "How
would you have him speak, pray?" — "In prose." Very good. A moment
later "How's this!" he will continue, if he is consistent; "the Cid is speaking French!" — "Well?" — "Nature demands that he speak his own language; he can't speak anything but Spanish."

We shall fail entirely to understand but again — very good. You imagine that this is all? By no means: before the tenth sentence in Castilian,
he is certain to rise and ask if the Cid who is speaking is the real Cid, in
flesh and blood. By what right does the actor, whose name is Pierre or
Jacques, take the name of the Cid? That is *false.* There is no reason why
he should not go on to demand that the sun should be substituted for
the footlights, *real* trees and *real* houses for those deceitful wings. For,
once started on that road, logic has you by the collar, and you cannot stop.

We must admit, therefore, or confess ourselves ridiculous, that the
domains of art and of nature are entirely distinct. Nature and art are two
things — were it not so, one or the other would not exist. Art, in addi-

tion to its idealistic side, has a terrestrial, material side. Let it do what it will, it is shut in between grammar and prosody, between Vaugelas and Richelet. For its most capricious creations, it has formulæ, methods of execution, a complete apparatus to set in motion. For genius there are delicate instruments, for mediocrity, tools.

It seems to us that someone has already said that the drama is a mirror wherein nature is reflected. But if it be an ordinary mirror, a smooth and polished surface, it will give only a dull image of objects, with no relief — faithful, but colourless; everyone knows that colour and light are lost in a simple reflection. The drama, therefore, must be a concentrating mirror, which, instead of weakening, concentrates and condenses the coloured rays, which make of a mere gleam a light, and of a light a flame. Then only is the drama acknowledged by art.

The stage is an optical point. Everything that exists in the world — in history, in life, in man — should be and can be reflected therein, but under the magic wand of art. Art turns the leaves of the ages, of nature, studies chronicles, strives to reproduce actual facts (especially in respect to manners and peculiarities, which are much less exposed to doubt and contradiction than are concrete facts), restores what the chroniclers have lopped off, harmonises what they have collected, divines and supplies their omissions, fills their gaps with imaginary scenes which have the colour of the time, groups what they have left scattered about, sets in motion anew the threads of Providence which work the human marionettes, clothes the whole with a form at once poetical and natural, and imparts to it that vitality of truth and brilliancy which gives birth to illusion, that prestige of reality which arouses the enthusiasm of the spectator, and of the poet first of all, for the poet is sincere. Thus the aim of art is almost divine: to bring to life again if it is writing history, to create if it is writing poetry.

.   .   .

It will readily be imagined that, for a work of this kind, if the poet must *choose* (and he must), he should choose, not the *beautiful,* but the *characteristic.* Not that it is advisable to "make local colour," as they say to-day; that is, to add as an afterthought a few discordant touches here and there to a work that is at best utterly conventional and false. The local colour should not be on the surface of the drama, but in its substance, in the very heart of the work, whence it spreads of itself, naturally, evenly, and, so to speak, into every corner of the drama, as the sap ascends from the root to the tree's topmost leaf. The drama should be thoroughly impregnated with this colour of the time, which should be, in some sort, in the air, so that one detects it only on entering the theatre, and that on going forth one finds one's self in a different period and atmosphere. It requires some study, some labour, to attain this end; so much the better. It is well that the avenues of art should be obstructed by those brambles from which everybody recoils except those of powerful will. Besides, it is this very study, fostered by an ardent inspiration, which will ensure the drama against a vice that kills it — the *commonplace*. To be commonplace is the failing of short-sighted, short-breathed poets. In this tableau of the stage, each figure must be held down to its most prominent, most individual, most precisely defined characteristic. Even the vulgar and the trivial should have an accent of their own. Like God, the true poet is present in every part of his work at once. Genius resembles the die which stamps the king's effigy on copper and golden coins alike.

.   .   .

If we were entitled to say what, in our opinion, the style of dramatic poetry should be, we would declare for a free, outspoken, sincere verse, which dares say everything without prudery, express its meaning without seeking for words; which passes naturally from comedy to tragedy, from the sublime to the grotesque; by turns practical and poetical, both artistic and inspired, profound and impulsive, of wide range and true; verse which is apt opportunely to displace the cæsura, in order to disguise the monotony of Alexandrines; more inclined to the *enjambement* that lengthens the line, than to the inversion of phrases that confuses the sense; faithful to rhyme, that enslaved queen, that supreme charm of our poetry, that creator of our metre; verse that is inexhaustible in the verity of its turns of thought, unfathomable in its secrets of composition and of grace; assuming, like Proteus, a thousand forms without changing its type and character; avoiding long speeches; taking delight in dialogue; always hiding behind the characters of the drama; intent, before everything, on being in its place, and when it falls to its lot to be *beautiful,* being so only by chance, as it were, in spite of itself and unconsciously; lyric, epic, dramatic, at need; capable of running through the whole gamut of poetry, of skipping from high notes to low, from the most exalted to the most trivial ideas, from the most extravagant to the most solemn, from the most superficial to the most abstract, without ever passing beyond the limits of a spoken scene; in a word, such verse as a man would write whom a fairy had endowed with Corneille's mind and Molière's brain. It seems to us that such verse would be *as fine as prose.*

There would be nothing in common between poetry of this sort and that of which we made a *post mortem* examination just now. The distinction will be easy to point out if a certain man of talent, to whom the author of this book is under personal obligation, will allow us to borrow his clever phrase: the other poetry was descriptive, this would be picturesque. . . .

.   .   .

Meanwhile, the first, the indispensable merit of a dramatic writer, whether he write in prose or verse, is correctness. Not a mere superficial correctness, the merit or defect of the descriptive school . . . but that intimate, deep-rooted, deliberate correctness, which is permeated with the genius of a language, which has sounded its roots and searched its etymology; always unfettered, because it is sure of its footing, and always more in harmony with the logic of the language. Our Lady Grammar leads the other in leading-strings; the other holds grammar in leash. It can venture anything, can create or invent its style; it has a right to do so. For, whatever certain men may have said who did not think what they were saying, and among whom we must place, notably, him who writes these lines, the French tongue is not *fixed* and never will be. A language does not become fixed. The human intellect is always on the march, or, if you prefer, in movement, and languages with it. Things are made so. When the body changes, how could the coat not change? The French of the nineteenth century can no more be the French of the eighteenth, than that is the French of the seventeenth, or than the French of the seventeenth is that of the sixteenth. Montaigne's language is not Rabelais's, Pascal's is not Montaigne's, Montesquieu's is not Pascal's. Each of the four languages, taken by itself, is admirable because it is original. Every age has its own ideas; it must have also words adapted to those ideas. Languages are like the sea, they move to and fro incessantly. At certain times they leave one shore of the world of thought and overflow another.

All that their waves thus abandon dries up and vanishes. It is in this wise that ideas vanish, that words disappear. It is the same with human tongues as with everything. Each age adds and takes away something. What can be done? It is the decree of fate. In vain, therefore, should we seek to petrify the mobile physiognomy of our idiom in a fixed form. In vain do our literary Joshuas cry out to the language to stand still; languages and the sun do not stand still. The day when they become *fixed,* they are dead. — That is why the French of a certain contemporary school is a dead language.

Such are, substantially, but without the more elaborate development which would make the evidence in their favour more complete, the *present* ideas of the author of this book concerning the drama. . . .

.   .   .

The author has soon come to the end of what he had to say to the reader. He has no idea how the critics will greet this drama and these thoughts, summarily set forth, stripped of their corollaries and ramifications, put together *currente calamo,* and in haste to have done with them. Doubtless they will appear to "the disciples of La Harpe" most impudent and strange. But if perchance, naked and undeveloped as they are, they should have the power to start upon the road of truth this public whose education is so far advanced, and whose minds so many notable writings, of criticism or of original thought, books or newspapers, have already matured for art, let the public follow that impulsion, caring naught whether it comes from a man unknown, from a voice with no authority, from a work of little merit. It is a copper bell which summons the people to the true temple and the true God.

There is to-day the old literary regime as well as the old political regime. The last century still weighs upon the present one at almost every point. It is notably oppressive in the matter of criticism. For instance, you find living men who repeat to you this definition of taste let fall by Voltaire: "Taste in poetry is no different from what it is in women's clothes." Taste, then, is coquetry. Remarkable words, which depict marvellously the painted, *moucheté,* powdered poetry of the eighteenth century — that literature in panniers, pompons and falbalas. They give an admirable résumé of an age with which the loftiest geniuses could not come in contact without becoming petty, in one respect or another; of an

age when Montesquieu was able and apt to produce *Le Temple de Gnide,*
Voltaire *Le Temple du Goût,* Jean-Jacques [Rousseau] *Le Devin du
Village.*

Taste is the common sense of genius. This is what will soon be demonstrated by another school of criticism; powerful, outspoken, well-informed,
— a school of the century which is beginning to put forth vigorous shoots
under the dead and withered branches of the old school. This youthful
criticism, as serious as the other is frivolous, as learned as the other is
ignorant, has already established organs that are listened to, and one is
sometimes surprised to find, even in the least important sheets, excellent
articles emanating from it. Joining hands with all that is fearless and
superior in letters, it will deliver us from two scourges: tottering *classi-
cism,* and false *romanticism,* which has the presumption to show itself at
the feet of the true. For modern genius already has its shadow, its copy,
its parasite, its *classic,* which forms itself upon it, smears itself with its
colours, assumes its livery, picks up its crumbs, and, like *the sorcerer's
pupil,* puts in play, with words retained by the memory, elements of
theatrical action of which its master many a time has much difficulty in
making good. But the thing that must be destroyed first of all is the old
false taste. Present-day literature must be cleansed of its rust. In vain does
the rust eat into it and tarnish it. It is addressing a young, stern, vigorous
generation, which does not understand it. The train of the eighteenth
century is still dragging in the nineteenth; but we, we young men who
have seen Bonaparte, are not the ones who will carry it.

We are approaching, then, the moment when we shall see the new
criticism prevail, firmly established upon a broad and deep foundation.
People generally will soon understand that writers should be judged, not
according to rules and species, which are contrary to nature and art, but
according to the immutable principles of the art of composition, and the
special laws of their individual temperaments. The sound judgment of
all men will be ashamed of the criticism which broke Pierre Corneille on
the wheel, gagged Jean Racine, and which ridiculously rehabilitated
John Milton only by virtue of the epic code of Père le Bossu. People will
consent to place themselves at the author's standpoint, to view the subject
with his eyes, in order to judge a work intelligently. They will lay aside
— and it is M. de Chateaubriand who speaks — "the paltry criticism of
defects for the noble and fruitful criticism of beauties." It is time that all
acute minds should grasp the thread that frequently connects what we,

following our special whim, call "defects" with what we call "beauty."
Defects — at all events those which we call by that name — are often the
inborn, necessary, inevitable conditions of good qualities.

    Scit genius, natale comes qui temperat astrum.
[The tutelar deity knows, the companion who regulates the star
of one's birth.]

Who ever saw a medal without its reverse? a talent that had not some
shadow with its brilliancy, some smoke with its flame? Such a blemish
can be only the inseparable consequence of such beauty. This rough
stroke of the brush, which offends my eye at close range, completes the
effect and gives relief to the whole picture. Efface one and you efface the
other. Originality is made up of such things. Genius is necessarily un-
even. There are no high mountains without deep ravines. Fill up the
valley with the mountain and you will have nothing but a steppe, a
plateau, the plain of Les Sablons instead of the Alps, swallows and not
eagles.

We must also take into account the weather, the climate, the local influences. The Bible, Homer, hurt us sometimes by their very sublimities.
Who would want to part with a word of either of them? Our infirmity
often takes fright at the inspired bold flights of genius, for lack of power
to swoop down upon objects with such vast intelligence. And then, once
again, there are *defects* which take root only in masterpieces; it is given
only to certain geniuses to have certain defects. Shakespeare is blamed
for his abuse of metaphysics, of wit, of redundant scenes, of obscenities,
for his employment of the mythological nonsense in vogue in his time,
for exaggeration, obscurity, bad taste, bombast, asperities of style. The
oak, that giant tree which we were comparing to Shakespeare just now,
and which has more than one point of resemblance to him, the oak has
an unusual shape, gnarled branches, dark leaves, and hard, rough bark;
but it is the oak.

And it is because of these qualities that it is the oak. If you would have
a smooth trunk, straight branches, satiny leaves, apply to the pale birch,
the hollow elder, the weeping willow; but leave the mighty oak in peace.
Do not stone that which gives you shade. . . .

      .   .   .

One last word. It may have been noticed that in this somewhat long journey through so many different subjects, the author has generally refrained from resting his personal views upon texts or citations of authorities. It is not, however, because he did not have them at his hand.

"If the poet establishes things that are impossible according to the rules of his art, he makes a mistake unquestionably; but it ceases to be a mistake when by this means he has reached the end that he aimed at; for he has found what he sought." — "They take for nonsense whatever the weakness of their intellects does not allow them to understand. They are especially prone to call absurd those wonderful passages in which the poet, in order the better to enforce his argument, departs, if we may so express it, from his argument. In fact, the precept which makes it a rule sometimes to disregard rules, is a mystery of the art which it is not easy to make men understand who are absolutely without taste and whom a sort of abnormality of mind renders insensible to those things which ordinarily impress men."

Who said the first? Aristotle. Who said the last? Boileau. By these two specimens you will see that the author of this drama might, as well as another, have shielded himself with proper names and taken refuge behind others' reputations. But he preferred to leave that style of argument to those who deem it unanswerable, universal and all-powerful. As for himself, he prefers reasons to authorities; he has always cared more for arms than for coats-of-arms.

[TRANSLATED BY GEORGE BURNHAM IVES]

The Lady of Shalott

ALFRED TENNYSON

(1809–1892)

This poem, published in 1832, is like The Ancient Mariner; *it is apparently a simple bit of medieval imaginative fantasy, but in actuality it creates a special symbolic language for referring to the psychic problems of the artist. The central problem is how the alienated artist shall re-enter society. He longs to do so, but he will be destroyed if he does. On the other hand, does not the contrast between weaving and singing suggest that only by a suicidal re-entry can he achieve truly sincere utterance? The irony of Lancelot's incapacity to understand what has happened should not be missed. Here the role confronts the anti-role.*

PART I.

On either side the river lie
Long fields of barley and of rye,
That clothe the wold and meet the sky;
And thro' the field the road runs by
      To many-tower'd Camelot;
And up and down the people go
Gazing where the lilies blow

Round an island there below,
    The island of Shalott.

Willows whiten, aspens quiver,
Little breezes dusk and shiver
Thro' the wave that runs for ever
By the island in the river
    Flowing down to Camelot.
Four gray walls, and four gray towers,
Overlook a space of flowers,
And the silent isle imbowers
    The Lady of Shalott.

By the margin, willow-veil'd,
Slide the heavy barges trail'd
By slow horses; and unhail'd
The shallop flitteth silken-sail'd
    Skimming down to Camelot:
But who hath seen her wave her hand?
Or at the casement seen her stand?
Or is she known in all the land,
    The Lady of Shalott?

Only reapers, reaping early
In among the bearded barley,
Hear a song that echoes cheerly
From the river winding clearly,
    Down to tower'd Camelot:
And by the moon the reaper weary,
Piling sheaves in uplands airy,
Listening, whispers " 'Tis the fairy
    Lady of Shalott."

PART II.

There she weaves by night and day
A magic web with colours gay.
She has heard a whisper say,
A curse is on her if she stay
    To look down to Camelot.

She knows not what the curse may be,
And so she weaveth steadily,
And little other care hath she,
   The Lady of Shalott.

And moving thro' a mirror clear
That hangs before her all the year,
Shadows of the world appear.
There she sees the highway near
   Winding down to Camelot:
There the river eddy whirls,
And there the surly village-churls,
And the red cloaks of market-girls,
   Pass onward from Shalott.

Sometimes a troop of damsels glad,
An abbot on an ambling pad,
Sometimes a curly shepherd-lad,
Or long-hair'd page in crimson clad,
   Goes by to tower'd Camelot;
And sometimes thro' the mirror blue
The knights come riding two and two:
She hath no loyal knight and true,
   The Lady of Shalott.

But in her web she still delights
To weave the mirror's magic sights,
For often thro' the silent nights
A funeral, with plumes and lights
   And music, went to Camelot:
Or when the moon was overhead,
Came two young lovers lately wed;
"I am half-sick of shadows," said
   The Lady of Shalott.

PART III.

A bow-shot from her bower-eaves,
He rode between the barley sheaves,

The sun came dazzling thro' the leaves,
And flamed upon the brazen greaves
      Of bold Sir Lancelot.
A redcross knight for ever kneel'd
To a lady in his shield,
That sparkled on the yellow field,
      Beside remote Shalott.

The gemmy bridle glitter'd free,
Like to some branch of stars we see
Hung in the golden Galaxy.
The bridle-bells rang merrily
      As he rode down to Camelot:
And from his blazon'd baldric slung
A mighty silver bugle hung,
And as he rode his armour rung,
      Beside remote Shalott.

All in the blue unclouded weather
Thick-jewell'd shone the saddle-leather,
The helmet and the helmet-feather
Burn'd like one burning flame together,
      As he rode down to Camelot.
As often thro' the purple night,
Below the starry clusters bright,
Some bearded meteor, trailing light,
      Moves over still Shalott.

His broad clear brow in sunlight glow'd;
On burnish'd hooves his war-horse trode;
From underneath his helmet flow'd
His coal-black curls as on he rode,
      As he rode down to Camelot.
From the bank and from the river
He flash'd into the crystal mirror,
"Tirra lirra," by the river
      Sang Sir Lancelot.

She left the web, she left the loom,
She made three paces thro' the room,

She saw the water-lily bloom,
She saw the helmet and the plume,
   She look'd down to Camelot.
Out flew the web and floated wide;
The mirror crack'd from side to side;
"The curse is come upon me," cried
   The Lady of Shalott.

PART IV.

In the stormy east-wind straining,
The pale-yellow woods were waning,
The broad stream in his banks complaining,
Heavily the low sky raining
   Over tower'd Camelot;
Down she came and found a boat
Beneath a willow left afloat,
And round about the prow she wrote
   The Lady of Shalott.

And down the river's dim expanse —
Like some bold seër in a trance,
Seeing all his own mischance —
With a glassy countenance
   Did she look to Camelot.
And at the closing of the day
She loosed the chain, and down she lay;
The broad stream bore her far away,
   The Lady of Shalott.

Lying, robed in snowy white
That loosely flew to left and right —
The leaves upon her falling light —
Thro' the noises of the night
   She floated down to Camelot:
And as the boat-head wound along
The willowy hills and fields among,
They heard her singing her last song,
   The Lady of Shalott.

Heard a carol, mournful, holy,
Chanted loudly, chanted lowly,
Till her blood was frozen slowly,
And her eyes were darken'd wholly,
   Turn'd to tower'd Camelot;
For ere she reach'd upon the tide
The first house by the water-side,
Singing in her song she died,
   The Lady of Shalott.

Under tower and balcony,
By garden-wall and gallery,
A gleaming shape she floated by,
A corse between the houses high,
   Silent into Camelot.
Out upon the wharfs they came,
Knight and burgher, lord and dame,
And round the prow they read her name,
   The Lady of Shalott.

Who is this? and what is here?
And in the lighted palace near
Died the sound of royal cheer;
And they cross'd themselves for fear,
   All the knights at Camelot:
But Lancelot mused a little space;
He said, "She has a lovely face;
God in his mercy lend her grace,
   The Lady of Shalott."

Sartor Resartus

THOMAS CARLYLE

(1795–1881)

The title means "The Tailor Re-Tailored." Man is the tailor;
his clothes are the ideas by which he organizes his relation to
a chaotic universe; but ideas, like clothes, wear out with use;
it is time to get a new set of ideas. Carlyle confronts the role
with the Self by pretending that an English magazine editor
is reviewing a German book, Clothes: Their Origin and Influence *by a Professor-of-Things-in-General, Diogenes Teufels-*
dröckh (God-born Devil-dung). Part II, from which the
following excerpts are taken, is a supposed biography of the
Professor, assembled from the miscellaneous contents of a set of
paper bags which the Professor left behind when he departed
to observe the French Revolution of 1830, and which a friend
has sent to the English editor. It contains the finest of all
accounts of the Romantic process of the loss and the recovery
of value. The emphasis on the act comes from Goethe, but it
has more striking affinities with Schopenhauer and Balzac.
Carlyle had great difficulty in getting so fantastic a book pub-
lished. It finally appeared as a magazine serial in 1832–33. Its
first book publication was in the United States, where it had
a profound influence. Subsequent American literature can
scarcely be understood without it, though most critics of nine-
teenth-century American literature ignore it.

THE EVERLASTING NO

.   .   .

"So had it lasted," concludes the Wanderer, "so had it lasted, as in bitter protracted Death-agony, through long years. The heart within me, unvisited by any heavenly dew-drop was smouldering in sulphurous, slow-consuming fire. Almost since earliest memory I had shed no tear; or once only when I, murmuring half-audibly, recited Faust's Death-song, that wild *Selig der den er im Siegesglanze findet* (Happy whom *he* finds in Battle's splendour), and thought that of this last Friend even I was not forsaken, that Destiny itself could not doom me not to die. Having no hope, neither had I any definite fear, were it of Man or of Devil: nay, I often felt as if it might be solacing, could the Arch-Devil himself, though in Tartarean terrors, but rise to me, that I might tell him a little of my mind. And yet, strangely enough, I lived in a continual, indefinite, pining fear; tremulous, pusillanimous, apprehensive of I knew not what; it seemed as if all things in the Heavens above and the Earth beneath would hurt me; as if the Heavens and the Earth were but boundless jaws of a devouring monster, wherein I, palpitating, waited to be devoured.

"Full of such humour, and perhaps the miserablest man in the whole French Capital or Suburbs, was I, one sultry Dog-day, after much perambulation, toiling along the dirty little *Rue Saint-Thomas de l'Enfer,* among civic rubbish enough, in a close atmosphere, and over pavements hot as Nebuchadnezzar's Furnace; whereby doubtless my spirits were little cheered; when, all at once, there rose a Thought in me, and I asked myself: 'What *art* thou afraid of? Wherefore, like a coward, dost thou forever pip and whimper, and go cowering and trembling? Despicable biped! what is the sum-total of the worst that lies before thee? Death? Well, Death; and say the pangs of Tophet too, and all that the Devil and Man may, will or can do against thee! Hast thou not a heart; canst thou not suffer whatsoever it be; and, as a Child of Freedom, though outcast, trample Tophet itself under thy feet, while it consumes thee? Let it come, then; I will meet it and defy it!' And as I so thought, there rushed like a stream of fire over my whole soul; and I shook base Fear away from me forever. I was strong, of unknown strength; a spirit, almost a god. Ever from that time, the temper of my misery was changed: not Fear or whining Sorrow was it, but Indignation and grim fire-eyed Defiance.

"Thus had the EVERLASTING NO (*das ewige Nein*) pealed authoritatively through all the recesses of my Being, of my ME; and then was it that my whole ME stood up, in native God-created majesty, and with emphasis recorded its Protest. Such a Protest, the most important transaction in Life, may that same Indignation and Defiance, in a psychological point of view, be fitly called. The Everlasting No had said: 'Behold, thou art fatherless, outcast, and the Universe is mine (the Devil's)'; to which my whole Me now made answer: 'I am not thine, but Free, and forever hate thee!'

"It is from this hour that I incline to date my Spiritual Newbirth, or Baphometic Fire-baptism; perhaps I directly thereupon began to be a Man."

CENTRE OF INDIFFERENCE

.   .   .

"At length, after so much roasting," thus writes our Autobiographer, "I was what you might name calcined. Pray only that it be not rather, as is the more frequent issue, reduced to a *caput-mortuum!* But in any case, by mere dint of practice, I had grown familiar with many things. Wretchedness was still wretched; but I could now partly see through it, and despise it. Which highest mortal, in this inane Existence, had I not found a Shadow-hunter, or Shadow-hunted; and, when I looked through his brave garnitures, miserable enough? Thy wishes have all been sniffed aside, thought I: but what, had they even been all granted! Did not the Boy Alexander weep because he had not two Planets to conquer; or a whole Solar System; or after that, a whole Universe? *Ach Gott,* when I gazed into these Stars, have they not looked-down on me as if with pity, from their serene spaces; like Eyes glistening with heavenly tears over the little lot of man! Thousands of human generations, all as noisy as our own, have been swallowed-up of Time, and there remains no wreck of them any more; and Arcturus and Orion and Sirius and the Pleiades are still shining in their courses, clear and young, as when the Shepherd first noted them in the plain of Shinar. Pshaw! what is this paltry little Dog-cage of an Earth; what art thou that sittest whining there? Thou art still Nothing, Nobody: true; but who, then, is Something, Somebody? For thee the Family of Man has no use; it rejects thee; thou art wholly as a dissevered limb: so be it; perhaps it is better so!"

Too-heavy-laden Teufelsdröckh! Yet surely his bands are loosening; one day he will hurl the burden far from him, and bound forth free and with a second youth.

"This," says our Professor, "was the CENTRE OF INDIFFERENCE I had now reached; through which whoso travels from the Negative Pole to the Positive must necessarily pass."

THE EVERLASTING YEA

"Temptations in the Wilderness!" exclaims Teufelsdröckh: "Have we not all to be tried with such? Not so easily can the old Adam, lodged in us by birth, be dispossessed. Our Life is compassed round with Necessity; yet is the meaning of Life itself no other than Freedom, than Voluntary Force; thus have we a warfare; in the beginning, especially, a hard-fought battle. For the God-given mandate, *Work thou in Welldoing,* lies mysteriously written, in Promethean Prophetic Characters, in our hearts; and leaves us no rest, night or day, till it be deciphered and obeyed; till it burn forth, in our conduct, a visible, acted Gospel of Freedom. And as the clay-given mandate, *Eat thou and be filled,* at the same time persuasively proclaims itself through every nerve, — must not there be a confusion, a contest, before the better Influence can become the upper?

"To me nothing seems more natural than that the Son of Man, when such God-given mandate first prophetically stirs within him, and the Clay must now be vanquished or vanquish, — should be carried of the spirit into grim Solitudes, and there fronting the Tempter do grimmest battle with him; defiantly setting him at naught, till he yield and fly. Name it as we choose: with or without visible Devil, whether in the natural Desert of rocks and sands, or in the populous moral Desert of selfishness and baseness, — to such Temptation are we all called. Unhappy if we are not! Unhappy if we are but Half-men, in whom that divine handwriting has never blazed forth, all-subduing, in true sun-splendour; but quivers dubiously amid meaner lights: or smoulders, in dull pain, in darkness, under earthly vapours! — Our Wilderness is the wide World in an Atheistic Century; our Forty Days are long years of suffering and fasting: nevertheless, to these also comes an end. Yes, to me also was given, if not Victory, yet the consciousness of Battle, and the resolve to persevere therein while life or faculty is left. To me also, entangled in the enchanted forests, demon-peopled, doleful of sight and of sound, it was given, after weariest wanderings, to work out my way into the higher sunlight slopes — of that Mountain which has no summit, or whose summit is in Heaven only!"

He says elsewhere, under a less ambitious figure; as figures are, once for all, natural to him: "Has not thy Life been that of most sufficient men (*tüchtigen Männer*) thou has known in this generation? An outflush of foolish young Enthusiasm, like the first fallow-crop, wherein are as many weeds as valuable herbs: this all parched away, under the Droughts of practical and spiritual Unbelief, as Disappointment, in thought and act, often-repeated gave rise to Doubt, and Doubt gradually settled into Denial! If I have had a second-crop, and now see the perennial greensward, and sit under umbrageous cedars, which defy all Drought (and Doubt); herein too, be the Heavens praised, I am not without examples, and even exemplars."

So that, for Teufelsdröckh also, there has been a "glorious revolution": these mad shadow-hunting and shadow-hunted Pilgrimings of his were but some purifying "Temptation in the Wilderness," before his apostolic work (such as it was) could begin; which Temptation is now happily over, and the Devil once more worsted! Was "that high moment in the *Rue de l'Enfer,*" then, properly the turning-point of the battle; when the Fiend said, *Worship me, or be torn in shreds;* and was answered valiantly with an *Apage Satana?* — Singular Teufelsdröckh, would thou hadst told thy singular story in plain words! But it is fruitless to look there, in those Paper-bags, for such. Nothing but innuendoes, figurative crotchets: a typical Shadow, fitfully wavering, prophetico-satiric; no clear logical Picture. "How paint to the sensual eye," asks he once, "what passes in the Holy-of-Holies of Man's Soul; in what words, known to these profane times, speak even afar-off of the unspeakable?" We ask in turn: Why perplex these times, profane as they are, with needless obscurity, by omission and by commission? Not mystical only is our Professor, but whimsical; and involves himself, now more than ever, in eye-bewildering *chiaroscuro.* Successive glimpses, here faithfully imparted, our more gifted readers must endeavour to combine for their own behoof.

He says: "The hot Harmattan wind had raged itself out; its howl went silent within me; and the long-deafened soul could now hear. I paused in my wild wanderings; and sat me down to wait, and consider; for it was as if the hour of change drew nigh. I seemed to surrender, to renounce utterly, and say: Fly, then, false shadows of Hope; I will chase you no more, I will believe you no more. And ye too, haggard spectres of Fear, I care not for you; ye too are all shadows and a lie. Let me rest here: for I am way-weary and life-weary; I will rest here, were it but to die: to die or to live is alike to me; alike insignificant." — And again: "Here, then, as I lay in that Centre of Indifference; cast, doubtless by benignant upper Influence, into a healing sleep, the heavy dreams rolled gradually away, and I awoke to a new Heaven and a new Earth. The first pre- liminary moral Act, Annihilation of Self (*Selbst-tödtung*), had been hap- pily accomplished; and my mind's eyes were now unsealed, and its hands ungyved."

Might we not also conjecture that the following passage refers to his Locality, during this same "healing sleep"; that his Pilgrim-staff lies cast aside here, on "the high table-land"; and indeed that the repose is already taking wholesome effect on him? If it were not that the tone, in some parts, has more of riancy, even of levity, than we could have expected! However, in Teufelsdröckh, there is always the strangest Dualism: light dancing, with guitar-music, will be going on in the forecourt, while by fits from within comes the faint whimpering of woe and wail. We tran- scribe the piece entire.

"Beautiful it was to sit there, as in my skyey Tent, musing and medi- tating; on the high table-land, in front of the Mountains; over me, as roof, the azure Dome, and around me, for walls, four azure-flowing cur- tains, — namely, of the Four azure Winds, on whose bottom-fringes also I have seen gilding. And then to fancy the fair Castles that stood sheltered in these Mountain hollows; with their green flower-lawns, and white dames and damosels, lovely enough: or better still, the straw-roofed Cot- tages, wherein stood many a Mother baking bread, with her children round her: — all hidden and protectingly folded-up in the valley-folds; yet there and alive, as sure as if I beheld them. Or to see, as well as fancy, the nine Towns and Villages, that lay round my mountain-seat, which, in still weather, were wont to speak to me (by their steeple-bells) with metal tongue; and, in almost all weather, proclaimed their vitality by repeated Smoke-clouds; whereon, as on a culinary horologe, I might read the hour of the day. For it was the smoke of cookery, as kind housewives at morning, midday, eventide, were boiling their husbands' kettles; and ever a blue pillar rose up into the air, successively or simultaneously, from each of the nine, saying, as plainly as smoke could say: Such and such a meal is getting ready here. Not uninteresting! For you have the whole Borough, with all its love-makings and scandal-mongeries, contentions and contentments, as in miniature, and could cover it all with your hat. — If, in my wide Wayfarings, I had learned to look into the business of the World in its details, here perhaps was the place for combining it into general propositions, and deducing inferences therefrom.

"Often also could I see the black Tempest marching in anger through the Distance: round some Schreckhorn, as yet grim-blue, would the eddying vapour gather, and there tumultuously eddy, and flow down like a mad witch's hair; till, after a space, it vanished, and, in the clear sun-beam, your Schreckhorn stood smiling grim-white, for the vapour had held snow. How thou fermentest and elaboratest, in thy great fermenting-vat and laboratory of an Atmosphere, of a World, O Nature! — Or what is Nature? Ha! why do I not name thee GOD? Art not thou the 'Living Garment of God'? O Heavens, is it, in very deed, HE, then, that ever speaks through thee; that lives and loves in thee, that lives and loves in me?

"Fore-shadows, call them rather fore-splendours, of that Truth, and Beginning of Truths, fell mysteriously over my soul. Sweeter than Day-spring to the Ship-wrecked in Nova Zembla; ah, like the mother's voice to her little child that strays bewildered, weeping, in unknown tumults; like soft streamings of celestial music to my too-exasperated heart, came that Evangel. The Universe is not dead and demoniacal, a charnel-house with spectres; but godlike, and my Father's!

"With other eyes, too, could I now look upon my fellow man: with an infinite Love, an infinite Pity. Poor, wandering, wayward man! Art thou not tried, and beaten with stripes, even as I am? Ever, whether thou bear the royal mantle or the beggar's gabardine, art thou not so weary, so heavy-laden; and thy Bed of Rest is but a Grave. O my Brother, my Brother, why cannot I shelter thee in my bosom, and wipe away all tears from thy eyes! — Truly, the din of many-voiced Life, which, in this soli-tude, with the mind's organ, I could hear, was no longer a maddening discord, but a melting one; like inarticulate cries, and sobbings of a dumb creature, which in the ear of Heaven are prayers. The poor Earth, with her poor joys, was now my needy Mother, not my cruel Stepdame; Man, with his so mad Wants and so mean Endeavours, had become the dearer to me; and even for his sufferings and his sins, I now first named him

Brother. Thus was I standing in the porch of that *'Sanctuary of Sorrow';* by strange, steep ways had I too been guided thither; and ere long its sacred gates would open, and the *'Divine Depth of Sorrow'* lie disclosed to me."

The Professor says, he here first got eye on the Knot that had been strangling him, and straightway could unfasten it, and was free. "A vain interminable controversy," writes he, "touching what is at present called Origin of Evil, or some such thing, arises in every soul, since the beginning of the world; and in every soul, that would pass from idle Suffering into actual Endeavouring, must first be put an end to. The most, in our time, have to go content with a simple, incomplete enough Suppression of this controversy; to a few some Solution of it is indispensable. In every new era, too, such Solution comes-out in different terms; and ever the Solution of the last era has become obsolete, and is found unserviceable. For it is man's nature to change his Dialect from century to century; he cannot help it though he would. The authentic *Church-Catechism* of our present century has not yet fallen into my hands: meanwhile, for my own private behoof, I attempt to elucidate the matter so. Man's Unhappiness, as I construe, comes of his Greatness; it is because there is an Infinite in him, which with all his cunning he cannot quite bury under the Finite. Will the whole Finance Ministers and Upholsterers and Confectioners of modern Europe undertake, in joint-stock company, to make one Shoeblack HAPPY? They cannot accomplish it, above an hour or two: for the Shoeblack also has a Soul quite other than his Stomach; and would require, if you consider it, for his permanent satisfaction and saturation, simply this allotment, no more, and no less: *God's infinite Universe altogether to himself,* therein to enjoy infinitely, and fill every wish as fast as it rose. Oceans of Hochheimer, a Throat like that of Ophiuchus: speak not of them; to the infinite Shoeblack they are as nothing. No sooner is your ocean filled, than he grumbles that it might have been of better vintage. Try him with half of a Universe, of an Omnipotence, he sets to quarrelling with the proprietor of the other half, and declares himself the most maltreated of men. — Always there is a black spot in our sunshine: it is even, as I said, the *Shadow of Ourselves.*"

.   .   .

"To me, in this our life," says the Professor, "which is an internecine

warfare with the Time-spirit, other warfare seems questionable. Hast
thou in any way a Contention with thy brother, I advise thee, think well
what the meaning thereof is. If thou gauge it to the bottom, it is simply
this: 'Fellow, see! thou art taking more than thy share of Happiness in
the world, something from *my* share: which, by the Heavens, thou shalt
not; nay I will fight thee rather.' — Alas, and the whole lot to be di-
vided is such a beggarly matter, truly a 'feast of shells,' for the substance
has been spilled out: not enough to quench one Appetite; and the collective human species clutching at them! — Can we not, in all such cases,
rather say: 'Take it, thou too-ravenous individual; take that pitiful addi-
tional fraction of a share, which I reckoned mine, but which thou so
wantest; take it with a blessing: would to Heaven I had enough for thee!'
— If Fichte's *Wissenschaftslehre* be, 'to a certain extent, Applied Christianity,' surely to a still greater extent, so is this. We have here not a
Whole Duty of Man, yet a Half Duty, namely the Passive half: could we
but do it, as we can demonstrate it!

"But indeed Conviction, were it never so excellent, is worthless till it
convert itself into Conduct. Nay properly Conviction is not possible till
then; inasmuch as all Speculation is by nature endless, formless, a vortex
amid vortices: only by a felt indubitable certainty of Experience does it
find any centre to revolve round, and so fashion itself into a system. Most
true is it, as a wise man teaches us, that 'Doubt of any sort cannot be
removed except by Action.' On which ground, too, let him who gropes
painfully in darkness or uncertain light, and prays vehemently that the
dawn may ripen into day, lay this other precept well to heart, which to
me was of invaluable service: *'Do the Duty which lies nearest thee,'*
which thou knowest to be a Duty! Thy second Duty will already have
become clearer.

"May we not say, however, that the hour of Spiritual Enfranchisement
is even this: When your Ideal World, wherein the whole man has been
dimly struggling and inexpressibly languishing to work, becomes revealed, and thrown open; and you discover, with amazement enough, like
the Lothario in *Wilhelm Meister,* that your 'America is here or nowhere'?
The Situation that has not its Duty, its Ideal, was never yet occupied by
man. Yes here, in this poor, miserable, hampered, despicable Actual,
wherein thou even now standest, here or nowhere is thy Ideal: work it
out therefrom; and working, believe, live, be free. Fool! the Ideal is in
thyself, the impediment too is in thyself: thy Condition is but the stuff

thou art to shape that same Ideal out of: what matters whether such stuff be of this sort or that, so the Form thou give it be heroic, be poetic? O thou that pinest in the imprisonment of the Actual, and criest bitterly to the gods for a kingdom wherein to rule and create, know this of a truth: the thing thou seekest is already with thee, 'here or nowhere,' couldst thou only see!

"But it is with man's Soul as it was with Nature: the beginning of Creation is — Light. Till the eye have vision, the whole members are in bonds. Divine moment, when over the tempest-tossed Soul, as once over the wild-weltering Chaos, it is spoken: Let there be Light! Ever to the greatest that has felt such moment, is it not miraculous and God-announcing; even as, under simpler figures, to the simplest and least. The mad primeval Discord is hushed; the rudely-jumbled conflicting elements bind themselves into separate Firmaments: deep silent rock-foundations are built beneath; and the skyey vault with its everlasting Luminaries above: instead of a dark wasteful Chaos, we have a blooming, fertile, heaven-encompassed World.

"I too could now say to myself: Be no longer a Chaos, but a World, or even Worldkin. Produce! Produce! Were it but the pitifullest infinitesi-mal fraction of a Product, produce it, in God's name! 'Tis the utmost thou hast in thee: out with it, then. Up, up! Whatsover thy hand findeth to do, do it with thy whole might. Work while it is called Today; for the Night cometh, wherein no man can work."

NOTE ON ILLUSTRATIONS: GROUP II
Numbers 17 to 28

The art of Transcendentalism was fantastic, exaggerated, explosive
— the art of the Virtuoso. Even a relatively conservative academician
like Couture exhibits this solution to the problem of the re-entry of the
Romantic into social reality by exploding the role. But the three follow-
ing pictures might be illustrations to the pianistic and orchestral works of
Liszt; and the landscape of John Martin is distinctly Tennysonian in its
misty vastness. Delacroix did with line and color what Martin achieved
with space, but Turner, the greatest European Transcendentalist painter,
surpassed them both, particularly in space, light, and color. Before the
end of the nineteenth century, no painter went so far in symbolizing the
explosive imagination of the Transcendentalist in re-creating and re-
deeming the world through the power of his unique vision, of a per-
sonality free from society, but above it and pointing to a new vision of
experience, a vision which, as I have pointed out in the Introduction, ran
into extreme difficulties. Daumier turned in what appears to be an oppo-
site direction, but is in fact identical in its intention, a direction which
reveals the other aspect of Transcendentalism, its fascination for the
domestic and its effort toward extreme simplification, the reduction to
essentials.

The greatest building in England at this time, and perhaps the greatest
in Europe, was Elmes' St. George's Hall in Liverpool; it still astonishes
by its enormous size, its truly Roman grandeur. The next two buildings
(Numbers 24 and 25) show an equally extravagant manipulation of
Gothic and late Italian Renaissance, even Mannerist, idioms. Isaac
Holden's design almost seems to be a late example of Analogist archi-
tecture; but the extremely powerful and bold handling of the wall

surface shows the Transcendental extravagance at work even in this utilitarian building. Egyptian architecture was by no means uncommon in the 1830's and 1840's; it corresponded to the use of the Etruscan idiom, which archaeology had recently made available. The inappropriateness of such a building for a debtor's prison is precisely to the point, and a comment upon the social system which is responsible. As suggested in my introduction, inappropriateness is one of the most interesting aspects of Romantic architecture. The interiors of the Harral house, now unfortunately destroyed, are even more fantastic than the exterior. Again, the exquisite absurdity of a Gothic mansion for an American businessman is precisely the point. The architect seems to imply that the businessman has a chance of achieving human decency if he conceives of himself in a profoundly different manner; in this sense, it is redemptive architecture, as was Thomas Walter's attempt to give dignity to the imprisoned debtors of Philadelphia.

17. Eugène Delacroix, *Abduction of Rebecca*, 1846.

18. Thomas Couture, *Romans of the Decadence,* 1847.

19. John Martin, *Manfred on the Jungfrau*, 1837.

20. Joseph Mallord William Turner, *Fire at Sea*, c. 1834.
Reproduced by courtesy of the Trustees, The National Gallery, London.

21. Honoré Daumier, *The Laundress*, 1861(?).

22. Harvey Lonsdale Elmes, *St. George's Hall*, Liverpool, 1842–1856.

23. Harvey Lonsdale Elmes, *St. George's Hall*, Liverpool.

24. Richard M. Upjohn, *Greenwood Cemetery*, Brooklyn, 1861.

25. Ludwig Ferdinand Hesse, *Orangery*, Potsdam, 1851–1856.

26. Isaac Holden, *Pennsylvania Hospital*, Philadelphia, 1836–1841.

27. Thomas U. Walter, *Debtors' Wing, Moyamensing Prison*, Philadelphia, 1835.

28. Alexander Jackson Davis, *Harral House*, Bridgeport.

III

Objectism

The two modern descendants of Transcendentalism, Communism and Fascism, show the weakness of this second attempt to solve the problem of Romanticism: To redeem others is to impose one's will upon them. But to do that is to violate others, to invade and deny the validity of other Selves. It is to reduce them from Selves to roles which exist only to serve the interests of heroic world-redemption. It is to turn them from Subjects into Objects. And to deny the validity of self-existent Subjects is to deny the validity of one's own self-existent subjectivity. It is to deny one's own Self, to turn oneself into an Object. Thus the sole ground of Romanticism was ultimately denied by following out the implications of Transcendentalism. One had to return either to Medieval Christianity or to the Enlightenment. But such solutions would merely precipitate the unsolved problem all over again. The only answer was to divest the Self of its Divine authority, to deny any Divine Ground to the world, and to define the Self as simply the conscious awareness which observed the full horror of Nature, Society, and Personality.

Sentimental Education

GUSTAVE FLAUBERT

(1821–1880)

In Madame Bovary *Flaubert had revealed the bitter failure of Transcendental values, but ironically had at the same time demonstrated that society, the world of roles, offered no values at all. In* Sentimental Education, *published in 1869 but begun long before, the hero experiences the illusory nature of all values, including love. The Subject and the Object cancel each other out, leaving only the naked Self. Not even Schopenhauer's consolation of denying the Will is available. The following excerpts form the conclusion of Flaubert's book.*

AFTER MANY YEARS

Frederick travelled a long time.

He experienced the melancholy associated with packet-boats, the chill feeling on waking up under tents, the dizzy effect of mountains and ruins, and the bitterness of broken sympathies.

He returned home.

He mingled in society, and he conceived attachments to many women. But the constant recollection of his first love made them all appear insipid; and besides, the vehemence of desire, the bloom of the sensation had gone. In like manner, his intellectual ambitions had grown weaker.

Years passed; and he was merely supporting the burthen of a life in which his mind was unoccupied and his heart bereft of energy.

Toward the end of March, 1867, just as the day was drawing to a close, he was sitting all alone in his study, when a woman suddenly entered.

"Madame Arnoux!"

"Frederick!"

She caught hold of his hands, and drew him gently toward the window. As she gazed into his face, she kept repeating:

" 'Tis he! Yes, indeed — 'tis he!"

In the lengthening shadows of the twilight, only her eyes were visible under the black lace veil that hid her face.

She laid down on the edge of the mantelpiece a little pocket-book bound in garnet velvet; she seated herself in front of him, and they both remained silent, unable to utter a word, smiling at each other.

At last he asked her a number of questions about herself and her husband.

They were living in a remote part of Brittany for the sake of economy, so as to be able to pay their debts. Arnoux, now almost a chronic invalid, had become quite an old man. Her daughter had been married and was living at Bordeaux, and her son was in garrison at Mostaganem.

Then she raised her head to look at him again:

"But I see you once more! I am happy!"

He did not fail to let her know that, as soon as he heard of their misfortune, he had hastened to their house.

"I knew it!"

"How?"

She had seen him in the street outside the house, and had hidden herself.

"Why did you do that?"

Then, in a trembling voice, and with long pauses between her words:

"I was afraid! Yes — afraid of you and of myself!"

This confession gave him a shock of voluptuous joy. His heart began to throb wildly. She went on:

"Forgive me for not having come sooner." And, pointing toward the little pocket-book covered with golden palm-branches:

"I embroidered it on your account expressly. It contains the amount for which the Belleville property was given as security."

Frederick thanked her, while chiding her at the same time for having given herself any trouble about it.

"No! 'tis not for this I came! I was determined to pay you this visit — then I would go back there again."

And she spoke about the place where they had taken up their abode.

It was a low-built house of only one story; and there was a garden full of huge box-trees, and a double avenue of chestnut-trees, reaching up to the top of the hill, from which there was a view of the sea.

"I go there and sit on a bench, which I have called 'Frederick's bench.'"

Then she gazed at the furniture, the objects of virtu, the pictures, with eager intentness, so that she might be able to carry away the impressions of them in her memory. The Maréchale's portrait was almost hidden behind a curtain. But the gilding and the white spaces of the picture, which showed their outlines through the midst of the surrounding darkness, attracted her attention.

"It seems to me I knew that woman?"

"Impossible!" said Frederick. "It is an old Italian painting."

She said that she would like to take a walk through the streets on his arm.

They went out.

The light from the shop-windows fell, now and then, on her pale profile; then once more she was wrapped in shadow, and in the midst of the carriages, the crowd, and the din, they walked on heedless to what was happening around them, hearing nothing, like those who walk across the fields over beds of dead leaves.

They talked about the days which they had formerly spent in each other's society, the dinners at the time when *L'Art Industriel* flourished, Arnoux's fads, his habit of drawing up the ends of his collar and of using cosmetic on his moustache, and other matters of a more intimate and serious character. What delight he experienced when he first heard her singing! How lovely she looked on her feast-day at Saint-Cloud! He recalled to her memory the little garden at Auteuil, evenings at the theatre, a chance meeting on the boulevard, and some of her old servants, including the negress.

She was astonished at his vivid recollection of these things.

"Sometimes your words come back to me like a distant echo, like the sound of a bell carried by the wind, and when I read love passages in books, it seems to me that it is you about whom I am reading."

"All that people have criticised as exaggerated in fiction you have made me feel," said Frederick. "I can understand Werther, who felt no disgust at his Charlotte for eating bread and butter."

"Poor, dear friend!"

She heaved a sigh; and, after a prolonged silence:

"No matter; we shall have loved each other truly!"

"And still without having ever belonged to each other!"

"That perhaps is all the better," she replied.

"No, no! What happiness we might have enjoyed!"

And it must have been very strong to endure after so long a separation. Frederick wished to know how she first discovered that he loved her.

"It was when you kissed my wrist one evening between the glove and the cuff. I said to myself, 'Ah! yes, he loves me — he loves me;' nevertheless, I was afraid of being assured of it. So charming was your reserve, that I felt myself the object, as it were, of an involuntary and continuous homage."

He regretted nothing now. He was compensated for all he had suffered in the past.

When they returned to the house, Madame Arnoux removed her bonnet. The lamp, placed on a bracket, threw its light on her white hair. Frederick felt as if some one had struck him in the middle of the chest.

In order to conceal from her his sense of disillusion, he flung himself on the floor at her feet, and seizing her hands, whispered in her ear words of tenderness:

"Your person, your slightest movements, seemed to me to have a more than human importance in the world. My heart was like dust under your feet. You produced on me the effect of moonlight on a summer's night, when around us we find nothing but perfumes, soft shadows, gleams of whiteness, infinity; and all the delights of the flesh and of the spirit were for me embodied in your name, which I kept repeating to myself while I tried to kiss it with my lips. I thought of nothing else. It was Madame Arnoux such as you were with your two children, tender, grave, dazzlingly beautiful, and yet so good! This image effaced every other. Did I not dream of it alone? for always, in the very depths of my soul, were the music of your voice and the brightness of your eyes!"

She accepted with transports of joy these tributes of adoration to the woman whom she could no longer claim to be. Frederick, becoming intoxicated with his own words, came to believe himself in the reality of what he said. Madame Arnoux, with her back to the light of the lamp, stooped toward him. He felt the caress of her breath on his forehead, and the undefined touch of her entire body through the garments that kept them apart. Their hands were clasped; the tip of her shoe peeped out from beneath her gown, and he said to her, as if ready to faint:

"The sight of your foot makes me lose my self-possession."

An impulse of modesty caused her to rise. Then, without any further movement, she said, with the strange intonation of a somnambulist:

"At my age! — he — Frederick! Ah! no woman has ever been loved as I have been. No! Where is the use in being young? What do I care about them, indeed? I despise them — all those women who come here!"

"Oh! very few women come to this place," he returned, in a complaisant fashion.

Her face brightened, and then she asked him whether he ever meant to marry.

He swore that he never would.

"Are you perfectly sure? Why should you not?"

" 'Tis on your account!" said Frederick, clasping her in his arms.

She remained thus pressed to his heart, with her head thrown back, her lips parted, and her eyes raised. Suddenly she pushed him away from her with a look of despair, and when he implored of her to say something to him in reply, she whispered:

"I would have liked to make you happy!"

Frederick had a suspicion that Madame Arnoux had come to offer herself to him, and once more he was seized with a desire to possess her — stronger, fiercer, more desperate than he had ever experienced before. And yet he felt, the next moment, an unaccountable repugnance to the thought of such a thing, and, as it were, a dread of incurring the guilt of incest. Another fear, too, affected him — lest disgust might afterward take possession of him. Besides, how embarrassing it would be! — and, abandoning the idea, partly through prudence, and partly through a resolve not to degrade his ideal, he walked away and proceeded to roll a cigarette between his fingers.

She watched him with admiration.

"How dainty you are! There is no one like you! No one!"

It struck eleven.

"Already!" she exclaimed; "at a quarter-past I must go."

She sat down again, but she kept looking at the clock, and he walked

up and down the room, puffing at his cigarette. Neither could think of
anything further to say. There is a moment at the hour of parting when
the person that we love is with us no longer.

At last, when the hands of the clock passed the twenty-five minutes, she
slowly took up her bonnet, holding it by the strings.

"Good-bye, my friend — my dear friend! I shall never see you again!
This is the last page in my life as a woman. My soul shall remain with
you even when you see me no more. May all the blessings of Heaven be
yours!"

And she kissed him on the forehead, like a mother.

But she appeared to be looking for something, and presently she asked
him for a pair of scissors.

She unfastened her comb, and all her white hair fell down.

With a quick movement of the scissors, she cut off a long lock from the
roots.

"Keep it! Good-bye!"

When she was gone, Frederick rushed to the window and threw it open.
On the footpath he saw Madame Arnoux beckoning a passing cab. She
stepped into it. The vehicle was soon out of sight.

And all was over.

WHEN A MAN'S FORTY

Frederick and Deslauriers were talking by the fireside one evening
about the beginning of winter. They were once more reconciled by the
fatality of their nature, which seemed to force them to reunite and be
friends again.

Frederick briefly explained his quarrel with Madame Dambreuse, who
had married again, her second husband being an Englishman.

Deslauriers, without telling how he had come to marry Mademoiselle
Roque, related how his wife had one day eloped with a singer. In order
to expunge to some extent the ridicule that this brought upon him, he
had compromised himself by an excess of governmental zeal in the exercise of his functions as prefect. He had been dismissed. After that, he
had been an agent for colonisation in Algeria, secretary to a pasha, editor
of a newspaper, and canvasser for advertisements, his latest employment
being the settling of disputed cases for a manufacturing company.

Frederick, having squandered two thirds of his means, was now living like a citizen of comparatively humble rank.

Then they questioned each other about their mutual friends.

Martinon was now a member of the Senate.

Hussonnet occupied a high position, in which he was fortunate enough to have all the theatres and entire press dependent upon him.

Cisy, given up to religion, and the father of eight children, was living in the château of his ancestors.

Pellerin, after turning his hand to Fourierism, homœopathy, table-turning, Gothic art, and humanitarian painting, had become a photographer; and he might be seen on every dead wall in Paris, where he was represented in a black coat with a very small body and a big head.

"And what about your chum, Sénécal?" asked Frederick.

"Disappeared — I don't know where! And yourself — what about the woman you were so passionately attached to, Madame Arnoux?"

"She is probably at Rome with her son, a lieutenant of chasseurs."

"And her husband?"

"He died a year ago."

"You don't say so?" exclaimed the advocate. Then, striking his forehead:

"Now that I think of it, the other day, in a shop, I met that worthy Maréchale, holding by the hand a little boy whom she has adopted. She is the widow of a certain Monsieur Oudry, and is now very stout. What a change! — she who formerly had such a slender waist!"

Deslauriers acknowledged that he had taken advantage of the other's despair to satisfy himself of that fact by personal experience.

"As you gave me permission, however."

This avowal was a compensation for the silence he had maintained with reference to his attempt with Madame Arnoux.

Frederick would have forgiven him, inasmuch as he had not succeeded.

Although a little annoyed at the discovery, he pretended to laugh at it; and the allusion to the Maréchale recalled the Vatnaz.

Deslauriers had not seen her, nor any of the others who used to come to the Arnoux's house; but he remembered Regimbart perfectly.

"Is he still living?"

"He is barely alive. Every evening regularly he drags himself from the Rue de Grammont to the Rue Montmartre, to the cafés, enfeebled, bent in two, emaciated, a spectre!"

"Well, and what about Compain?"

Frederick uttered a cry of joy, and begged of the ex-delegate of the provisional government to explain to him the mystery of the calf's head.

" 'Tis an English importation. In order to parody the ceremony which the Royalists celebrated on the thirtieth of January, some Independents founded an annual banquet, at which they have been accustomed to eat calves' head, and at which they drank red wine out of calves' skulls while giving toasts in favour of the extermination of the Stuarts. After Thermidor, the Terrorists organised a brotherhood of a similar description, which proves how universally prolific folly is."

"You appear to be dispassionate about politics?"

"Effect of age," said the advocate.

Then they each proceeded to summarise their lives.

They had both failed in their objects — the one who dreamed only of love, and the other of power.

What was the reason of this?

" 'Tis perhaps on account of not having taken up the proper line," said Frederick.

"In your case that may be so. I, on the contrary, have sinned through excess of rectitude, without giving due weight to a thousand secondary things more important than any. I had too much logic, and you too much sentiment."

Then they blamed luck, circumstances, the epoch at which they were born.

Frederick went on:

"We have never done what we thought of doing long ago at Sens, when you wished to write a critical history of Philosophy and I a great mediæval romance about Nogent, the subject of which I had found in Froissart: 'How Messire Brokars de Fenestranges and the Archbishop of Troyes attacked Messire Eustache d'Ambrecicourt.' Do you remember?"

And, exhuming their youth with every sentence, they continually said to each other:

"Do you remember?"

They saw once more the college playground, the chapel, the parlour, the fencing-school at the bottom of the staircase, the faces of the ushers and of the pupils — one named Angelmare, from Versailles, who used to cut off trousers-straps from old boots, M. Mirbal and his red whiskers, the two professors of linear drawing and large drawing, who were always wrangling, and the Pole, the fellow-countryman of Copernicus, with his planetary system on pasteboard, an itinerant astronomer whose lecture had been paid for by a dinner in the refectory, then a terrible debauch while they were out on a walking excursion, the first pipes they had smoked, the distribution of prizes, and the delightful sensation of going home for the holidays.

It was during the vacation of 1837 that they had called at the house of the Turkish woman.

This was a phrase used to designate a woman whose real name was Zoraide Turc; and many persons believed her to be a Mohammedan, a Turk; this added to the poetic character of her establishment, situated at the water's edge behind the rampart. Even in the middle of summer there was a shadow around her house, which was distinguished by a glass bowl of goldfish near a pot of mignonette at a window. Women in white negligées, with painted cheeks and long earrings, used to tap at the panes as the students passed; and as it grew dark, their custom was to hum softly in their hoarse voices as they stood on the doorsteps.

This home of perdition spread its fantastic notoriety over all the arrondissement. References were made to it in a circumlocutory style: "The place you know — a certain street — at the bottom of the Bridges." It made the farmers' wives of the district tremble for their husbands, and the ladies grow apprehensive as to their servants' virtue, inasmuch as the sub-prefect's cook had been found there; and, of course, it exercised a fascination over the minds of all the young lads of the place.

One Sunday, during vesper-time, Frederick and Deslauriers, having previously curled their hair, gathered some flowers in Madame Moreau's garden, then went out through the gate leading into the fields, and, after taking a wide circuit round the vineyards, came back through the Fishery, and stole into the Turkish woman's house with their big bouquets in their hands.

Frederick presented his as a lover does to his betrothed. But the heat, the fear of the unknown, and even the very pleasure of seeing at one glance so many women at his disposal, excited him so strangely that he turned exceedingly pale, and stood there without advancing a single step or uttering a word. All the girls burst out laughing, amused at his embarrassment. Fancying that they were ridiculing him, he ran away; and, as Frederick had the money, Deslauriers was obliged to follow him.

They were observed leaving the house; and the episode furnished material for a bit of local gossip which was remembered three years later.

They related the story to each other in a prolix fashion, each supplementing the narrative where the other's memory failed; and when they had finished the tale:

"I believe that was the best time we ever had!" said Frederick.

"Well, perhaps! Yes, I, too, believe that was the best time we ever had," said Deslauriers.

[ANONYMOUS TRANSLATION, EDITED BY DORA KNOWLES RANOUS]

Flowers of Evil

CHARLES BAUDELAIRE

(1821–1867)

*Long before Freud, Baudelaire revealed that hell is person-
ality. Like Flaubert, and Wagner (in* The Ring of the Nibelung *and* Tristan and Isolde*), he wishes to deprive man of all
refuge. Paradise is not merely illusion; to attempt to inhabit
it turns it into hell. He agrees with Carlyle that the spot on
the world is cast by oneself, but Carlyle's methods of transcending that spot are no longer available to Baudelaire. When life
does not bore, it disgusts. The only value is to face that fact.*

TO THE READER

Folly and error, avarice and vice,
Employ our souls and waste our bodies' force.
As mangy beggars incubate their lice,
We nourish our innocuous remorse.

Our sins are stubborn, craven our repentance.
For our weak vows we ask excessive prices.
Trusting our tears will wash away the sentence,
We sneak off where the muddy road entices.

Cradled in evil, that Thrice-Great Magician,
The Devil, rocks our souls, that can't resist;
And the rich metal of our own volition
Is vaporized by that sage alchemist.

The Devil pulls the strings by which we're worked:
By all revolting objects lured, we slink
Hellwards; each day down one more step we're jerked
Feeling no horror, through the shades that stink.

Just as a lustful pauper bites and kisses
The scarred and shrivelled breast of an old whore,
We steal, along the roadside, furtive blisses,
Squeezing them like stale oranges for more.

Packed tight, like hives of maggots, thickly seething,
Within our brains a host of demons surges.
Deep down into our lungs at every breathing,
Death flows, an unseen river, moaning dirges.

If rape or arson, poison, or the knife
Has wove no pleasing patterns in the stuff
Of this drab canvas we accept as life —
It is because we are not bold enough!

Amongst the jackals, leopards, mongrels, apes,
Snakes, scorpions, vultures, that with hellish din,
Squeal, roar, writhe, gambol, crawl, with monstrous shapes,
In each man's foul menagerie of sin —

There's one more damned than all. He never gambols,
Nor crawls, nor roars, but, from the rest withdrawn,
Gladly of this whole earth would make a shambles
And swallow up existence with a yawn. . .

Boredom! He smokes his hookah, while he dreams
Of gibbets, weeping tears he cannot smother.
You know this dainty monster, too, it seems —
Hypocrite reader! — You! — My twin! — My brother!

VOYAGE TO CYTHERA

My heart, a bird, seemed joyfully to fly
And round the rigging cruised with nimble gyre.
The vessel rolled beneath the cloudless sky
Like a white angel, drunk with solar fire.

"What is that sad, black island like a pall?"
— "Why, it's Cythera, famed in many a book,
The Eldorado of old playboys. Look:
It's but a damned poor country after all!"

(Isle of sweet secrets and heart-feasting fire!
Of antique Venus the majestic ghost
Rolls like a storm of fragrance from your coast
Filling our souls with languor and desire!

Isle of green myrtles where each flower uncloses,
Adored by nations till the end of time:
Sighs of adoring hearts, like incense, climb
And pour their perfume over sheaves of roses,

Like groves of turtles in an endless coo!)
But no! it was a waste where nothing grows,
Torn only by the raucous cries of crows:
Yet there a curious object rose in view.

This was no temple hid in bosky trees,
Where the young priestess, amorous of flowers,
Whom secretly a loving flame devours,
Walks with her robe half-open to the breeze.

For as we moved inshore to coast the shallows
And our white canvas scared the crows to fly,
Like a tall cypress, blackened on the sky,
We saw it was a gaunt three-forking gallows.

Fierce birds, perched on their meal, began to slash
And rip with rage a rotten corpse that swung.
Each screwed and chiselled with its beak among
The crisp and bleeding crannies of the hash.

His eyes were holes. His paunch, ripped open quite,
Drooped to his thighs its thick festoons of gut.
Gorged with the ghastly treats their beaks had cut,
His torturers had gelded him outright.

Beneath, some jealous prowling quadrupeds,
With lifted muzzles, for the leavings scrambled.
The largest seemed, as in the midst he gambolled,
An executioner among his aides.

Native of Cythera's cloudless clime,
In silent suffering you paid the price,
And expiated ancient cults of vice
With generations of forbidden crime.

Ridiculous hanged man! Your griefs I know.
I felt, to see you swing above the heath,
Like nausea slowly rising to my teeth,
The bilious stream of ancient human woe.

Poor devil, dear to memory! before me
I seemed to feel each talon, fang, and beak
Of all the stinking crows and panthers sleek
That in my lifetime ever chewed and tore me.

— The sky was charming and the sea unclouded,
But all was black and bloody to my mind.
As in a dismal winding-sheet entwined,
My heart was in this allegory shrouded.

A gallows where my image hung apart
Was all I found on Venus' isle of sighs.
— O God, give me the strength to scrutinise,
Without disgust, my body and my heart!

THE VOYAGE

I

For children crazed with maps and prints and stamps —
The universe can sate their appetite.

How vast the world is by the light of lamps,
But in the eyes of memory how slight!

One morning we set sail, with brains on fire,
And hearts swelled up with rancorous emotion,
Balancing, to the rhythm of its lyre,
Our infinite upon the finite ocean.

Some wish to leave their venal native skies,
Some flee their birthplace, others change their ways,
Astrologers who've drowned in Beauty's eyes,
Tyrannic Circe with the scent that slays.

Not to be changed to beasts, they have their fling
With space, and splendour, and the burning sky,
The suns that bronze them and the frosts that sting
Efface the mark of kisses by and by.

But the true travellers are those who go
Only to get away: hearts like balloons
Unballasted, with their own fate aglow,
Who know not why they fly with the monsoons:

Those whose desires are in the shape of clouds,
Who dream, as raw recruits of shot and shell,
Of mighty raptures in strange, transient crowds
Of which no human soul the name can tell.

                                II

Horror! We imitate the top and bowl
In swerve and bias. Through our sleep it runs.
It's Curiosity that makes us roll,
As the fierce Angel whips the whirling suns.

Singular game! where the goal changes places;
The winning-post is nowhere, yet all round;
Where Man tires not of the mad hope he races
Thinking, some day, that respite will be found.

Our soul's like a three-master, where one hears
A voice that from the bridge would warn all hands.
Another from the foretop madly cheers
"Love, joy, and glory" . . . Hell! we're on the sands!

The watchmen think each isle that heaves in view
An Eldorado, shouting their belief;
Imagination riots in the crew
Who in the morning only find a reef.

The fool that dotes on far, chimeric lands —
Put him in irons, or feed him to the shark!
The drunken sailor's visionary lands
Can only leave the bitter truth more stark.

So some old vagabond, in mud who grovels,
Dreams, nose in air, of Edens sweet to roam;
Wherever smoky wicks illumine hovels
He sees another Capua or Rome.

III

Amazing travellers, what noble stories
We read in the deep oceans of your gaze!
Show us your memory's casket, and the glories
Streaming from gems made out of stars and rays!

We, too, would roam without a sail or steam,
And to combat the boredom of our jail,
Would stretch, like canvas on our souls, a dream,
Framed in horizons, of the seas you sail.

What have you seen?

IV

"We have seen stars and waves,
We have seen sands and shores and oceans too,
In spite of shocks and unexpected graves,
We have been bored, at times, the same as you.

The solar glories on the violet ocean
And those of spires that in the sunset rise,
Lit, in our hearts, a yearning, fierce emotion
To plunge into those ever-luring skies.

The richest cities and the scenes most proud
In nature, have no magic to enamour

Like those which hazard traces in the cloud
While wistful longing magnifies their glamour.

(Enjoyment adds more fuel for desire,
Old tree, to which all pleasure is manure;
As the bark hardens, so the boughs shoot higher,
And nearer to the sun would grow mature.

Tree, will you always flourish, more vivacious
Than cypress?) None the less, these views are yours:
We took some photographs for your voracious
Album, who only care for distant shores.

We have seen idols elephantine-snouted,
And thrones with living gems bestarred and pearled,
And palaces whose riches would have routed
The dreams of all the bankers in the world.

We have seen wonder-striking robes and dresses,
Women whose nails and teeth the betel stains
And jugglers whom the rearing snake caresses."

V

What then? What then?

VI

"O childish little brains,
Not to forget the greatest wonder there —
We've seen in every country, without searching,
From top to bottom of the fatal stair
Immortal sin ubiquitously lurching:

Woman, a vile slave, proud in her stupidity,
Self-worshipping, without the least disgust:
Man, greedy, lustful, ruthless in cupidity,
Slave to a slave, and sewer to her lust:

The torturer's delight, the martyr's sobs,
The feasts where blood perfumes the giddy rout:

Power sapping its own tyrants: servile mobs
In amorous obeisance to the knout:

Some similar religions to our own,
All climbing skywards: Sanctity who treasures,
As in his downy couch some dainty drone,
In horsehair, nails, and whips, his dearest pleasures.

Prating Humanity, with genius raving,
As mad today as ever from the first,
Cries in fierce agony, its Maker braving,
'O God, my Lord and likeness, be thou cursed!'

But those less dull, the lovers of Dementia,
Fleeing the herd which fate has safe impounded,
In opium seek for limitless adventure.
— That's all the record of the globe we rounded."

VII

It's bitter knowledge that one learns from travel.
The world so small and drab, from day to day,
The horror of our image will unravel,
A pool of dread in deserts of dismay.

Must we depart, or stay? Stay if you can.
Go if you must. One runs: another hides
To baffle Time, that fatal foe to man.
And there are runners, whom no rest betides,

Like the Apostles or the Wandering Jew,
Whom neither ship nor waggon can enable
To cheat the retiary. But not a few
Have killed him without stirring from their cradle.

But when he sets his foot upon our nape
We still can hope and cry "Leave all behind!"
As in old times to China we'd escape
With eyes turned seawards, hair that fans the wind,

We'll sail once more upon the sea of Shades
With heart like that of a young sailor beating.

I hear the rich, sad voices of the Trades
Who cry "This Way! all you who would be eating

The scented Lotus. Here it is they range
The piles of magic fruit. O hungry friend,
Come here and swoon away into the strange
Trance of an afternoon that has no end."

In the familiar tones we sense the spectre;
Our Pylades stretch arms across the seas.
"To salve your heart, now swim to your Electra,"
She cries, of whom we used to kiss the knees.

VIII

O Death, old Captain, it is time. Weigh anchor!
To sail beyond the doldrums of our days.
Though black as pitch the sea and sky, we hanker
For space; you know our hearts are full of rays.

Pour us your poison to revive our soul!
It cheers the burning quest that we pursue,
Careless if Hell or Heaven be our goal,
Beyond the known world to seek out the New!

[TRANSLATED BY ROY CAMPBELL]

The Ring and the Book

ROBERT BROWNING

(1812–1888)

Browning is far from being the witless optimist most people imagine him. He is an Objectist, as deeply engaged with penetrating illusion as were Baudelaire and Flaubert, but with a tougher mind. He was one of the most subtle and complex of nineteenth-century writers. The meaning of his dramatic monologues is so structured that every position — even his own, on those rare occasions when he offers one — is ironically destroyed. The following excerpts are from a poem which tells the same murder story eleven times from eleven differing points of view — two of them by the same man. It can be understood only if one realizes that the poet is exploring the various overlapping and inconsistent meanings of "truth." The work was published in 1868–69.

Do you see this Ring?
                    'T is Rome-work, made to match
(By Castellani's imitative craft)
Etrurian circlets found, some happy morn,
After a dropping April; found alive
Spark-like 'mid unearthed slope-side figtree-roots

That roof old tombs at Chiusi: soft, you see,
Yet crisp as jewel-cutting. There's one trick,
(Craftsmen instruct me) one approved device
And but one, fits such slivers of pure gold
As this was, — such mere oozings from the mine,
Virgin as oval tawny pendent tear
At beehive-edge when ripened combs o'erflow, —
To bear the file's tooth and the hammer's tap:
Since hammer needs must widen out the round,
And file emboss it fine with lily-flowers,
Ere the stuff grow a ring-thing right to wear.
That trick is, the artificer melts up wax
With honey, so to speak; he mingles gold
With gold's alloy, and, duly tempering both,
Effects a manageable mass, then works:
But his work ended, once the thing a ring,
Oh, there's repristination! Just a spirt
O' the proper fiery acid o'er its face,
And forth the alloy unfastened flies in fume;
While, self-sufficient now, the shape remains,
The rondure brave, the lilied loveliness,
Gold as it was, is, shall be evermore:
Prime nature with an added artistry —
No carat lost, and you have gained a ring.
What of it? 'T is a figure, a symbol, say;
A thing's sign: now for the thing signified.

Do you see this square old yellow Book, I toss
I' the air, and catch again, and twirl about
By the crumpled vellum covers, — pure crude fact
Secreted from man's life when hearts beat hard,
And brains, high-blooded, ticked two centuries since?
Examine it yourselves! I found this book,
Gave a *lira* for it, eightpence English just,
(Mark the predestination!) when a Hand,
Always above my shoulder, pushed me once,
One day still fierce 'mid many a day struck calm,

Across a Square in Florence, crammed with booths,
Buzzing and blaze, noontide and market-time,
Toward Baccio's marble, — ay, the basement-ledge
O' the pedestal where sits and menaces
John of the Black Bands with the upright spear,
'Twixt palace and church, — Riccardi where they lived,
His race, and San Lorenzo where they lie.
This book, — precisely on that palace-step
Which, meant for lounging knaves o' the Medici,
Now serves re-venders to display their ware, —
Mongst odds and ends of ravage, picture-frames
White through the worn gilt, mirror-sconces chipped,
Bronze angel-heads once knobs attached to chests,
(Handled when ancient dames chose forth brocade)
Modern chalk drawings, studies from the nude,
Samples of stone, jet, breccia, porphyry
Polished and rough, sundry amazing busts
In baked earth, (broken, Providence be praised!)
A wreck of tapestry, proudly-purposed web
When reds and blues were indeed red and blue,
Now offered as a mat to save bare feet
(Since carpets constitute a cruel cost)
Treading the chill scagliola bedward: then
A pile of brown-etched prints, two *crazie* each,
Stopped by a conch a-top from fluttering forth
— Sowing the Square with works of one and the same
Master, the imaginative Sienese
Great in the scenic backgrounds — (name and fame
None of you know, nor does he fare the worse:)
From these . . . Oh, with a Lionard going cheap
If it should prove, as promised, that Joconde
Whereof a copy contents the Louvre! — these
I picked this book from. Five compeers in flank
Stood left and right of it as tempting more —
A dogseared Spicilegium, the fond tale
O' the Frail One of the Flower, by young Dumas,
Vulgarized Horace for the use of schools,
The Life, Death, Miracles of Saint Somebody,

Saint Somebody Else, his Miracles, Death and Life, —
With this, one glance at the lettered back of which,
And "Stall!" cried I: a *lira* made it mine.

Here it is, this I toss and take again;
Small-quarto size, part print part manuscript:
A book in shape but, really, pure crude fact
Secreted from man's life when hearts beat hard,
And brains, high-blooded, ticked two centuries since.
Give it me back! The thing's restorative
I' the touch and sight.

　　　　　　That memorable day,
(June was the month, Lorenzo named the Square)
I leaned a little and overlooked my prize
By the low railing round the fountain-source
Close to the statue, where a step descends:
While clinked the cans of copper, as stooped and rose
Thick-ankled girls who brimmed them, and made place
For marketmen glad to pitch basket down,
Dip a broad melon-leaf that holds the wet,
And whisk their faded fresh. And on I read
Presently, though my path grew perilous
Between the outspread straw-work, piles of plait
Soon to be flapping, each o'er two black eyes
And swathe of Tuscan hair, on festas fine:
Through fire-irons, tribes of tongs, shovels in sheaves,
Skeleton bedsteads, wardrobe-drawers agape,
Rows of tall slim brass lamps with dangling gear, —
And worse, cast clothes a-sweetening in the sun:
None of them took my eye from off my prize.
Still read I on, from written title-page
To written index, on, through street and street,
At the Strozzi, at the Pillar, at the Bridge;
Till, by the time I stood at home again
In Casa Guidi by Felice Church,
Under the doorway where the black begins
With the first stone-slab of the staircase cold,
I had mastered the contents, knew the whole truth

Gathered together, bound up in this book,
Print three-fifths, written supplement the rest.
"Romana Homicidiorum" — nay,
Better translate — "A Roman murder-case:
"Position of the entire criminal cause
"Of Guido Franceschini, nobleman,
"With certain Four the cutthroats in his pay,
"Tried, all five, and found guilty and put to death
"By heading or hanging as befitted ranks,
"At 'Rome on February Twenty Two,
"Since our salvation Sixteen Ninety Eight:
"Wherein it is disputed if, and when,
"Husbands may kill adulterous wives, yet 'scape
"The customary forfeit."

                              Word for word,
So ran the title-page: murder, or else
Legitimate punishment of the other crime,
Accounted murder by mistake, — just that
And no more, in a Latin cramp enough
When the law had her eloquence to launch,
But interfilleted with Italian streaks
When testimony stooped to mother-tongue, —
That, was this old square yellow book about.

Now, as the ingot, ere the ring was forged,
Lay gold, (beseech you, hold that figure fast!)
So, in this book lay absolutely truth,
Fanciless fact, the documents indeed,
Primary lawyer-pleadings for, against,
The aforesaid Five; real summed-up circumstance
Adduced in proof of these on either side,
Put forth and printed, as the practice was,
At Rome, in the Apostolic Chamber's type,
And so submitted to the eye o' the Court
Presided over by His Reverence
Rome's Governor and Criminal Judge, — the trial
Itself, to all intents, being then as now
Here in the book and nowise out of it;

Seeing, there properly was no judgment-bar,
No bringing of accuser and accused,
And whoso judged both parties, face to face
Before some court, as we conceive of courts.
There was a Hall of Justice; that came last:
For Justice had a chamber by the hall
Where she took evidence first, summed up the same,
Then sent accuser and accused alike,
In person of the advocate of each,
To weigh its worth, thereby arrange, array
The battle.

. . .

This is the bookful; thus far take the truth,
The untempered gold, the fact untampered with,
The mere ring-metal ere the ring be made!
And what has hitherto come of it? Who preserves
The memory of this Guido, and his wife
Pompilia, more than Ademollo's name,
The etcher of those prints, two *crazie* each,
Saved by a stone from snowing broad the Square
With scenic backgrounds? Was this truth of force?
Able to take its own part as truth should,
Sufficient, self-sustaining? Why, if so —
Yonder's a fire, into it goes my book,
As who shall say me nay, and what the loss?

. . .

Well, British Public, ye who like me not,
(God love you!) and will have your proper laugh
At the dark question, laugh it! I laugh first.
Truth must prevail, the proverb vows; and truth
— Here is it all i' the book at last, as first
There it was all i' the heads and hearts of Rome
Gentle and simple, never to fall nor fade
"And waive what's wanting! Take a friend's advice!

"It's not the custom of the country. Mend
"Your ways indeed and we may stretch a point:
"Go get you manned by Manning and new-manned
"By Newman and, mayhap, wise-manned to boot
"By Wiseman, and we'll see or else we won't!
"Thanks meantime for the story, long and strong,
"A pretty piece of narrative enough,
"Which scarce ought so to drop out, one would think,
"From the more curious annals of our kind.
"Do you tell the story, now, in off-hand style,
"Straight from the book? Or simply here and there,
"(The while you vault it through the loose and large)
"Hang to a hint? Or is there book at all,
"And don't you deal in poetry, make-believe,
"And the white lies it sounds like?"

                                        Yes and no!
From the book, yes; thence bit by bit I dug
The lingot truth, that memorable day,
Assayed and knew my piecemeal gain was gold, —
Yes; but from something else surpassing that,
Something of mine which, mixed up with the mass,
Made it bear hammer and be firm to file.
Fancy with fact is just one fact the more;
To-wit, that fancy has informed, transpierced,
Nor be forgotten. Yet, a little while,
The passage of a century or so,
Decads thrice five, and here's time paid his tax,
Oblivion gone home with her harvesting,
And all left smooth again as scythe could shave.
Far from beginning with you London folk,
I took my book to Rome first, tried truth's power
On likely people. "Have you met such names?
"Is a tradition extant of such facts?
"Your law-courts stand, your records frown a-row:
"What if I rove and rummage?" " — Why, you'll waste
"Your pains and end as wise as you began!"
Everyone snickered: "names and facts thus old

"Are newer much than Europe news we find
"Down in to-day's *Diario*. Records, quotha?
"Why, the French burned them, what else do the French?
"The rap-and-rending nation! And it tells
"Against the Church, no doubt, — another gird
"At the Temporality, your Trial, of course?"
" — Quite otherwise this time," submitted I;
"Clean for the Church and dead against the world,
"The flesh and the devil, does it tell for once."
" — The rarer and the happier! All the same,
"Content you with your treasure of a book,
Thridded and so thrown fast the facts else free,
As right through ring and ring runs the djereed
And binds the loose, one bar without a break.
I fused my live soul and that inert stuff,
Before attempting smithcraft, on the night
After the day when, — truth thus grasped and gained, —
The book was shut and done with and laid by
On the cream-coloured massive agate, broad
'Neath the twin cherubs in the tarnished frame
O' the mirror, tall thence to the ceiling-top.

.   .   .

This was it from, my fancy with those facts,
I used to tell the tale, turned gay to grave,
But lacked a listener seldom; such alloy,
Such substance of me interfused the gold
Which, wrought into a shapely ring therewith,
Hammered and filed, fingered and favoured, last
Lay ready for the renovating wash
O' the water. "How much of the tale was true?"
I disappeared; the book grew all in all;
The lawyers' pleadings swelled back to their size, —
Doubled in two, the crease upon them yet,
For more commodity of carriage, see! —
And these are letters, veritable sheets
That brought posthaste the news to Florence, writ

At Rome the day Count Guido died, we find,
To stay the craving of a client there,
Who bound the same and so produced my book.
Lovers of dead truth, did ye fare the worse?
Lovers of live truth, found ye false my tale?

Well, now; there's nothing in nor out o' the world
Good except truth: yet this, the something else,
What's this then, which proves good yet seems untrue?
This that I mixed with truth, motions of mine
That quickened, made the inertness malleolable
O' the gold was not mine, — what's your name for this?
Are means to the end, themselves in part the end?
Is fiction which makes fact alive, fact too?
The somehow may be thishow.
                                   I find first
Writ down for very A B C of fact,
"In the beginning God made heaven and earth;"
From which, no matter with what lisp, I spell
And speak you out a consequence — that man,
Man, — as befits the made, the inferior thing, —
Purposed, since made, to grow, not make in turn,
Yet forced to try and make, else fail to grow, —
Formed to rise, reach at, if not grasp and gain
The good beyond him, — which attempt is growth, —
Repeats God's process in man's due degree,
Attaining man's proportionate result, —
Creates, no, but resuscitates, perhaps.
Inalienable, the arch-prerogative
Which turns thought, act — conceives, expresses too!
No less, man, bounded, yearning to be free,
May so project his surplusage of soul
In search of body, so add self to self
By owning what lay ownerless before, —
So find, so fill full, so appropriate forms —
That, although nothing which had never life
Shall get life from him, be, not having been,
Yet, something dead may get to live again,

Something with too much life or not enough,
Which, either way imperfect, ended once:
An end whereat man's impulse intervenes,
Makes new beginning, starts the dead alive,
Completes the incomplete and saves the thing.
Man's breath were vain to light a virgin wick, —
Half-burned-out, all but quite-quenched wicks o' the lamp
Stationed for temple-service on this earth,
These indeed let him breathe on and relume!
For such man's feat is, in the due degree,
— Mimic creation, galvanism for life,
But still a glory portioned in the scale.
Why did the mage say, — feeling as we are wont
For truth, and stopping midway short of truth,
And resting on a lie, — "I raise a ghost"?
"Because," he taught adepts, "man makes not man.
"Yet by a special gift, an art of arts,
"More insight and more outsight and much more
"Will to use both of these than boast my mates,
"I can detach from me, commission forth
"Half of my soul; which in its pilgrimage
"O'er old unwandered waste ways of the world,
"May chance upon some fragment of a whole,
"Rag of flesh, scrap of bone in dim disuse,
"Smoking flax that fed fire once: prompt therein
"I enter, spark-like, put old powers to play,
"Push lines out to the limit, lead forth last
"(By a moonrise through a ruin of a crypt)
"What shall be mistily seen, murmuringly heard,
"Mistakenly felt: then write my name with Faust's!"
Oh, Faust, why Faust? Was not Elisha once? —
Who bade them lay his staff on a corpse-face.
There was no voice, no hearing: he went in
Therefore, and shut the door upon them twain,
And prayed unto the Lord: and he went up
And lay upon the corpse, dead on the couch,
And put his mouth upon its mouth, his eyes
Upon its eyes, his hands upon its hands,

And stretched him on the flesh; the flesh waxed warm:
And he returned, walked to and fro the house,
And went up, stretched him on the flesh again,
And the eyes opened. 'T is a credible feat
With the right man and way.
                              Enough of me!
The Book! I turn its medicinable leaves
In London now till, as in Florence erst,
A spirit laughs and leaps through every limb,
And lights my eye, and lifts me by the hair,
Letting me have my will again with these
— How title I the dead alive once more?

                    .   .   .

Let this old woe step on the stage again!
Act itself o'er anew for men to judge,
Not by the very sense and sight indeed —
(Which take at best imperfect cognizance,
Since how heart moves brain, and how both move hand,
What mortal ever in entirety saw?)
— No dose of purer truth than man digests,
But truth with falsehood, milk that feeds him now,
Not strong meat he may get to bear some day —
To-wit by voices we call evidence,
Uproar in the echo, live fact deadened down,
Talked over, bruited abroad, whispered away,
Yet helping us to all we seem to hear:
For how else know we save by worth of word?

                    .   .   .

Finally, even as thus by step and step
I led you from the level of to-day
Up to the summit of so long ago,
Here, whence I point you the wide prospect round —
Let me, by like steps, slope you back to smooth,
Land you on mother-earth, no whit the worse,
To feed o' the fat o' the furrow: free to dwell,

Taste our time's better things profusely spread
For all who love the level, corn and wine,
Much cattle and the many-folded fleece.
Shall not my friends go feast again on sward,
Though cognizant of country in the clouds
Higher than wistful eagle's horny eye
Ever unclosed for, 'mid ancestral crags,
When morning broke and Spring was back once more,
And he died, heaven, save by his heart, unreached?
Yet heaven my fancy lifts to, ladder-like, —
As Jack reached, holpen of his beanstalk-rungs!

A novel country: I might make it mine
By choosing which one aspect of the year
Suited mood best, and putting solely that
On panel somewhere in the House of Fame,
Landscaping what I saved, not what I saw:
— Might fix you, whether frost in goblin-time
Startled the moon with his abrupt bright laugh,
Or, August's hair afloat in filmy fire,
She fell, arms wide, face foremost on the world,
Swooned there and so singed out the strength of things.
Thus were abolished Spring and Autumn both,
The land dwarfed to one likeness of the land,
Life cramped corpse-fashion. Rather learn and love
Each facet-flash of the revolving year! —
Red, green and blue that whirl into a white,
The variance now, the eventual unity,
Which make the miracle. See it for yourselves,
This man's act, changeable because alive!
Action now shrouds, nor shows the informing thought;
Man, like a glass ball with a spark a-top,
Out of the magic fire that lurks inside,
Shows one tint at a time to take the eye:
Which, let a finger touch the silent sleep,
Shifted a hair's-breadth shoots you dark for bright,
Suffuses bright with dark, and baffles so
Your sentence absolute for shine or shade.

Once set such orbs, — white styled, black stigmatized, —
A-rolling, see them once on the other side
Your good men and your bad men every one
From Guido Franceschini to Guy Faux,
Oft would you rub your eyes and change your names.

Such, British Public, ye who like me not,
(God love you!) — whom I yet have laboured for,
Perchance more careful whoso runs may read
Than erst when all, it seemed, could read who ran, —
Perchance more careless whoso reads may praise
Than late when he who praised and read and wrote
Was apt to find himself the self-same me, —
Such labour had such issue, so I wrought
This arc, by furtherance of such alloy,
And so, by one spirt, take away its trace
Till, justifiably golden, rounds my ring.

.   .   .

Such, then, the final state o' the story. So
Did the Star Wormwood in a blazing fall
Frighten awhile the waters and lie lost.
So did this old woe fade from memory:
Till after, in the fulness of the days,
I needs must find an ember yet unquenched,
And, breathing, blow the spark to flame. It lives,
If precious be the soul of man to man.

So, British Public, who may like me yet,
(Marry and amen!) learn one lesson hence
Of many which whatever lives should teach:
This lesson, that our human speech is naught,
Our human testimony false, our fame
And human estimation words and wind.
Why take the artistic way to prove so much?
Because, it is the glory and good of Art,
That Art remains the one way possible

Of speaking truth, to mouths like mine at least.
How look a brother in the face and say
"Thy right is wrong, eyes hast thou yet art blind.
"Thine ears are stuffed and stopped, despite their length:
"And, oh, the foolishness thou countest faith!"
Say this as silverly as tongue can troll —
The anger of the man may be endured,
The shrug, the disappointed eyes of him
Are not so bad to bear — but here's the plague
That all this trouble comes of telling truth,
Which truth, by when it reaches him, looks false,
Seems to be just the thing it would supplant,
Nor recognizable by whom it left:
While falsehood would have done the work of truth.
But Art, — wherein man nowise speaks to men,
Only to mankind, — Art may tell a truth
Obliquely, do the thing shall breed the thought,
Nor wrong the thought, missing the mediate word.
So may you paint your picture, twice show truth,
Beyond mere imagery on the wall, —
So, note by note, bring music from your mind,
Deeper than ever e'en Beethoven dived, —
So write a book shall mean beyond the facts,
Suffice the eye and save the soul beside.
And save the soul! If this intent save mine, —
If the rough ore be rounded to a ring,
Render all duty which good ring should do,
And, failing grace, succeed in guardianship, —
Might mine but lie outside thine, Lyric Love,
Thy rare gold ring of verse (the poet praised)
Linking our England to his Italy!

NOTE ON ILLUSTRATIONS: GROUP III
Numbers 29 to 46

The first three pictures are representative of one tradition of what in the Introduction I have called Objectism, the confrontation of the naked Self with the Object, so that, as in Baudelaire, even the personality is now conceived of as part of the Object, the Subject being only the self-conscious perceiver, or Self. The result of this tradition was Naturalism in the novel, and extreme realism in painting, though in various modes. One mode is presented in Work (Number 29), the early pre-Raphaelite determination to make a rendering of phenomena so precise it had scientific value. This was above all literary painting; the painter was controlled by something outside of his art. Böcklin and Rossetti are in this way highly similar. Courbet and Menzel, the latter apparently, like Manet, influenced by the literalism of photography, show a more purely "painterly" or non-illustrative mode of encountering the Object. Yet they were as much under the control of extra-painting conceptions and values as was the literary tradition. Manet, in particular, modeled his paintings, in a half-parodic way, on famous masterpieces of the past. The earlier interest of Impressionism was in a quasi-scientific rendering of the world through colored light. It is well known that Pissarro and Renoir, as well as Monet, became dissatisfied with this program in the 1880's. A similar dissatisfaction is perhaps to be seen in the work of Leibl (Number 35). On the one hand the extreme literalism suggests an Objectist interest, but on the other the elevated perspective and the intense preoccupation with the purely formal properties of the dresses and of the carvings suggest a Stylistic aim. There is even a hint of Art Nouveau, the last Stylistic architectural and decorative mode before the breakthrough into Modern or post-Nietzschean art.

This period produced most of what are still known as Victorian architectural horrors. These are the buildings which have been mocked for seventy years. Some of them were even mocked at the time by people of advanced taste who had entered into the next stage of Romanticism, Stylism. The mark of all these buildings (Numbers 36 to 46) is an extreme expressivity which almost seems a willful seeking for the ugly, or at least the outrageous. Again, there is an affinity with Baudelaire and Browning. The emotional expressiveness of a building is to be found in its manipulation of light and shadow and in the three-dimensional manipulation of the screen or wall. It is the emotional nakedness of these buildings that astounds and offends, their deliberate sacrifice of the ingratiating. Yet if we think of the recent work of Louis Kahn or Paul Rudolph, with their extreme expressiveness and brutalization of architectural forms, these buildings become much more understandable and acceptable. The first group (Numbers 36 to 42) are more historically minded than the second group (Numbers 43 to 46). Here clearly something new has begun. The historical correctness is sacrificed to the expressive architectural symbol. I have included two buildings by Frank Furness, because he was one of the most remarkable architects of the nineteenth century, in Europe or America. Inspired by Ruskin, Furness was the founder of the line that ran through Sullivan to Wright.

29. Ford Madox Brown, *Work*, 1852–1865.

30. Arnold Böcklin, *The Isle of the Dead*, 1880.

31. Dante Gabriel Rossetti, *Mnemosyne*, 1879.

32. Gustave Courbet, *The Seashore at Palavas,* 1854.

33. Adolf von Menzel, *Room with a Balcony,* 1845.

34. Édouard Manet, *The Dead Christ with Angels*, 1864.

35. Wilhelm Leibl, *Three Women in Church*, 1878–1881.

36. Sir Gilbert Scott, *Albert Memorial*, London, 1872.

37. George Edmund Street, *Royal Courts of Justice*, London, 1871–1872.

38. T. J. Visconti and H. M. Lefuel, *Pavillon Sully, Louvre*, Paris, 1852–1872.

39. Jean Louis Charles Garnier, *Opera House*, Paris, 1861–1874.

40. John McArthur, Jr., *U.S. Post Office*, Philadelphia, 1873–1884.

41. Joseph Poelaert, *Palace of Justice*, Brussels, 1883–1886.

42. John McArthur, Jr. and Thomas U. Walter, *City Hall*, Philadelphia, 1871–1881.

43. Gabriel Darriaud and Jules Bourdais, *Palais du Trocadéro*, Paris, 1878.

44. Richard M. Hunt, *Studio Building*, New York, 1856.

45. Frank Furness, *Provident Life and Trust Co.,* Philadelphia, 1879.

46. Frank Furness, *Pennsylvania Academy of Fine Arts,* Philadelphia, 1871–1876.

PART

IV

Stylism

*Objectism could only be a temporary solution, for it pro-
vided no means of realizing the Self other than self-
awareness and courage. The Self could see through the
illusions with which men protect themselves from the
horror of existence, but it could not maintain itself. Value
had only a negative existence. The maelstrom of the world
threatened to dissolve the Self into the flux of experience
and to reduce Romanticism again to mere Negative Romanticism. Clearly the Self needed not only protective
armor but also a means of symbolizing the radiance of
Self-discovered and Self-created value without compromis-
ing the vision of illusion and horror. Stylism was the
resolution to this problem. The history of the arts was
ransacked to create a symbolization of the positive value
of the Self — of the Self as the very source of value — as
opposed to the negative value of the world.*

Atalanta in Calydon

ALGERNON CHARLES SWINBURNE

(1837–1909)

This dramatic poem, published in 1865, is modeled on Greek tragedy. It is the first great example of Stylism to appear in English. It is not only an extraordinarily violent attack upon the institution of the family; it is also a revelation of the failure of the trustful as well as of the suspicious and untrusting attitude towards experience. What marks a new stage in the development of Romanticism is the absolute sundering between subject-matter and style, the totally nonfunctional and "beautiful" surface through which is seen the horror of human life.

CHORUS

Who hath given man speech? or who hath set therein
A thorn for peril and a snare for sin?
For in the word his life is and his breath,
   And in the word his death,
That madness and the infatuate heart may breed
   From the word's womb the deed
And life bring one thing forth ere all pass by,

Even one thing which is ours yet cannot die —
Death. Hast thou seen him ever anywhere,
Time's twin-born brother, imperishable as he
Is perishable and plaintive, clothed with care
     And mutable as sand,
But death is strong and full of blood and fair
And perdurable and like a lord of land?
Nay, time thou seest not, death thou wilt not see
Till life's right hand be loosened from thine hand
     And thy life-days from thee.
For the gods very subtly fashion
     Madness with sadness upon earth:
Not knowing in any wise compassion,
     Nor holding pity of any worth;
And many things they have given and taken,
     And wrought and ruined many things;
The firm land have they loosed and shaken,
     And sealed the sea with all her springs;
They have wearied time with heavy burdens
     And vexed the lips of life with breath:
Set men to labour and given them guerdons,
     Death, and great darkness after death:
Put moans into the bridal measure
     And on the bridal wools a stain;
And circled pain about with pleasure,
     And girdled pleasure about with pain;
And strewed one marriage-bed with tears and fire
For extreme loathing and supreme desire.

What shall be done with all these tears of ours?
     Shall they make watersprings in the fair heaven
To bathe the brows of morning? or like flowers
Be shed and shine before the starriest hours,
     Or made the raiment of the weeping Seven?
Or rather, O our masters, shall they be
Food for the famine of the grievous sea,
     A great well-head of lamentation
Satiating the sad gods? or fall and flow

Among the years and seasons to and fro,
    And wash their feet with tribulation
And fill them full with grieving ere they go?
    Alas, our lords, and yet alas again,
Seeing all your iron heaven is gilt as gold
    But all we smite thereat in vain;
Smite the gates barred with groanings manifold,
    But all the floors are paven with our pain.
Yea, and with weariness of lips and eyes,
With breaking of the bosom, and with sighs,
    We labour, and are clad and fed with grief
And filled with days we would not fain behold
And nights we would not hear of; we wax old,
    All we wax old and wither like a leaf.
We are outcast, strayed between bright sun and moon;
    Our light and darkness are as leaves of flowers,
Black flowers and white, that perish; and the noon
    As midnight, and the night as daylight hours.
    A little fruit a little while is ours,
        And the worm finds it soon.

But up in heaven the high gods one by one
    Lay hands upon the draught that quickeneth,
Fulfilled with all tears shed and all things done,
    And stir with soft imperishable breath
    The bubbling bitterness of life and death,
And hold it to our lips and laugh; but they
Preserve their lips from tasting night or day,
    Lest they too change and sleep, the fates that spun,
The lips that made us and the hands that slay;
    Lest all these change, and heaven bow down to none,
Change and be subject to the secular sway
    And terrene revolution of the sun.
Therefore they thrust it from them, putting time away.

I would the wine of time, made sharp and sweet
    With multitudinous days and nights and tears
    And many mixing savours of strange years,
Where no more trodden of them under feet,

Cast out and split about their holy places:
That life were given them as a fruit to eat
And death to drink as water; that the light
Might ebb, drawn backward from their eyes, and night
    Hide for one hour the imperishable faces;
That they might rise up sad in heaven, and know
Sorrow and sleep, one paler than young snow,
    One cold as blight of dew and ruinous rain;
Rise up and rest and suffer a little, and be
Awhile as all things born with us and we,
    And grieve as men, and like slain men be slain.

For now we know not of them; but one saith
    The gods are gracious, praising God; and one,
When hast thou seen? or hast thou felt his breath
    Touch, nor consume thine eyelids as the sun,
Nor fill thee to the lips with fiery death?
    None hath beheld him, none
Seen above other gods and shapes of things,
Swift without feet and flying without wings,
Intolerable, not clad with death or life,
    Insatiable, not known of night or day,
The lord of love and loathing and of strife
    Who gives a star and takes a sun away;
Who shapes the soul, and makes her a barren wife
    To the earthly body and grievous growth of clay;
Who turns the large limbs to a little flame
    And binds the great sea with a little sand;
Who makes desire, and slays desire with shame;
    Who shakes the heaven as ashes in his hand;
Who, seeing the light and shadow for the same,
    Bids day waste night as fire devours a brand,
Smites without sword, and scourges without rod;
    The supreme evil, God.
Yea, with thine hate, O God, thou hast covered us,
    One saith, and hidden our eyes away from sight,
And made us transitory and hazardous,
    Light things and slight;

Yet have men praised thee, saying, He hath made man thus,
  And he doeth right.
Thou hast kissed us, and hast smitten; thou hast laid
Upon us with thy left hand life, and said,
Live: and again thou hast said, Yield up your breath,
And with thy right hand laid upon us death.
Thou hast sent us sleep, and stricken sleep with dreams,
  Saying, Joy is not, but love of joy shall be;
Thou hast made sweet springs for all the pleasant streams,
  In the end thou hast made them bitter with the sea.
Thou hast fed one rose with dust of many men;
  Thou hast marred one face with fire of many tears;
Thou hast taken love, and given us sorrow again;
  With pain thou hast filled us full to the eyes and ears.
Therefore because thou art strong, our father, and we
  Feeble; and thou art against us, and thine hand
Constrains us in the shallows of the sea
  And breaks us at the limits of the land;
Because thou hast bent thy lightnings as a bow,
  And loosed the hours like arrows; and let fall
Sins and wild words and many a wingèd woe
  And wars among us, and one end of all;
Because thou hast made the thunder, and thy feet
  Are as a rushing water when the skies
Break, but thy face as an exceeding heat
  And flames of fire the eyelids of thine eyes;
Because thou art over all who are over us;
  Because thy name is life and our name death;
Because thou art cruel and men are piteous,
  And our hands labour and thine hand scattereth;
Lo, with hearts rent and knees made tremulous,
  Lo, with ephemeral lips and casual breath,
    At least we witness of thee ere we die
That these things are not otherwise, but thus;
  That each man in his heart sigheth, and saith,
    That all men even as I,
All we are against thee, against thee, O God most high.

But ye, keep ye on earth
Your lips from over-speech,
Loud words and longing are so little worth;
And the end is hard to reach.
For silence after grievous things is good,
And reverence, and the fear that makes men whole,
And shame, and righteous governance of blood,
And lordship of the soul.
But from sharp words and wits men pluck no fruit,
And gathering thorns they shake the tree at root;
For words divide and rend;
But silence is most noble till the end.

The Drunken Boat

ARTHUR RIMBAUD

(1854–1891)

Among other strategies developed by Stylism to confirm and stabilize the Self while simultaneously looking at the world in its horror, was the sustained metaphor. This device creates a work of two separate levels, held together not by fusion but by disturbing tension. Thus the point of view of the speaker was kept separate from both the author and the subject matter. In the novel, Henry James is the great exemplar of this technique. Using this strategy, Rimbaud created a revolution in poetry. Hence, the following poem, written in 1871 but not published until 1883 from Verlaine's copy, has an extraordinarily modern character.

As I proceeded down along impassive rivers,
I lost my crew of haulers; they'd been seized by hosts
Of whooping Redskins, who had emptied out their quivers
Against these naked targets, nailed to coloured posts.

Little I cared for any crew I bore, a rover
With Flemish wheat or English cottons in my hold.
When once the tribulations of my crew were over,
The rivers let me go where my own fancy told.

Amid the fury of the loudly chopping tide,
I, just last winter, with a child's insensate brain,
Ah, how I raced! And no Peninsulas untied
Were ever tossed in more triumphant hurricane.

The blessing of the storm on my sea-watch was shed.
More buoyant than a cork I darted for ten nights
Over the waves, those famed old trundlers of the dead,
Nor missed the foolish blink of homely warning lights.

The wash of the green water on my shell of pine,
Sweeter than apples to a child its pungent edge;
It cleansed me of the stains of vomits and blue wine
And carried off with it the rudder and the kedge.

And afterwards down through the poem of the sea,
A milky foam infused with stars, frantic I dive
Down through green heavens where, descending pensively,
Sometimes the pallid remnants of the drowned arrive;

Where suddenly the bluish tracts dissolve, desires
And rhythmic languors stir beneath the day's full glow.
Stronger than alcohol and vaster than your lyres,
The bitter humours of fermenting passion flow!

I know how lightning splits the skies, the current roves;
I know the surf and waterspouts and evening's fall;
I've seen the dawn arisen like a flock of doves;
Sometimes I've seen what men believe they can recall.

I've seen the low sun blotched with blasphemies sublime,
Projecting vividly long, violet formations
Which, like tragedians in very ancient mime
Bestride the latticed waves, that speed remote vibrations.

My dreams were of green night and its bedazzled snow,
Of kisses slowly mounting up to the sea's eyes,
Of winding courses where unheard-of fluids go,
Flares blue and yellow that from singing phosphors rise.

For whole months at a time I've ridden with the surge
That like mad byres a-toss keeps battering the reefs,

Nor thought that the bright touch of Mary's feet could urge
A muzzle on the seas, muting their wheezy griefs.

And, yes, on Floridas beyond belief I've fetched,
Where flowers and eyes of panthers mingle in confusion,
Panthers with human skin, rainbows like bridles stretched
Controlling glaucous herds beneath the sea's horizon.

I've seen fermenting marshes like huge lobster-traps
Where in the rushes rots a whole Leviathan,
Or in the midst of calm the water's face collapse
And cataracts pour in from all the distant span.

Glaciers, silver suns, pearl waves and skies afire,
Brown gulfs with loathsome strands in whose profundities
Huge serpents, vermin-plagued, drop down into the mire
With black effluvium from the contorted trees!

I longed to show the children how the dolphins sport
In the blue waves, these fish of gold, these fish that sing.
Flowers of foam have blessed my puttings-out from port,
Winds from I know not where at times have lent me wing.

And often, weary martyr of the poles and zones,
Dark blooms with yellow mouths reached towards me from the seas
On which I gently rocked, in time to their soft moans;
And I was left there like a woman on her knees.

Trembling peninsula, upon my decks I tossed
The dung of pale-eyed birds and clacking, angry sound;
And on I sailed while down through my frail cordage crossed
The sleeping, backwards falling bodies of the drowned.

I, lost boat in the hair of estuaries caught,
Hurled by the cyclone to a birdless apogee,
I, whom the Monitors and Hansamen had thought
Nor worth the fishing up — a carcase drunk with sea;

Free, smoking, touched with mists of violet above,
I, who the lurid heavens breached like some rare wall
Which boasts — confection that the goodly poets love —
Lichens of sunlight on a mucoid azure pall;

Who, with electric moons bedaubed, sped on my way,
A plank gone wild, black hippocamps my retinue,
When in July, beneath the cudgels of the day
Down fell the heavens and the craters of the blue;

I, trembling at the mutter, fifty leagues from me,
Of rutting Behemoths, the turbid Maelstrom's threats,
Spinning a motionless and blue eternity
I long for Europe, land of ancient parapets.

Such starry archipelagoes! Many an isle
With heavens fiercely to the wanderer wide-thrown;
Is it these depthless nights that your lone sleep beguile,
A million golden birds, O Vigour not yet known?

And yet, I've wept too much. The dawns are sharp distress,
All moons are baleful and all sunlight harsh to me
Swollen by acrid love, sagging with drunkenness —
Oh, that my keel might rend and give me to the sea!

If there's a water in all Europe that I crave,
It is the cold, black pond where 'neath the scented sky
Of eve a crouching infant, sorrowfully grave,
Launches a boat as frail as a May butterfly.

Soaked in your languors, waves, I can no more go hunting
The cotton-clippers' wake, no more can enterprise
Amid the proud displays of lofty flags and bunting,
Nor swim beneath the convict-hulks' appalling eyes!

[TRANSLATED BY NORMAN CAMERON]

Sebastian Van Storck

WALTER PATER

(1839–1894)

This is one of the Imaginary Portraits *published in 1887. It shares with Swinburne the nonfunctional and exquisite surface and the disturbing content; with Rimbaud the sustained metaphor, here historical rather than geographical; with Mallarmé the use of philosophy as a technique of withdrawal; and with Thomas Mann the use of disease as a metaphor for alienation. The ending seems at first sentimental but is in fact ironic.*

It was a winter-scene, by Adrian van de Velde, or by Isaac van Ostade. All the delicate poetry together with all the delicate comfort of the frosty season was in the leafless branches turned to silver, the furred dresses of the skaters, the warmth of the red-brick house-fronts under the gauze of white fog, the gleams of pale sunlight on the cuirasses of the mounted soldiers as they receded into the distance. Sebastian van Storck, confessedly the most graceful performer in all that skating multitude, moving in endless maze over the vast surface of the frozen water-meadow, liked best this season of the year for its expression of a perfect impassivity, or at least of a perfect repose. The earth was, or seemed to be, at rest, with a breathlessness of slumber which suited the young man's peculiar temper. The heavy summer, as it dried up the meadows now lying dead below the ice, set free a crowded and competing world of life, which, while it gleamed very pleasantly russet and yellow for the painter Albert Cuyp, seemed wellnigh to suffocate Sebastian van Storck. Yet with all his appreciation of the national winter, Sebastian was not altogether a Hollander. His mother, of Spanish descent and Catholic, had given a richness of tone and form to the healthy freshness of the Dutch physiognomy, apt to preserve its youthfulness of aspect far beyond the period of life usual with other peoples. This mixed expression charmed the eye of Isaac van Ostade, who had painted his portrait from a sketch taken at one of those skating parties, with his plume of squirrel's tail and fur muff, in all the modest pleasantness of boyhood. When he returned home lately from his studies at a place far inland, at the proposal of his tutor, to recover, as the tutor suggested, a certain loss of robustness, something more than that cheerful indifference of early youth had passed away. The learned man, who held, as was alleged, the doctrines of a surprising new philosophy, reluctant to disturb too early the fine intelligence of the pupil entrusted to him, had found it, perhaps, a matter of honesty to send back to his parents one likely enough to catch from others any sort of theoretic light; for the letter he wrote dwelt much on the lad's intellectual fearlessness. "At present," he had written, "he is influenced more by curiosity than by a care for truth, according to the character of the young. Certainly, he differs strikingly from his equals in age, by his passion for a vigorous intellectual gymnastic, such as the supine character of their minds renders distasteful to most young·men, but in which he shows a fearlessness that at times makes me fancy that his ultimate destination may be the military life; for indeed the rigidly logical tendency of his mind always leads him out upon the practical. Don't misunderstand me! At present, he is strenuous only intellectually; and has given no definite sign of preference, as regards a vocation in life. But he seems to me to be one practical in this sense, that his theorems will shape life for him, directly; that he will always seek, as a matter of course, the effective equivalent to — the line of being which shall be the proper continuation of — his line of thinking. This intellectual rectitude, or candour, which to my mind has a kind of beauty in it, has reacted upon myself, I confess, with a searching quality." That "searching quality," indeed, many others also, people far from being intellectual, had experienced — an agitation of mind in his neighbourhood, oddly at variance with the composure of the young man's manner and surrounding, so jealously preserved.

In the crowd of spectators at the skating, whose eyes followed, so well-satisfied, the movements of Sebastian van Storck, were the mothers of marriageable daughters, who presently became the suitors of this rich and distinguished youth, introduced to them, as now grown to man's estate, by his delighted parents. Dutch aristocracy had put forth all its graces to become the winter morn: and it was characteristic of the period that the artist tribe was there, on a grand footing, — in waiting, for the lights and shadows they liked best. The artists were, in truth, an important body just then, as a natural consequence of the nation's hard-won prosperity; helping it to a full consciousness of the genial yet delicate homeliness it loved, for which it had fought so bravely, and was ready at any moment to fight anew, against man or the sea. Thomas de Keyser, who understood better than any one else the kind of quaint new Atticism which had found its way into the world over those waste salt marshes, wondering whether quite its finest type as he understood it could ever actually be seen there, saw it at last, in lively motion, in the person of Sebastian van Storck, and desired to paint his portrait. A little to his surprise, the young man declined the offer; not graciously, as was thought.

Holland, just then, was reposing on its laurels after its long contest with Spain, in a short period of complete wellbeing, before troubles of another kind should set in. That a darker time might return again, was clearly enough felt by Sebastian the elder — a time like that of William the Silent, with its insane civil animosities, which would demand similarly energetic personalities, and offer them similar opportunities. And then, it was part of his honest geniality of character to admire those who "get on" in the world. Himself had been, almost from boyhood, in contact with great affairs. A member of the States-General which had taken so hardly the kingly airs of Frederick Henry, he had assisted at the Congress of Munster, and figures conspicuously in Terburgh's picture of that assembly, which had finally established Holland as a first-rate power. The heroism by which the national wellbeing had been achieved was still of recent memory — the air full of its reverberation, and great movement. There was a tradition to be maintained; the sword by no means resting in its sheath. The age was still fitted to evoke a generous ambition; and this son, from whose natural gifts there was so much to hope for, might play his part, at least as a diplomatist, if the present quiet continued. Had not the learned man said that his natural disposition would lead him out always upon practice? And in truth, the memory of that Silent hero had its fascination for the youth. When, about this time, Peter de

Keyser, Thomas's brother, unveiled at last this tomb of wrought bronze and marble in the *Nieuwe Kerk* at Delft, the young Sebastian was one of a small company present, and relished much the cold and abstract simplicity of the monument, so conformable to the great, abstract, and unuttered force of the hero who slept beneath.

In complete contrast to all that is abstract or cold in art, the home of Sebastian, the family mansion of the Storcks — a house, the front of which still survives in one of those patient architectural pieces by Jan van der Heyde — was, in its minute and busy wellbeing, like an epitome of Holland itself with all the good-fortune of its "thriving genius" reflected, quite spontaneously, in the national taste. The nation had learned to content itself with a religion which told little, or not at all, on the outsides of things. But we may fancy that something of the religious spirit had gone, according to the law of the transmutation of forces, into the scrupulous care for cleanliness, into the grave, old-world, conservative beauty of Dutch houses, which meant that the life people maintained in them was normally affectionate and pure.

The most curious florists of Holland were ambitious to supply the Burgomaster van Storck with the choicest products of their skill for the garden spread below the windows on either side of the portico, and along the central avenue of hoary beeches which led to it. Naturally this house, within a mile of the city of Haarlem, became a resort of the artists, then mixing freely in great society, giving and receiving hints as to the domestic picturesque. Creatures of leisure — of leisure on both sides — they were the appropriate complement of Dutch prosperity, as it was understood just then. Sebastian the elder could almost have wished his son to be one of them: it was the next best thing to being an influential publicist or statesman. The Dutch had just begun to see what a picture their country was — its canals, and *boompjis,* and endless, broadly-lighted meadows, and thousands of miles of quaint water-side: and their painters, the first true masters of landscape for its own sake, were further informing them in the matter. They were bringing proof, for all who cared to see, of the wealth of colour there was all around them in this, supposably, sad land. Above all, they developed the old Low-country taste for interiors. Those innumerable *genre* pieces — conversation, music, play — were in truth the equivalent of novel-reading for that day; its own actual life, in its own proper circumstances, reflected in various degrees of idealisation, with no diminution of the sense of reality (that is to say) but with more and more purged and perfected delightfulness of interest. Themselves illustrating, as every student of their history knows, the good-fellowship of family life, it was the ideal of that life which these artists depicted; the ideal of home in a country where the preponderant interest of life, after all, could not well be out of doors. Of the earth earthy — genuine red earth of the old Adam — it was an ideal very different from that which the sacred Italian painters had evoked from the life of Italy, yet, in its best types, was not without a kind of natural religiousness. And in the achievement of a type of beauty so national and vernacular, the votaries of purely Dutch art might well feel that the Italianisers, like Berghem, Boll, and Jan Weenix went so far afield in vain.

The fine organisation and acute intelligence of Sebastian would have made him an effective connoisseur of the arts, as he showed by the justice of his remarks in those assemblies of the artists which his father so much loved. But in truth the arts were a matter he could but just tolerate. Why add, by a forced and artificial production, to the monotonous tide of competing, fleeting existence? Only, finding so much fine art actually about him, he was compelled (so to speak) to adjust himself to it; to ascertain and accept that in it which should least collide with, or might even carry forward a little, his own characteristic tendencies. Obviously somewhat jealous of his intellectual interests, he loved inanimate nature, it might have been thought, better than man. He cared nothing, indeed, for the warm sandbanks of Wynants, nor for those eerie relics of the ancient Dutch woodland which survive in Hobbema and Ruysdael, still less for the highly-coloured sceneries of the academic band at Rome, in spite of the escape they provide one into clear breadth of atmosphere. For though Sebastian van Storck refused to travel, he loved the distant — enjoyed the sense of things seen from a distance, carrying us, as on wide wings of space itself, far out of one's actual surrounding. His preference in the matter of art was, therefore, for those prospects *à vol a'oiseau* — of the caged bird on the wing at last — of which Rubens had the secret, and still more Philip de Koninck, four of whose choicest works occupied the four walls of his chamber; visionary escapes, north, south, east, and west, into a wide-open, though it must be confessed, a somewhat sullen land. For the fourth of them he had exchanged with his mother a marvellously vivid Metsu, lately bequeathed to him, in which she herself was presented. They were the sole ornaments he permitted himself. From the midst of the busy and busy-looking house, crowded with the furni-

ture and the pretty little toys of many generations, a long passage led
the rare visitor up a winding staircase, and (again at the end of a long
passage) he found himself as if shut off from the whole talkative Dutch
world, and in the embrace of that wonderful quiet which is also possible
in Holland at its height all around him. It was here that Sebastian
could yield himself, with the only sort of love he had ever felt, to the
supremacy of his difficult thoughts. — A kind of *empty* place! Here, you
felt, all had been mentally put to rights by the working-out of a long
equation, which had zero is equal to zero for its result. Here one did,
and perhaps felt, nothing; one only thought. Of living creatures only
birds came there freely, the sea-birds especially, to attract and detain
which there were all sorts of ingenious contrivances about the windows,
such as one may see in the cottage sceneries of Jan Steen and others.
There was something, doubtless, of his passion for distance in this
welcoming of the creatures of the air. An extreme simplicity in their
manner of life was, indeed, characteristic of many a distinguished Hollander — William the Silent, Baruch de Spinosa, the brothers de Witt.
But the simplicity of Sebastian van Storck was something different from
that, and certainly nothing democratic. His mother thought him like
one disembarrassing himself carefully, and little by little, of all impedi-
ments, habituating himself gradually to make shift with as little as
possible, in preparation for a long journey.

The Burgomaster van Storck entertained a party of friends, consisting chiefly of his favourite artists, one summer evening. The guests
were seen arriving on foot in the fine weather, some of them accompanied by their wives and daughters, against the light of the low sun,
falling red on the old trees of the avenue and the faces of those who
advanced along it: — Willem van Aelst, expecting to find hints for a
flower-portrait in the exotics which would decorate the banqueting-
room; Gerard Dow, to feed his eye, amid all that glittering luxury, on
the combat between candle-light and the last rays of the departing sun;
Thomas de Keyser, to catch by stealth the likeness of Sebastian the
younger. Albert Cuyp was there, who, developing the latent gold in
Rembrandt, had brought into his native Dordrecht a heavy wealth of
sunshine, as exotic as those flowers or the eastern carpets on the Burgomaster's tables, with Hooch, the indoor Cuyp, and Willem van de
Velde, who painted those shore-pieces with gay ships of war, such as
he loved, for his patron's cabinet. Thomas de Keyser came, in company

with his brother Peter, his niece, and young Mr. Nicholas Stone from England, pupil of that brother Peter, who afterwards married the niece. For the life of Dutch artists, too, was exemplary in matters of domestic relationship, its history telling many a cheering story of mutual faith in misfortune. Hardly less exemplary was the comradeship which they displayed among themselves, obscuring their own best gifts sometimes, one in the mere accessories of another man's work, so that they came together to-night with no fear of falling out, and spoiling the musical interludes of Madame van Storck in the large back parlour. A little way behind the other guests, three of them together, son, grandson, and the grandfather, moving slowly, came the Hondecoeters — Giles, Gybrecht, and Melchior. They led the party before the house was entered, by fading light, to see the curious poultry of the Burgomaster go to roost; and it was almost night when the supper-room was reached at last. The occasion was an important one to Sebastian, and to others through him. For (was it the music of the duets? he asked himself next morning, with a certain distaste as he remembered it all, or the heady Spanish wines poured out so freely in those narrow but deep Venetian glasses?) on this evening he approached more nearly than he had ever yet done to Mademoiselle van Westrheene, as she sat there beside the *clavecin* looking very ruddy and fresh in her white satin, trimmed with glossy crimson swans-down.

So genially attempered, so warm, was life become, in the land of which Pliny had spoken as scarcely dry land at all. And, in truth, the sea which Sebastian so much loved, and with so great a satisfaction and sense of wellbeing in every hint of its nearness, is never far distant in Holland. Invading all places, stealing under one's feet, insinuating itself everywhere along an endless network of canals (by no means such formal channels as we understand by the name, but picturesque rivers, with sedgy banks and haunted by innumerable birds), its incidents present themselves oddly even in one's park or woodland walks; the ship in full sail appearing suddenly among the great trees or above the garden wall, where we had no suspicion of the presence of water. In the very conditions of life in such a country there was a standing force of pathos. The country itself shared the uncertainty of the individual human life; and there was pathos also in the constantly renewed, heavily-taxed labour, necessary to keep the native soil, fought for so unselfishly, there at all, with a warfare that must still be maintained when that other struggle with the Spaniard was over. But though Sebastian liked to breathe, so nearly, the sea and its influences, those were considerations he scarcely entertained. In his passion for *Schwindsucht* — we haven't the word — he found it pleasant to think of the resistless element which left one hardly a foot-space amidst the yielding sand; of the old beds of lost rivers, surviving now only as deeper channels in the sea; of the remains of a certain ancient town, which within men's memory had lost its few remaining inhabitants, and, with its already empty tombs, dissolved and disappeared in the flood.

It happened, on occasion of an exceptionally low tide, that some remarkable relics were exposed to view on the coast of the island of Vleeland. A countryman's waggon overtaken by the tide, as he returned with merchandise from the shore! you might have supposed, but for a touch of grace in the construction of the thing — lightly wrought timber-work, united and adorned by a multitude of brass fastenings, like the work of children for their simplicity, while the rude, stiff chair, or throne, set upon it, seemed to distinguish it as a chariot of state. To some antiquarians it told the story of the overwhelming of one of the chiefs of the old primeval people of Holland, amid all his gala array, in a great storm. But it was another view which Sebastian preferred; that this object was sepulchral, namely, in its motive — the one surviving relic of a grand burial, in the ancient manner, of a king or hero, whose very tomb was wasted away. — *Sunt metis metæ!* There came with it the odd fancy that he himself would like to have been dead and gone as long ago, with a kind of envy of those whose deceasing was so long since over.

On more peaceful days he would ponder Pliny's account of those primeval forefathers, but without Pliny's contempt for them. A cloyed Roman might despise their humble existence, fixed by necessity from age to age, and with no desire of change, as "the ocean poured in its flood twice a day, making it uncertain whether the country was a part of the continent or of the sea." But for his part Sebastian found something of poetry in all that, as he conceived what thoughts the old Hollander might have had at his fishing, with nets themselves woven of seaweed, waiting carefully for his drink on the heavy rains, and taking refuge, as the flood rose, on the sand-hills, in a little hut constructed but airily on tall stakes, conformable to the elevation of the highest tides, like a navigator, thought the learned writer, when the sea was risen, like a shipwrecked mariner when it was retired. For the fancy of Sebastian he lived with great breadths of calm light above and around him, influenced by, and, in a sense, living upon them, and surely might well complain, though to Pliny's so infinite surprise, on being made a Roman citizen.

And certainly Sebastian van Storck did not felicitate his people on the luck which, in the words of another old writer, "hath disposed them to so thriving a genius." Their restless ingenuity in making and maintaining dry land where nature had willed the sea, was even more like the industry of animals than had been that life of their forefathers. Away with that tetchy, feverish, unworthy agitation! with this and that, all too importunate, motive of interest! And then, "My son!" said his father, "be stimulated to action!" he, too, thinking of that heroic industry which had triumphed over nature precisely where the contest had been most difficult.

Yet, in truth, Sebastian was forcibly taken by the simplicity of a great affection, as set forth in an incident of real life of which he heard just then. The eminent Grotius being condemned to perpetual imprisonment, his wife determined to share his fate, alleviated only by the reading of books sent by friends. The books, finished, were returned in a great chest. In this chest the wife enclosed the husband, and was able to reply to the objections of the soldiers who carried it complaining of its weight, with a self-control, which she maintained till the captive was in safety, herself remaining to face the consequences; and there was a kind of absoluteness of affection in that, which attracted Sebastian for a while to ponder on the practical forces which shape men's lives. Had he turned, indeed, to a practical career it would have been less in the direction of the military or political life than of another form of enterprise popular with his countrymen. In the eager, gallant life of that age, if the sword fell for a moment into its sheath, they were for starting off on perilous voyages to the regions of frost and snow in search after that "North-Western passage," for the discovery of which the States-General had offered large rewards. Sebastian, in effect, found a charm in the thought of that still, drowsy, spellbound world of perpetual ice, as in art and life he could always tolerate the sea. Admiral-general of Holland, as painted by Van der Helst, with a marine background by Backhuizen: — at moments his father could fancy him so.

There was still another very different sort of character to which

Sebastian would let his thoughts stray, without check, for a time. His mother, whom he much resembled outwardly, a Catholic from Brabant, had had saints in her family, and from time to time the mind of Sebastian had been occupied on the subject of monastic life, its quiet, its negation. The portrait of a certain Carthusian prior, which, like the famous statue of Saint Bruno, the first Carthusian, in the church of Santa Maria degli Angeli at Rome, could it have spoken, would have said, "Silence!" kept strange company with the painted visages of men of affairs. A great theological strife was then raging in Holland. Grave ministers of religion assembled sometimes, as in the painted scene by Rembrandt, in the Burgomaster's house, and once, not however in their company, came a renowned young Jewish divine, Baruch de Spinosa, with whom, most unexpectedly, Sebastian found himself in sympathy, meeting the young Jew's far-reaching thoughts half-way, to the confirmation of his own; and he did not know that his visitor, very ready with the pencil, had taken his likeness as they talked on the fly-leaf of his note-book. Alive to that theological disturbance in the air all around him, he refused to be moved by it, as essentially a strife on small matters, anticipating a vagrant regret which may have visited many other minds since, the regret, namely, that the old, pensive, use-and-wont Catholicism, which had accompanied the nation's earlier struggle for existence, and consoled it therein, had been taken from it. And for himself, indeed, what impressed him in that old Catholicism was a kind of lull in it — a lulling power — like that of the monotonous organ-music, which Holland, Catholic or not, still so greatly loves. But what he could not away with in the Catholic religion was its unfailing drift towards the concrete — the positive imageries of a faith, so richly beset with persons, things, historical incidents.

Rigidly logical in the method of his inferences, he attained the poetic quality only by the audacity with which he conceived the whole sublime extension of his premises. The contrast was a strange one between the careful, the almost petty fineness of his personal surrounding — all the elegant conventionalities of life, in that rising Dutch family — and the mortal coldness of a temperament, the intellectual tendencies of which seemed to necessitate straightforward flight from all that was positive. He seemed, if one may say so, in love with death; preferring winter to summer; finding only a tranquillising influence in the thought of the earth beneath our feet cooling down for ever from its old cosmic heat; watching pleasurably how their colours fled out of things, and the long sand-bank in the sea, which had been the rampart of a town, was washed down in its turn. One of his acquaintance, a penurious young poet, who, having nothing in his pockets but the imaginative or otherwise barely potential gold of manuscript verses, would have grasped so eagerly, had they lain within his reach, at the elegant outsides of life, thought the fortunate Sebastian, possessed of every possible opportunity of that kind, yet bent only on dispensing with it, certainly a most puzzling and comfortless creature. A few only, half discerning what was in his mind, would fain have shared his intellectual clearness, and found a kind of beauty in this youthful enthusiasm for an abstract theorem. Extremes meeting, his cold and dispassionate detachment from all that is most attractive to ordinary minds came to have the impressiveness of a great passion. And for the most part, people had loved him; feeling instinctively that somewhere there must be the justification of his difference from themselves. It was like being in love: or it was an intellectual malady, such as pleaded for forbearance, like bodily sickness, and gave at times a resigned and touching sweetness to what he did and said. Only once, at a moment of the wild popular excitement which at that period was easy to provoke in Holland, there was a certain group of persons who would have shut him up as no well-wisher to, and perhaps a plotter against, the common-weal. A single traitor might cut the dykes in an hour, in the interest of the English or the French. Or, had he already committed some treasonable act, who was so anxious to expose no writing of his that he left his very letters unsigned, and there were little stratagems to get specimens of his fair manuscript? For with all his breadth of mystic intention, he was persistent, as the hours crept on, to leave all the inevitable details of life at least in order, in equation. And all his singularities appeared to be summed up in his refusal to take his place in the life-sized family group (*très distingué et très soigné,* remarks a modern critic of the work) painted about this time. His mother expostulated with him on the matter: — she must needs feel, a little icily, the emptiness of hope, and something more than the due measure of cold in things for a woman of her age, in the presence of a son who desired but to fade out of the world like a breath — and she suggested filial duty. "Good mother," he answered, "there are duties towards the intellect also, which women can but rarely understand."

The artists and their wives were come to supper again, with the

Burgomaster van Storck. Mademoiselle van Westrheene was also come,
with her sister and mother. The girl was by this time fallen in love with
Sebastian; and she was one of the few who, in spite of his terrible coldness, really loved him for himself. But though of good birth she was
poor, while Sebastian could not but perceive that he had many suitors
of his wealth. In truth, Madame van Westrheene, her mother, did wish to
marry this daughter into the great world, and plied many arts to that
end, such as "daughterful" mothers use. Her healthy freshness of mien
and mind, her ruddy beauty, some showy presents that had passed, were
of a piece with the ruddy colouring of the very house these people lived
in; and for a moment the cheerful warmth that may be felt in life seemed
to come very close to him, — to come forth, and enfold him. Meantime
the girl herself taking note of this, that on a former occasion of their
meeting he had seemed likely to respond to her inclination, and that
his father would readily consent to such a marriage, surprised him on the
sudden with those coquetries and importunities, all those little arts of
love, which often succeed with men. Only, to Sebastian they seemed
opposed to that absolute nature we suppose in love. And while, in the
eyes of all around him to-night, this courtship seemed to promise him,
thus early in life, a kind of quiet happiness, he was coming to an
estimate of the situation, with strict regard to that ideal of a calm, intellectual indifference, of which he was the sworn chevalier. Set in the
cold, hard light of that ideal, this girl, with the pronounced personal
views of her mother, and in the very effectiveness of arts prompted by a
real affection, bringing the warm life they prefigured so close to him,
seemed vulgar! And still he felt himself bound in honour; or judged from
their manner that she and those about them thought him thus bound.
He did not reflect on the inconsistency of the feeling of honour (living, as
it does essentially, upon the concrete and minute detail of social relationship) for one who, on principle, set so slight a value on anything whatever that is merely relative in its character.

The guests, lively and late, were almost pledging the betrothed in the
rich wine. Only Sebastian's mother knew; and at that advanced hour,
while the company were thus intently occupied, drew away the Burgomaster to confide to him the misgivings she felt, grown to a great height
just then. The young man had slipped from the assembly; but certainly
not with Mademoiselle van Westrheene, who was suddenly withdrawn
also. And she never appeared again in the world. Already, next day, with

the rumour that Sebastian had left his home, it was known that the expected marriage would not take place. The girl, indeed, alleged some-thing in the way of a cause on her part; but seemed to fade away con-tinually afterwards, and in the eyes of all who saw her was like one perishing of wounded pride. But to make a clean breast of her poor girlish worldliness, before she became a *béguine,* she confessed to her mother the receipt of the letter — the cruel letter that had killed her. And in effect, the first copy of this letter, written with a very deliberate fineness, rejecting her — accusing her, so natural, and simply loyal! of a vulgar coarseness of character — was found, oddly tacked on, as their last word, to the studious record of the abstract thoughts which had been the real business of Sebastian's life, in the room whither his mother went to seek him next day, littered with the fragments of the one portrait of him in existence.

The neat and elaborate manuscript volume, of which this letter formed the final page (odd transition! by which a train of thought so abstract drew its conclusion in the sphere of action) afforded at length to the few who were interested in him a much-coveted insight into the curiosity of his existence; and I pause just here to indicate in outline the kind of reasoning through which, making the "Infinite" his beginning and his end, Sebastian had come to think all definite forms of being, the warm pressure of life, the cry of nature itself, no more than a troublesome irritation of the surface of the one absolute mind, a passing vexatious thought or uneasy dream there, at its height of petulant importunity in the eager, human creature.

The volume was, indeed, a kind of treatise to be: — a hard, systematic, well-concatenated train of thought, still implicated in the circumstances of a journal. Freed from the accidents of that particular literary form with its unavoidable details of place and occasion, the theoretic strain would have been found mathematically continuous. The already so weary Sebastian might perhaps never have taken in hand, or succeeded in, this detachment of his thoughts; every one of which, beginning with himself, as the peculiar and intimate apprehension of this or that par-ticular day and hour, seemed still to protest against such disturbance, as if reluctant to part from those accidental associations of the personal his-tory which had prompted it, and so become a purely intellectual abstrac-tion.

The series began with Sebastian's boyish enthusiasm for a strange, fine

saying of Doctor Baruch de Spinosa, concerning the Divine Love: —
That whoso loveth God truly must not expect to be loved by him in
return. In mere reaction against an actual surrounding of which every
circumstance tended to make him a finished egotist, that bold assertion
defined for him the ideal of an intellectual disinterestedness, of a domain
of unimpassioned mind, with the desire to put one's subjective side out
of the way, and let pure reason speak.

And what pure reason affirmed in the first place, as the "beginning of
wisdom," was that the world is but a thought, or a series of thoughts:
that it exists, therefore, solely in mind. It showed him, as he fixed the
mental eye with more and more of self-absorption on the phenomena
of his intellectual existence, a picture or vision of the universe as
actually the product, so far as he really knew it, of his own lonely thinking power — of himself, there, thinking: as being zero without him: and
as possessing a perfectly homogeneous unity in that fact. "Things that
have nothing in common with each other," said the axiomatic reason,
"cannot be understood or explained by means of each other." But to
pure reason things discovered themselves as being, in their essence,
thoughts: — all things, even the most opposite things, mere transmutations of a single power, the power of thought. All was but conscious
mind. Therefore, all the more exclusively, he must minister to mind,
to the intellectual power, submitting himself to the sole direction of
that, whithersoever it might lead him. Everything must be referred
to, and, as it were, changed into the terms of that, if its essential
value was to be ascertained. "Joy," he said, anticipating Spinosa — that,
for the attainment of which men are ready to surrender all beside — "is
but the name of a passion in which the mind passes to a greater perfection or power of thinking; as grief is the name of the passion in
which it passes to a less."

Looking backward for the generative source of that creative power of
thought in him, from his own mysterious intellectual being to its first
cause, he still reflected, as one can but do, the enlarged pattern of himself into the vague region of hypothesis. In this way, some, at all events,
would have explained his mental process. To him that process was
nothing less than the apprehension, the revelation, of the greatest and
most real of ideas — the true substance of all things. He, too, with his
vividly-coloured existence, with this picturesque and sensuous world of
Dutch art and Dutch reality all around that would fain have made him

the prisoner of its colours, it genial warmth, its struggle for life, its selfish and crafty love, was but a transient perturbation of the one absolute mind; of which, indeed, all finite things whatever, time itself, the most durable achievements of nature and man, and all that seems most like independent energy, are no more than petty accidents or affections. Theorem and corollary! Thus they stood:

"*There can be only one substance*: (corollary) it is the greatest of errors to think that the non-existent, the world of finite things seen and felt, really is: (theorem): *for, whatever is, is but in that:* (practical corollary): one's wisdom, therefore, consists in hastening, so far as may be, the action of those forces which tend to the restoration of equilibrium, the calm surface of the absolute, untroubled mind, to *tabula rasa,* by the extinction in one's self of all that is but correlative to the finite illusion — by the suppression of ourselves."

In the loneliness which was gathering round him, and, oddly enough, as a somewhat surprising thing, he wondered whether there were, or had been, others possessed of like thoughts, ready to welcome any such as his veritable compatriots. And in fact he became aware just then, in readings difficult indeed, but which from their all-absorbing interest seemed almost like an illicit pleasure, a sense of kinship with certain older minds. The study of many an earlier adventurous theorist satisfied his curiosity as the record of daring physical adventure, for instance, might satisfy the curiosity of the healthy. It was a tradition — a constant tradition — that daring thought of his; an echo, or haunting recurrent voice of the human soul itself, and as such sealed with natural truth, which certain minds would not fail to heed; discerning also, if they were really loyal to themselves, its practical conclusion. — The one alone is: and all things beside are but its passing affections, which have no necessary or proper right to be.

As but such "accidents" or "affections," indeed, there might have been found, within the circumference of that one infinite creative thinker, some scope for the joy and love of the creature. There have been dispositions in which that abstract theorem has only induced a renewed value for the finite interests around and within us. Centre of heat and light, truly nothing has seemed to lie beyond the touch of its perpetual summer. It has allied itself to the poetical or artistic sympathy, which feels challenged to acquaint itself with and explore the various forms of finite existence all the more intimately, just because of that sense of one lively spirit circulating through all things — a tiny particle of the one soul, in the sunbeam, or the leaf. Sebastian van Storck, on the contrary, was determined, perhaps by some inherited satiety or fatigue in his nature, to the opposite issue of the practical dilemma. For him, that one abstract being was as the pallid Arctic sun, disclosing itself over the dead level of a glacial, a barren and absolutely lonely sea. The lively purpose of life had been frozen out of it. What he must admire, and love if he could, was "equilibrium," the void, the *tabula rasa,* into which, through all those apparent energies of man and nature, that in truth are but forces of disintegration, the world was really settling. And, himself a mere circumstance in a fatalistic series, to which the clay of the potter was no sufficient parallel, he could not expect to be "loved in return." At first, indeed, he had a kind of delight in his thoughts — in the eager pressure forward, to whatsoever conclusion, of a rigid intellectual gymnastic, which was like the making of Euclid. Only, little by little, under the freezing influence of such propositions, the theoretic energy itself, and with it his old eagerness for truth, the care to track it from proposition to proposition, was chilled out of him. In fact, the conclusion was there already, and might have been foreseen, in the premises. By a singular perversity, it seemed to him that every one of those passing "affections" — he too, alas! at times — was for ever trying to be, to assert *itself,* to maintain its isolated and petty self, by a kind of practical lie in things; although through every incident of its hypothetic existence it had protested that its proper function was to die. Surely! those transient affections marred the freedom, the truth, the beatific calm, of the absolute selfishness, which could not, if it would, pass beyond the circumference of itself; to which, at times, with a fantastic sense of wellbeing, he was capable of a sort of fanatical devotion. And those, as he conceived, were his moments of genuine theoretic insight, in which, under the abstract "perpetual light," he died to self; while the intellect, after all, had attained a freedom of its own through the vigorous act which assured him that, as nature was but a thought of his, so himself also was but the passing thought of God.

No! rather a puzzle only, an anomaly, upon that one, white, unruffled consciousness! His first principle once recognised, all the rest, the whole array of propositions down to the heartless practical conclusion, must follow of themselves. Detachment: to hasten hence: to fold up one's whole self, as a vesture put aside: to anticipate, by such individual force

as he could find in him, the slow disintegration by which nature herself is levelling the eternal hills: — here would be the secret of peace, of
such dignity and truth as there could be in a world which after all was
essentially an illusion. For Sebastian at least, the world and the individual alike had been divested of all effective purpose. The most vivid
of finite objects, the dramatic episodes of Dutch history, the brilliant
personalities which had found their parts to play in them, that golden
art, surrounding us with an ideal world, beyond which the real world is
discernible indeed, but etherealised by the medium through which it
comes to one: all this, for most men so powerful a link to existence,
only set him on the thought of escape — means of escape — into a formless and nameless infinite world, quite evenly grey. The very emphasis
of those objects, their importunity to the eye, the ear, the finite intelligence, was but the measure of their distance from what really is. One's
personal presence, the presence, such as it is, of the most incisive things
and persons around us, could only lessen by so much, that which really
is. To restore *tabula rasa,* then, by a continual effort at self-effacement!
Actually proud at times of his curious, well-reasoned nihilism, he could
but regard what is called the business of life as no better than a trifling
and wearisome delay. Bent on making sacrifice of the rich existence possible for him, as he would readily have sacrificed that of other people, to
the bare and formal logic of the answer to a query (never proposed at
all to entirely healthy minds) regarding the remote conditions and
tendencies of that existence, he did not reflect that if others had inquired
as curiously as himself the world could never have come so far at all
— that the fact of its having come so far was itself a weighty exception
to his hypothesis. His odd devotion, soaring or sinking into fanaticism,
into a kind of religious mania, with what was really a vehement assertion
of his individual will, he had formulated duty as the principle to hinder
as little as possible what he called the restoration of equilibrium, the
restoration of the primary consciousness to itself — its relief from that
uneasy, tetchy, unworthy dream of a world, made so ill, or dreamt so
weakly — to forget, to be forgotten.

And at length this dark fanaticism, losing the support of his pride in
the mere novelty of a reasoning so hard and dry, turned round upon
him, as our fanaticism will, in black melancholy. The theoretic or
imaginative desire to urge Time's creeping footsteps, was felt now as the
physical fatigue which leaves the book or the letter unfinished, or

finishes eagerly out of hand, for mere finishing's sake, unimportant business. Strange! that the presence to the mind of a metaphysical abstraction should have had this power over one so fortunately endowed for the reception of the sensible world. It could hardly have been so with him but for the concurrence of physical causes with the influences proper to a mere thought. The moralist, indeed, might have noted that a meaner kind of pride, the morbid fear of vulgarity, lent secret strength to the intellectual prejudice, which realised duty as the renunciation of all finite objects, the fastidious refusal to be or do any limited thing. But besides this it was legible in his own admissions from time to time, that the body, following, as it does with powerful temperaments, the lead of mind and the will, the intellectual consumption (so to term it) had been concurrent with, had strengthened and been strengthened by, a vein of physical *phthisis* — by a merely physical accident, after all, of his bodily constitution, such as might have taken a different turn, had another accident fixed his home among the hills instead of on the shore. Is it only the result of disease? he would ask himself sometimes with a sudden suspicion of his intellectual cogency — this persuasion that myself, and all that surrounds me, are but a diminution of that which really is? — this unkindly melancholy?

The journal, with that "cruel" letter to Mademoiselle van Westrheene coming as the last step in the rigid process of theoretic deduction, circulated among the curious; and people made their judgments upon it. There were some who held that such opinions should be suppressed by law; that they were, or might become, dangerous to society. Perhaps it was the confessor of his mother who thought of the matter most justly. The aged man smiled, observing how, even for minds by no means superficial, the mere dress it wears alters the look of a familiar thought; with a happy sort of smile, as he added (reflecting that such truth as there was in Sebastian's theory was duly covered by the propositions of his own creed, and quoting Sebastian's favourite pagan wisdom from the lips of Saint Paul) "in Him, we live, and move, and have our being."

Next day, as Sebastian escaped to the sea under the long, monotonous line of wind-mills, in comparative calm of mind — reaction of that pleasant morning from the madness of the night before — he was making light, or trying to make light, with some success, of his late distress. He would fain have thought it a small matter, to be adequately set at rest for him by certain well-tested influences of external nature, in a long visit to the place he liked best: a desolate house, amid the sands of the Helder, one of the old lodgings of his family, property now, rather, of the sea-birds, and almost surrounded by the encroaching tide, though there were still relics enough of hardy, sweet things about it, to form what was to Sebastian the most perfect garden in Holland. Here he could make "equation" between himself and what was not himself, and set things in order, in preparation towards such deliberate and final change in his manner of living as circumstances so clearly necessitated.

As he stayed in this place, with one or two silent serving people, a sudden rising of the wind altered, as it might seem, in a few dark, tempestuous hours, the entire world around him. The strong wind changed not again for fourteen days, and its effect was a permanent one; so that people might have fancied that an enemy had indeed cut the dykes somewhere — a pin-hole enough to wreck the ship of Holland, or at least this portion of it, which underwent an inundation of the sea the like of which had not occurred in that province for half a century. Only, when the body of Sebastian was found, apparently not long after death, a child lay asleep, swaddled warmly in his heavy furs, in an upper room of the old tower, to which the tide was almost risen; though the building still stood firmly, and still with the means of life in plenty. And it was in the saving of this child, with a great effort, as certain circumstances seemed to indicate, that Sebastian had lost his life.

His parents were come to seek him, believing him bent on self-destruction, and were almost glad to find him thus. A learned physician, moreover, endeavoured to comfort his mother by remarking that in any case he must certainly have died ere many years were passed, slowly, perhaps painfully, of a disease then coming into the world; disease begotten by the fogs of that country — waters, he observed, not in their place, "above the firmament" — on people grown somewhat over-delicate in their nature by the effects of modern luxury.

Hérodiade

STÉPHANÉ MALLARMÉ

(1842–1898)

*The tendencies of Stylism achieve their maximum exaltation
in the poetry of Mallarmé. He creates an almost impermeable
surface, ravishingly beautiful, and consisting of metaphors
which glide one into the other to create so seamless a surface
that the poem lacks the information which would enable us
to decide what the metaphors are metaphors of. And in fact,
they are metaphors of nothing, or more precisely, of Nothingness. The greatness of Mallarmé is the greatness of a perfect
style suspended over a void. The poem was published in 1887.*

I. Ouverture ancienne d'Hérodiade

LA NOURRICE

(Incantation)

Abolished, and her frightful wings in the tears
of the pool, abolished, that mirrors her alarms,
the naked golds thrashing crimson space,
an Aurora has, heraldic plumage, chosen
our cinerary and sacrificial tower,
heavy tomb whence a beautiful bird has fled,

solitary caprice of dawn with vain black plumage . . .
ah, the manorhouse of sad and fallen lands!
No plashing! The gloomy water is resigned,
no longer visited by plume or swan
never forgotten: the water reflects the yielding
of autumn extinguishing therein his torch:
of the swan when amid the pallid mausoleum
where he plunged his feathery head, in grief
for the pure diamond of some star, but long
ago, a star that never scintillated.

Crime! pyre! ancient dawn! torture!
Purple of a sky! Pool of accomplice purple!
And on the rose-tints, wide-open, this stained-glass window.
The bizarre chamber in this frame, the pomp
of warring centuries, with the tarnished goldwork,
is like old snows instead of its former color,
and its tapestry, with nacrous luster, futile
folds with the shrouded eyes of sibyls offering
their aged fingernails to the Mages.
One of them, with embroideries of flowers
on my robe bleached in the closed ivory
with a sky of birds strewn on the blackened silver,
seems, garbed in risen flights and like a phantom,
an aroma reaching, O roses! an aroma,
far from the empty bed hidden by a snuffed candle,
an aroma of cold bones lingering on the sachet,
a bunch of flowers unfaithful to the moon
(by the dead candle it still sheds its petals),
flowers whose long regret and stems are steeped
in a lone vase whose brightness is bedimmed . . .
a Dawn was dragging her wings among the tears!

Sorcerer-shadow with symbolic charms!
A voice, long-drawn, evocative of the past,
(Is it mine ready for the incantation?)
languishing among the yellowed folds
of thought, and agèd as a cloth perfumed
with incense over a pile of cold church vessels,

arises through the ancient holes and through
the stiffened folds matching the rhythm and pure
lacework of the shroud that lets the desperate
old veiled brilliance mount through its meshes;
(oh, what distance hidden in these calls!)
the old veiled brilliance of a strange vermilion
of the languishing voice, toneless, without acolyte,
will it cast its gold among the final splendors,
still the antiphony of petitioning verses,
in the hour of agony and the death-struggles?
and, such is the power of silence and black darkness,
all return likewise to the ancient past,
monotonous, prophetic, weary, vanquished,
as the water of ancient basins grows resigned.

She has sung, sometimes incoherently,
lamentable sign!
                    the bed with vellum pages,
such, useless and so claustral, it's not linen!
No more the dear gramarye of dreams from wrinkled
sheets, the sepulchral dais with the abandoned moire,
the fragrance of sleeping hair. Did it have that?
Cold girl, to indulge her subtle pleasure
when on a felled heap of corpses without coffins
and when the spiteful evening has cut the pomegranates!
The new moon, yes the only one's on the iron
face of the clock, with Lucifer for its weight,
always wounds, always another hour,
that she, forsaken, wanders, and on her shadow
never an angel escorts her ineffable steps!
He does not know of this, the king who pays
in walks at daybreak shivering with flowers
for this long time the dried and aged breasts.
wept by the clepsydra with its dark drops,
odorous with resin, enigmatic, he offers
Her father does not know this, nor the fierce
glacier reflecting the steel of armor and weapons,
his trumpets of black silver to the old pines!

Will he return some day from Cisalpine lands?
Soon enough? for all is bad omens and evil dreams!
On the fingernail lifted in this stained-glass window
as if remembering the trumpets, the old sky
burns, and changes a finger to an envious taper.
And soon the red light of this sorrowful dawn
will penetrate the shrinking body of wax!
Not of dawn, no, but of the red awakening,
sunrise of the last day when all will be ended,
so sadly it struggles, one knows not the hour
the redness of this prophetic time that weeps
over the girl, exiled in her insolent heart
like a swan hiding his eyes among his plumage,
as the old swan buries them in his feathers, gone,
these rumpled feathers, in the eternal blotting
of any hope to behold the chosen diamonds
of a star, dying, and which shines no more!

II. Scène

LA NOURRICE — HÉRODIADE

N.

You're still alive! or do I see here the shade of a princess?
Your fingers and their rings to my lips and cease
moving in a bygone age . . .

H.

    Stand back.
The flaxen torrent of my immaculate hair
when it bathes my lonely body turns it ice
with horror, and my locks enlaced with light
become immortal. O woman, a mere kiss
would kill me were not beauty death . . .

        How should
I know: enticed by what spell and what morning
forgotten by prophets pours, on the dying distance,
its dreary festivals? O nurse of winter,
you have seen me go down to the massive prison

of iron and stone where my old lions draw
the tawny centuries, and I walked there, doomed,
with hands inviolable, in the desert perfume
of those former kings: but did you notice my fears?
Dreaming of banishments I stand, and I strip,
as if by a basin whose fountain welcomes me,
my pallid lilies, while the enamoured lions,
following with their gaze the languid spoils
slipping in silence through my reverie,
disregarding my robe's indolence,
watch my feet that would make calm the sea.
Calm the shudderings of your anile flesh.
Come, and my hair imitating the manner
too ferocious that makes you afraid of manes,
help me, since you no longer dare look at me,
to comb it listlessly before a mirror.

N.

If not the cheerful myrrh in its closed bottles,
will you not try, my child, the gloomy strength
of the essence ravished from roses that are old
and faded?

H.

     Leave the perfumes! You know I hate them.
Would you have me feel their intoxication drowning
my languid head? I want my hair (not flowers
diffusing oblivion on human sorrows,
but gold) forever pure of aromatics,
with its cruel lightning and dull pallor,
to be like the sterile and metallic coldness
of having reflected you, armor and vases,
gems of my natal walls from my lonely childhood.

N.

Forgive, queen! Age was blotting your command
from my memory, dim as an ancient or black book . .

H.

Enough! Hold up this glass for me.
       O mirror!

cold water frozen by ennui in your frame,
how many times and through what hours, distressed
by dreams and searching my memories, like leaves
under your ice in the deep hole, have I
appeared in you like a shadow far away,
but, horror! in the dusk, in your austere pool
I have known the nakedness of my scattered dreams!

Nurse, am I beautiful?

N.

Truly, a star
but this lock's slipping down . . .

H.

Restrain your crime
that chills my blood back to its source, hold back
the notorious profanation of this gesture:
ah, say what certain demon casts this sinister
emotion over you, that kiss, those perfumes
offered and, shall I say, O my heart,
this hand more sacrilegious still? because
I think you wanted to touch me — it is a day
will end on the tower not without disaster . . .
Oh, day Herodias looks on with dread!

N.

Outlandish times, indeed, from which heaven guard you!
You wander, solitary shade, new furor,
examining yourself, precocious with terror;
but always adorable as an immortal,
O my child, and lovely, terribly, and such
that . . .

H.

But were you not about to touch me?

N.

I'd love to be one for whom fate reserves your secrets.

H.

Silence!

N.

Will he come sometime?

H.

Pure stars,
heed not!

N.

How then, if not among obscure
terrors, to dream still more implacable
and like a suppliant the god for whom
your favor's treasure waits! for whom do you,
devoured by anguish, keep the unknown splendor
and the vain mystery of your being?

H.

For me.

N.

Sad flower that grows alone, not a flutter of feeling
but its shadow seen on the water languidly.

H.

Go, save your pity with your irony.

N.

Oh no, my naïve child! Only explain.
Some day this triumphant scorn will wane . . .

H.

But who would touch me whom the lions spared?
Besides, I want nothing human, and should you see me,
sculptured, the eyes lost in paradise,
it is when I remember your milk drunk of old.

N.

Lamentable victim offered to its doom!

H.

Yes, it's for me I bloom, for me, deserted!
You know that, amethystine gardens, hidden
without end in dazzling erudite abysses,
unknown golds, keeping your ancient light
under the somber sleep of primeval earth,
you stones from which my eyes like pure jewels
borrow their melodious clarity,
metals that give to my young locks a fatal
splendor and their flowing massive charm!

As for you, woman born in malignant times
for the wicked spitefulness of sibylline caves,
who speak of a mortal! for whom, from the chalices
of my robes, should come forth the white shuddering
of my nakedness, the aroma of fierce delights,
prophesy that if the warm azure of summer,
toward which woman instinctively unveils,
behold my shivering star of chastity,
I die!
       I love the horror of being virgin
and I wish to live in the terror my tresses make
thus, at evening, on my couch, a snake
inviolate, to feel in my useless flesh
the frigid scintillations of your pale glow,
you who die as yourself, who burn with chastity,
white night of icicles and cruel snow!

And your lonely sister, O my sister eternal
my dream will rise toward you: already such
rare limpidity of a heart that dreamed it,
I think I'm alone in my monotonous country,
and all, around me, lives in idolatry
of a mirror that reflects in its slumbering calm
Herodias with the lucid diamond look . . .
O supreme enchantment! I feel it, yes, I am alone.
               N.
Milady, you will die then?
               H.
         No, poor grandam,
be calm and, leaving, pardon this hard heart,
but close the shutters first, please, for the azure
seraphically smiles in the profound panes,
and I, I hate the beautiful azure!

                Yonder
the waves are tossing; if you know a land
where the sinister sky has the hateful look
of Venus burning, at evening, among the leaves,
I'd like to go there.

And though you say it's childish,
kindle those links where wax with frivolous fire
weeps an alien tear in the vain gold
and . . .

N.

And now?

H.

Farewell.

O naked flower
of my lips, you lie!

I await a thing unknown
or perhaps, unaware of the mystery and your cries
you give, O lips, the supreme tortured moans
of a childhood groping among its reveries
to sort out finally its cold precious stones.

III. CANTIQUE DE SAINT JEAN

The sun that is exalted
by its supernatural halt
forthwith redescends
     incandescent

I feel how vertebrae
in the dark give way
all of them together
     in a shudder

and in lonely vigil
among flights triumphal
of this scythe's swings
     my head springs

as the downright rupture
represses or cuts rather
the primordial clash
     with the flesh

Drunken with abstinence
may it stubbornly advance

in some haggard flight
   its pure sight

up where the infinite
cold does not permit
that you be its surpassers
   O all glaciers

but, thanks to a baptism
shining from the chrism
of that consecration
   my head bows salutation.

[TRANSLATED BY C. F. MACINTYRE]

The Decay of Lying

OSCAR WILDE

(1856–1900)

Although he may not have fully realized the implications of this essay, published in 1889, the position Wilde was reaching for is that all perceptions, scientific as well as aesthetic, are governed by conventions, or more directly, are conventions. This, the necessary consequence of Romantic thinking, was the great achievement of Stylism. It is hardly necessary to say that it has been asserted over and over again by philosophy and science in the twentieth century.

CYRIL (*coming in through the open window from the terrace*). My dear Vivian, don't coop yourself up all day in the library. It is a perfectly lovely afternoon. The air is exquisite. There is a mist upon the woods like the purple bloom upon a plum. Let us go and lie on the grass, and smoke cigarettes, and enjoy Nature.

VIVIAN. Enjoy Nature! I am glad to say that I have entirely lost that faculty. People tell us that Art makes us love Nature more than we loved her before; that it reveals her secrets to us; and that after a careful study of Corot and Constable we see things in her that had escaped our observation. My own experience is that the more we study Art, the less we care for Nature. What Art really reveals to us is Nature's lack of design, her curious crudities, her extraordinary monotony, her absolutely unfinished condition. Nature has good intentions, of course, but, as Aristotle once said, she cannot carry them out. When I look at a landscape I cannot help seeing all its defects. It is fortunate for us, however, that Nature is so imperfect, as otherwise we should have had no art at all. Art is our spirited protest, our gallant attempt to teach Nature her proper place. As for the infinite variety of Nature, that is a pure myth. It is not to be found in Nature herself. It resides in the imagination, or fancy, or cultivated blindness of the man who looks at her.

CYRIL. Well, you need not look at the landscape. You can lie on the grass and smoke and talk.

VIVIAN. But Nature is so uncomfortable. Grass is hard and lumpy and damp, and full of dreadful black insects. Why, even Morris' poorest workman could make you a more comfortable seat than the whole of Nature can. Nature pales before the furniture of "the street which from Oxford has borrowed its name," as the poet you love so much once vilely phrased it. I don't complain. If Nature had been comfortable, mankind would never have invented architecture, and I prefer houses to the open air. In a house we all feel of the proper proportions. Everything is subordinated to us, fashioned for our use and our pleasure. Egotism itself, which is so necessary to a proper sense of human dignity, is entirely the result of indoor life. Out of doors one becomes abstract and impersonal. One's individuality absolutely leaves one. And then Nature is so indifferent, so unappreciative. Whenever I am walking in the park here, I always feel that I am no more to her than the cattle that browse on the slope, or the burdock that blooms in the ditch. Nothing is more evident than that Nature hates Mind. Thinking is the most unhealthy thing in the world, and people die of it just as they die of any other disease. Fortunately, in England at any rate, thought is not catching. Our splendid physique as a people is entirely due to our national stupidity. I only hope we shall be able to keep this great historic bulwark of our happiness for many years to come; but I am afraid that we are beginning to be over-educated; at least everybody who is incapable of learning has taken to teaching — that is really what our enthusiasm for education has come to. In the meantime, you had better go back to your wearisome, uncomfortable Nature, and leave me to correct my proofs.

CYRIL. Writing an article! That is not very consistent after what you have just said.

VIVIAN. Who wants to be consistent? The dullard and the doctrinaire, the tedious people who carry out their principles to the bitter end of action, to the *reductio ad absurdum* of practice. Not I. Like Emerson, I write over the door of my library the word "Whim." Besides, my article is really a most salutary and valuable warning. If it is attended to, there may be a new Renaissance of Art.

CYRIL. What is the subject?

VIVIAN. I intend to call it "The Decay of Lying: A Protest."

.   .   .

"One of the chief causes that can be assigned for the curiously commonplace character of most of the literature of our age is undoubtedly the decay of Lying as an art, a science, and a social pleasure. The ancient historians gave us delightful fiction in the form of fact; the modern novelist presents us with dull facts under the guise of fiction. The Blue-Book is rapidly becoming his ideal both for method and manner. He has his tedious *'document humain,'* his miserable little *'coin de la création,'* into which he peers with his microscope. He is to be found at the Librairie Nationale, or at the British Museum, shamelessly reading up his subject. He has not even the courage of other people's ideas, but insists on going directly to life for everything, and ultimately, between encyclopædias and personal experience, he comes to the ground, having drawn his types from the family circle or from the weekly washerwoman, and having acquired an amount of useful information from which never, even in his most meditative moments, can he thoroughly free himself.

"The loss that results to literature in general from this false ideal of our time can hardly be overestimated. People have a careless way of talking about a 'born liar,' just as they talk about a 'born poet.' But in both cases they are wrong. Lying and poetry are arts — arts, as Plato saw, not unconnected with each other — and they require the most careful study, the most disinterested devotion. Indeed, they have their technique, just as the more material arts of painting and sculpture have, their subtle secrets of form and colour, their craft-mysteries, their deliberate artistic methods. As one knows the poet by his fine music, so one can recognise the liar by his rich rhythmic utterance, and in neither case will the casual inspiration of the moment suffice. Here, as elsewhere, practice must precede perfection. But in modern days while the fashion of writing poetry has become far too common, and should, if possible, be discouraged, the fashion of lying has almost fallen into disrepute. Many a young man starts in life with a natural gift for exaggeration which, if nurtured in congenial and sympathetic surroundings, or by the imitation of the best models, might grow into something really great and wonderful. But, as a rule, he comes to nothing. He either falls into careless habits of accuracy —— "

CYRIL. My dear fellow!

VIVIAN. Please don't interrupt in the middle of a sentence. "He either falls into careless habits of accuracy, or takes to frequenting the society of the aged and the well-informed. Both things are equally fatal to his imagination, as indeed they would be fatal to the imagination of anybody, and in a short time he develops a morbid and unhealthy faculty of truth-telling, begins to verify all statements made in his presence, has no hesitation in contradicting people who are much younger than himself, and often ends by writing novels which are so like life that no one can possibly believe in their probability. This is no isolated instance that we are giving. It is simply one example out of many; and if something cannot be done to check, or at least to modify, our monstrous worship of facts, Art will become sterile and Beauty will pass away from the land.

"Even Mr. Robert Louis Stevenson, that delightful master of delicate and fanciful prose, is tainted with this modern vice, for we know positively no other name for it. There is such a thing as robbing a story of its reality by trying to make it too true, and *The Black Arrow* is so inartistic as not to contain a single anachronism to boast of, while the transformation of Dr. Jekyll reads dangerously like an experiment out of the *Lancet*. As for Mr. Rider Haggard, who really has, or had once, the makings of a perfectly magnificent liar, he is now so afraid of being suspected of genius that when he does tell us anything marvellous, he feels bound to invent a personal reminiscence, and to put it into a footnote as a kind of cowardly corroboration. Nor are our other novelists much better. Mr. Henry James writes fiction as if it were a painful duty, and wastes upon mean motives and imperceptible 'points of view' his neat literary style, his felicitous phrases, his swift and caustic satire. . . .

.   .   .

"In France . . . things are not much better. M. Guy de Maupassant, with his keen mordant irony and his hard vivid style, strips life of the few poor rags that still cover her, and shows us foul sore and festering wound. He writes lurid little tragedies in which everybody is ridiculous; bitter comedies at which one cannot laugh for very tears. M. Zola, true to the lofty principle that he lays down in one of his pronunciamientos on literature, 'L'homme de génie n'a jamais d'esprit,' is determined to show that, if he has not got genius, he can at least be dull. And how well he succeeds! He is not without power. Indeed at times, as in *Germinal,* there is something almost epic in his work. But his work is entirely wrong from beginning to end, and wrong not on the ground of morals, but on the ground of art. From any ethical standpoint it is just what it should be. The author is perfectly truthful, and describes things exactly as they happen. What more can any moralist desire? We have no sympathy at all with the moral indignation of our time against M. Zola. It is simply the indignation of Tartuffe on being exposed. But from the standpoint of art, what can be said in favour of the author of *L'Assommoir, Nana,* and *Pot-Bouille?* Nothing. Mr. Ruskin once described the characters in George Eliot's novels as being like the sweepings of a Pentonville omnibus, but M. Zola's characters are much worse. They have their dreary vices, and their drearier virtues. The record of their lives is absolutely without interest. Who cares what happens to them? In literature we require distinction, charm, beauty, and imaginative power. We don't want to be harrowed and disgusted with an account of the doings of the lower orders. . . .''

.   .   .

"It is a humiliating confession, but we are all of us made out of the same stuff. In Falstaff there is something of Hamlet, in Hamlet there is not a little of Falstaff. The fat knight has his moods of melancholy, and the young prince his moments of coarse humour.

Where we differ from each other is purely in accidentals: in dress, manner, tone of voice, religious opinions, personal appearance, tricks of habit, and the like. The more one analyses people, the more all reasons for analysis disappear. Sooner or later one comes to that dreadful universal thing called human nature. Indeed, as any one who has ever worked among the poor knows only too well, the brotherhood of man is no mere poet's dream, it is a most depressing and humiliating reality; and if a writer insists upon analysing the upper classes, he might just as well write of match-girls and coster-mongers at once." However, my dear Cyril, I will not detain you any further just here. I quite admit that modern novels have many good points. All I insist on is that, as a class, they are quite unreadable.

.   .   .

Meredith! Who can define him? His style is chaos illumined by flashes of lightning. As a writer he has mastered everything except language: as a novelist he can do everything, except tell a story: as an artist he is everything, except articulate.

.   .   .

As for Balzac, he was a most wonderful combination of the artistic temperament with the scientific spirit. The latter he bequeathed to his disciples: the former was entirely his own. The difference between such a book as M. Zola's *L'Assommoir* and Balzac's *Illusions Perdues* is the difference between unimaginative realism and imaginative reality. "All Balzac's characters," said Baudelaire, "are gifted with the same ardour of life that animated himself. All his fictions are as deeply coloured as dreams. Each mind is a weapon loaded to the muzzle with will. The very scullions have genius." A steady course of Balzac reduces our living friends to shadows, and our acquaintances to the shadows of shades. His characters have a kind of fervent fiery-coloured existence. They dominate us, and defy scepticism. One of the greatest tragedies of my life is the death of Lucien de Rubempré. It is a grief from which I have never been able to completely rid myself. It haunts me in my moments of pleasure. I remember it when I laugh. But Balzac is no more a realist than Holbein was. He created life, he did not copy it. I admit, however, that he set far too high a value on modernity of form and that, consequently, there is no book of his that, as an artistic masterpiece, can rank with *Salammbô* or *Esmond*, or *The Cloister and the Hearth*, or the *Vicomte de Bragelonne*.

CYRIL. Do you object to modernity of form, then?

VIVIAN. Yes. It is a huge price to pay for a very poor result. Pure modernity of form is always somewhat vulgarising. It cannot help being so. The public imagine that, because they are interested in their immediate surroundings, Art should be interested in them also, and should take them as her subject-matter. But the mere fact that they are interested in these things makes them unsuitable subjects for Art. The only beautiful things, as somebody once said, are the things that do not concern us. As long as a thing is useful or necessary to us, or affects us in any way, either for pain or for pleasure, or appeals strongly to our sympathies, or is a vital part of the environment in which we live, it is outside the proper sphere of art. To art's subject-matter we should be more or less indifferent. We should, at any rate, have no preferences, no prejudices, no partisan feeling of any kind. It is exactly because Hecuba is nothing to us that her sorrows are such an admirable motive for a tragedy. . . .

.   .   .

"The popular cry of our time is 'Let us return to Life and Nature; they will recreate Art for us, and send the red blood coursing through her veins; they will shoe her feet with swiftness and make her hand strong.' But, alas! we are mistaken in our amiable and well-meaning efforts. Nature is always behind the age. And as for Life, she is the solvent that breaks up Art, the enemy that lays waste her house."

CYRIL. What do you mean by saying that Nature is always behind the age?

VIVIAN. Well, perhaps that is rather cryptic. What I mean is this. If we take Nature to mean natural simple instinct as opposed to self-conscious culture, the work produced under this influence is always old-fashioned, antiquated, and out of date. One touch of Nature may make the whole world kin, but two touches of Nature will destroy

any work of Art. If, on the other hand, we regard Nature as the collection of phenomena external to man, people only discover in her
what they bring to her. She has no suggestions of her own. Wordsworth went to the lakes, but he was never a lake poet. He found in
stones the sermons he had already hidden there. He went moralising
about the district, but his good work was produced when he returned, not to Nature but to poetry. Poetry gave him *Laodamia,*
and the fine sonnets, and the great Ode, such as it is. Nature gave
him *Martha Ray* and *Peter Bell,* and the address to Mr. Wilkinson's
spade.

CYRIL. I think that view might be questioned. I am rather inclined to
believe in the "impulse from a vernal wood," though of course the
artistic value of such an impulse depends entirely on the kind of
temperament that receives it, so that the return to Nature would
come to mean simply the advance to a great personality. You would
agree with that, I fancy. However, proceed with your article.

VIVIAN (*reading*). "Art begins with abstract decoration with purely imaginative and pleasurable work dealing with what is unreal and non-
existent. This is the first stage. Then Life becomes fascinated with
this new wonder, and asks to be admitted into the charmed circle.
Art takes life as part of her rough material, recreates it, and re-
fashions it in fresh forms, is absolutely indifferent to fact, invents,
imagines, dreams, and keeps between herself and reality the im-
penetrable barrier of beautiful style, of decorative or ideal treatment.
The third stage is when Life gets the upper hand, and drives Art
out into the wilderness. This is the true decadence, and it is from
this that we are now suffering.

"Take the case of the English drama. At first in the hands of the
monks Dramatic Art was abstract, decorative, and mythological.
Then she enlisted Life in her service, and using some of life's external forms, she created an entirely new race of beings, whose sorrows were more terrible than any sorrow man has ever felt, whose
joys were keener than lover's joys, who had the rage of the Titans
and the calm of the gods, who had monstrous and marvellous sins,
monstrous and marvellous virtues. To them she gave a language different from that of actual use, a language full of resonant music and
sweet rhythm, made stately by solemn cadence, or made delicate by
fanciful rhyme, jewelled with wonderful words, and enriched with

lofty diction. She clothed her children in strange raiment and gave
them masks, and at her bidding the antique world rose from its
marble tomb. A new Cæsar stalked through the streets of risen Rome,
and with purple sail and flute-led oars another Cleopatra passed up
the river to Antioch. Old myth and legend and dream took shape
and substance. History was entirely rewritten, and there was hardly
one of the dramatists who did not recognise that the object of Art
is not simple truth but complex beauty. In this they were perfectly
right. Art itself is really a form of exaggeration; and selection, which
is the very spirit of art, is nothing more than an intensified mode of
over-emphasis.

"But Life soon shattered the perfection of the form. Even in
Shakespeare we can see the beginning of the end. It shows itself by
the gradual breaking up of the blank-verse in the later plays, by the
predominance given to prose, and by the over-importance assigned
to characterisation. The passages in Shakespeare — and they are many
— where the language is uncouth, vulgar, exaggerated, fantastic,
obscene even, are entirely due to Life calling for an echo of her own
voice, and rejecting the intervention of beautiful style, through
which alone should Life be suffered to find expression. Shakespeare
is not by any means a flawless artist. He is too fond of going directly
to life, and borrowing life's natural utterance. He forgets that when
Art surrenders her imaginative medium she surrenders everything.
Goethe says, somewhere —

> In der Beschränkung zeigt sich erst der Meister,

'It is in working within limits that the master reveals himself,' and
the limitation, the very condition of any art is style. However, we
need not linger any longer over Shakespeare's realism. *The Tempest*
is the most perfect of palinodes. All that we desired to point out
was, that the magnificent work of the Elizabethan and Jacobean
artists contained within itself the seeds of its own dissolution, and
that, if it drew some of its strength from using life as rough material,
it drew all its weakness from using life as an artistic method. As the
inevitable result of this substitution of an imitative for a creative
medium, this surrender of an imaginative form, we have the modern
English melodrama. The characters in these plays talk on the stage
exactly as they would talk off it; they have neither aspirations nor

aspirates; they are taken directly from life and reproduce its vulgarity down to the smallest detail; they present the gait, manner, costume, and accent of real people; they would pass unnoticed in a third-class railway carriage. And yet how wearisome the plays are! They do not succeed in producing even that impression of reality at which they aim, and which is their only reason for existing. As a method, realism is a complete failure.

"What is true about the drama and the novel is no less true about those arts that we call the decorative arts. The whole history of these arts in Europe is the record of the struggle between Orientalism, with its frank rejection of imitation, its love of artistic convention, its dislike to the actual representation of any object in Nature, and our own imitative spirit. Wherever the former has been paramount, as in Byzantium, Sicily, and Spain, by actual contact, or in the rest of Europe by the influence of the Crusades, we have had beautiful and imaginative work in which the visible things of life are transmuted into artistic conventions, and the things that Life has not are invented and fashioned for her delight. But wherever we have returned to Life and Nature, our work has always become vulgar, common, and uninteresting. Modern tapestry, with its aërial effects, its elaborate perspective, its broad expanses of waste sky, its faithful and laborious realism, has no beauty whatsoever. The pictorial glass of Germany is absolutely detestable. We are beginning to weave possible carpets in England, but only because we have returned to the method and spirit of the East. Our rugs and carpets of twenty years ago, with their solemn depressing truths, their inane worship of Nature, their sordid reproductions of visible objects, have become, even to the Philistine, a source of laughter. A cultured Mahomedan once remarked to us, 'You Christians are so occupied in misinterpreting the fourth commandment that you have never thought of making an artistic application of the second.' He was perfectly right, and the whole truth of the matter is this: The proper school to learn art in is not Life but Art."

And now let me read you a passage which seems to me to settle the question very completely.

"It was not always thus. We need not say anything about the poets, for they, with the unfortunate exception of Mr. Wordsworth, have been really faithful to their high mission, and are universally

recognised as being absolutely unreliable. But in the works of
Herodotus, who, in spite of the shallow and ungenerous attempts
of modern sciolists to verify his history, may justly be called the
'Father of Lies'; in the published speeches of Cicero and the bio-
graphies of Suetonius; in Tacitus at his best; in Pliny's *Natural
History;* in Hanno's *Periplus;* in all the early chronicles; in the Lives
of the Saints; in Froissart and Sir Thomas Mallory; in the travels of
Marco Polo; in Olaus Magnus, and Aldrovandus, and Conrad
Lycosthenes, with his magnificent *Prodigiorum et Ostentorum
Chronicon;* in the autobiography of Benvenuto Cellini; in the
memoirs of Casanuova; in Defoe's *History of the Plague;* in Boswell's
Life of Johnson; in Napoleon's despatches, and in the works of our
own Carlyle, whose *French Revolution* is one of the most fascinating
historical novels ever written, facts are either kept in their proper
subordinate position, or else entirely excluded on the general ground
of dulness. Now, everything is changed. Facts are not merely finding
a footing-place in history, but they are usurping the domain of
Fancy, and have invaded the kingdom of Romance. Their chilling
touch is over everything. They are vulgarising mankind. The crude
commercialism of America, its materialising spirit, its indifference to
the poetical side of things, and its lack of imagination and of high
unattainable ideals, are entirely due to that country having adopted
for its national hero a man, who according to his own confession,
was incapable of telling a lie, and it is not too much to say that the
story of George Washington and the cherry-tree has done more harm,
and in a shorter space of time, than any other moral tale in the
whole of literature."

CYRIL. My dear boy!

VIVIAN. I assure you it is the case, and the amusing part of the whole
thing is that the story of the cherry-tree is an absolute myth. However, you must not think that I am too despondent about the artistic
future either of America or of our own country. Listen to this: —
　　"That some change will take place before this century has drawn
to its close we have no doubt whatsoever. Bored by the tedious and
improving conversation of those who have neither the wit to exag-
gerate nor the genius to romance, tired of the intelligent person
whose reminiscences are always based upon memory, whose statements are invariably limited by probability, and who is at any time

liable to be corroborated by the nearest Philistine who happens to be present, Society sooner or later must return to its lost leader, the cultured and fascinating liar. Who he was who first, without ever having gone out to the rude chase, told the wondering cavemen at sunset how he had dragged the Megatherium from the purple darkness of its jasper cave, or slain the Mammoth in single combat and brought back its gilded tusks, we cannot tell, and not one of our modern anthropologists, for all their much-boasted silence, has had the ordinary courage to tell us. Whatever was his name or race, he certainly was the true founder of social intercourse. For the aim of the liar is simply to charm, to delight, to give pleasure. He is the very basis of civilised society, and without him a dinner party, even at the mansions of the great, is as dull as a lecture at the Royal Society, or a debate at the Incorporated Authors, or one of Mr. Burnand's farcical comedies.

"Nor will he be welcomed by society alone. Art, breaking from the prison-house of realism, will run to greet him, and will kiss his false, beautiful lips, knowing that he alone is in possession of the great secret of all her manifestations, the secret that Truth is entirely and absolutely a matter of style; while Life — poor, probable, uninteresting human life — tired of repeating herself for the benefit of Mr. Herbert Spencer, scientific historians, and the compilers of statistics in general, will follow meekly after him, and try to reproduce, in her own simple and untutored way, some of the marvels of which he talks.

"No doubt there will always be critics who, like a certain writer in the *Saturday Review,* will gravely censure the teller of fairy tales for his defective knowledge of natural history, who will measure imaginative work by their own lack of any imaginative faculty, and will hold up their inkstained hands in horror if some honest gentleman, who has never been farther than the yew-trees of his own garden, pens a fascinating book of travels like Sir John Mandeville, or, like great Raleigh, writes a whole history of the world, without knowing anything whatsoever about the past. To excuse themselves they will try and shelter under the shield of him who made Prospero the magician, and gave him Caliban and Ariel as his servants, who heard the Tritons blowing their horns round the coral reefs of the Enchanted Isle, and the fairies singing to each other in a wood near Athens, who led the phantom kings in dim procession across the misty Scottish heath, and hid Hecate in a cave with the weird sister. They will call upon Shakespeare — they always do — and will quote that hackneyed passage about Art holding the mirror up to Nature, forgetting that this unfortunate aphorism is deliberately said by Hamlet in order to convince the bystanders of his absolute insanity in all art-matters."

CYRIL. Ahem! Another cigarette, please.

VIVIAN. My dear fellow, whatever you may say, it is merely a dramatic utterance, and no more represents Shakespeare's real views upon art than the speeches of Iago represent his real views upon morals. But let me get to the end of the passage:

"Art finds her own perfection within, and not outside of, herself. She is not to be judged by any external standard of resemblance. She is a veil, rather than a mirror. She has flowers that no forests know of, birds that no woodland possesses. She makes and unmakes many worlds, and can draw the moon from heaven with a scarlet thread. Hers are the 'forms more real than living man,' and hers the great archetypes of which things that have existence are but unfinished copies. Nature has, in her eyes, no laws, no uniformity. She can work miracles at her will, and when she calls monsters from the deep they come. She can bid the almond tree blossom in winter, and send the snow upon the ripe cornfield. At her word the frost lays its silver finger on the burning mouth of June, and the winged lions creep out from the hollows of the Lydian hills. The dryads peer from the thicket as she passes by, and the brown fauns smile strangely at her when she comes near them. She has hawk-faced gods that worship her, and the centaurs gallop at her side."

CYRIL. I like that. I can see it. Is that the end?

VIVIAN. No. There is one more passage, but it is purely practical. It simply suggests some methods by which we could revive this lost art of Lying.

CYRIL. Well, before you read it to me, I should like to ask you a question. What do you mean by saying that life, "poor, probable, uninteresting human life," will try to reproduce the marvels of art? I can quite understand your objection to art being treated as a mirror. You think it would reduce genius to the position of a cracked looking-glass. But you don't mean to say that you seriously believe that Life imitates Art, that Life in fact is the mirror, and Art the reality?

VIVIAN. Certainly I do. Paradox though it may seem — and paradoxes are always dangerous things — it is none the less true that Life imitates art far more than Art imitates life. We have all seen in our own day in England how a certain curious and fascinating type of beauty, invented and emphasised by two imaginative painters, has so influenced Life that whenever one goes to a private view or to an artistic salon one sees, here the mystic eyes of Rossetti's dream, the long ivory throat, the strange square-cut jaw, the loosened shadowy hair that he so ardently loved, there the sweet maidenhood of *The Golden Stair*, the blossom-like mouth and weary loveliness of the *Laus Amoris, the passion-pale* face of Andromeda, the thin hands and lithe beauty of the Vivien in *Merlin's Dream*. And it has always been so. A great artist invents a type, and Life tries to copy it, to reproduce it in a popular form, like an enterprising publisher. Neither Holbein nor Vandyck found in England what they have given us. They brought their types with them, and Life, with her keen imitative faculty, set herself to supply the master with models. The Greeks, with their quick artistic instinct, understood this, and set in the bride's chamber the statue of Hermes or of Apollo, that she might bear children as lovely as the works of art that she looked at in her rapture or her pain. They knew that Life gains from Art not merely spirituality, depth of thought and feeling, soul-turmoil or soul-peace, but that she can form herself on the very lines and colours of art and can reproduce the dignity of Pheidias as well as the grace of Praxiteles. Hence came their objection to realism. They disliked it on purely social grounds. They felt that it inevitably makes people ugly, and they were perfectly right. We try to improve the conditions of the race by means of good air, free sunlight, wholesome water, and hideous bare buildings for the better housing of the lower orders. But these things merely produce health; they do not produce beauty. For this, Art is required, and the true disciples of the great artist are not his studio-imitators, but those who become like his works of art, be they plastic as in Greek days, or pictorial as in modern times; in a word, Life is Art's best, Art's only pupil.

As it is with the visible arts, so it is with literature. The most obvious and the vulgarest form in which this is shown is in the case of the silly boys who, after reading the adventures of Jack Sheppard or Dick Turpin, pillage the stalls of unfortunate apple-women, break into sweet-shops at night, and alarm old gentlemen who are returning home from the city by leaping out on them in suburban lanes, with black masks and unloaded revolvers. This interesting phenomenon, which always occurs after the appearance of a new edition of either of the books I have alluded to, is usually attributed to the influence of literature on the imagination. But this is a mistake. The imagination is essentially creative and always seeks for a new form. The boy-burglar is simply the inevitable result of life's imitative instinct. He is Fact, occupied as Fact usually is with trying to reproduce Fiction, and what we see in him is repeated on an extended scale throughout the whole of life. Schopenhauer has analysed the pessimism that characterises modern thought, but Hamlet invented it. The world has become sad because a puppet was once melancholy. The Nihilist, that strange martyr who has no faith, who goes to the stake without enthusiasm, and dies for what he does not believe in, is a purely literary product. He was invented by Tourgénieff, and completed by Dostoieffski. Robespierre came out of the pages of Rousseau as surely as the People's Palace rose out of the débris of a novel. Literature always anticipates life. It does not copy it, but moulds it to its purpose. The nineteenth century, as we know it, is largely an invention of Balzac. Our Luciens de Rubempré, our Rastignacs, and De Marsays made their first appearance on the stage of the *Comédie Humaine*. We are merely carrying out, with footnotes and unnecessary additions, the whim or fancy or creative vision of a great novelist. I once asked a lady, who knew Thackeray intimately, whether he had had any model for Becky Sharp. She told me that Becky was an invention, but that the idea of the character had been partly suggested by a governess who lived in the neighbourhood of Kensington Square, and was the companion of a very selfish and rich old woman. I inquired what became of the governess, and she replied that, oddly enough, some years after the appearance of *Vanity Fair,* she ran away with the nephew of the lady with whom she was living, and for a short time made a great splash in society, quite in Mrs. Rawdon Crawley's style, and entirely by Mrs. Rawdon Crawley's methods. Ultimately she came to grief, disappeared to the Continent, and used to be occasionally seen at Monte Carlo and other gambling places.

.   .   .

However, I do not wish to dwell any further upon individual
instances. Personal experience is a most vicious and limited circle.
All that I desire to point out is the general principle that Life
imitates Art far more than Art imitates Life, and I feel sure that
if you think seriously about it you will find that it is true. Life holds
the mirror up to Art, and either reproduces some strange type
imagined by painter or sculptor, or realises in fact what has been
dreamed in fiction. Scientifically speaking, the basis of life — the
energy of life, as Aristotle would call it — is simply the desire for
expression, and Art is always presenting various forms through
which this expression can be attained. Life seizes on them and uses
them, even if they be to her own hurt. Young men have committed
suicide because Rolla did so, have died by their own hand because
by his own hand Werther died. Think of what we owe to the imitation of Christ, of what we owe to the imitation of Cæsar.

CYRIL. The theory is certainly a very curious one, but to make it complete you must show that Nature, no less than Life, is an imitation of
Art. Are you prepared to prove that?

VIVIAN. My dear fellow, I am prepared to prove anything.

CYRIL. Nature follows the landscape painter then, and takes her effects
from him?

VIVIAN. Certainly. Where, if not from the Impressionists, do we get those
wonderful brown fogs that come creeping down our streets, blurring
the gas-lamps and changing the houses into monstrous shadows? To
whom, if not to them and their master, do we owe the lovely silver
mists that brood over our river, and turn to faint forms of fading
grace curved bridge and swaying barge? The extraordinary change
that has taken place in the climate of London during the last ten
years is entirely due to this particular school of Art. You smile.
Consider the matter from a scientific or a metaphysical point of
view, and you will find that I am right. For what is Nature? Nature
is no great mother who has borne us. She is our creation. It is in
our brain that she quickens to life. Things are because we see them,
and what we see, and how we see it, depends on the Arts that have
influenced us. To look at a thing is very different from seeing a
thing. One does not see anything until one sees its beauty. Then,
and then only, does it come into existence. At present, people see
fogs, not because there are fogs, but because poets and painters

have taught them the mysterious loveliness of such effects. There
may have been fogs for centuries in London. I dare say there were.
But no one saw them, and so we do not know anything about them.
They did not exist till Art had invented them. Now, it must be
admitted, fogs are carried to excess. They have become the mere
mannerism of a clique, and the exaggerated realism of their method
gives dull people bronchitis. Where the cultured catch an effect, the
uncultured catch cold. And so, let us be humane, and invite Art to
turn her wonderful eyes elsewhere. She has done so already, indeed.
That white quivering sunlight that one sees now in France, with
its strange blotches of mauve, and its restless violet shadows, is
her latest fancy, and, on the whole, Nature reproduces it quite
admirably. Where she used to give us Corots and Daubignys, she
gives us now exquisite Monets and entrancing Pissarros. Indeed
there are moments, rare, it is true, but still to be observed from time
to time, when Nature becomes absolutely modern. Of course she
is not always to be relied upon. The fact is that she is in this unfortunate position. Art creates an incomparable and unique effect, and,
having done so, passes on to other things. Nature, upon the other
hand, forgetting that imitation can be made the sincerest form of
insult, keeps on repeating this effect until we all become absolutely
wearied of it. Nobody of any real culture, for instance, ever talks
now-a-days about the beauty of a sunset. Sunsets are quite old-
fashioned. They belong to the time when Turner was the last note
in art. To admire them is a distinct sign of provincialism of temperament. Upon the other hand they go on. Yesterday evening Mrs.
Arundel insisted on my coming to the window, and looking at the
glorious sky, as she called it. Of course I had to look at it. She is
one of those absurdly pretty Philistines, to whom one can deny
nothing. And what was it? It was simply a very second-rate Turner,
a Turner of a bad period, with all the painter's worst faults
exaggerated and over-emphasized. Of course, I am quite ready to
admit that Life very often commits the same error. She produces her
false Renés and her sham Vautrins, just as Nature gives us, on one
day a doubtful Cuyp, and on another a more than questionable
Rousseau. Still, Nature irritates one more when she does things
of that kind. It seems so stupid, so obvious, so unnecessary. A false
Vautrin might be delightful. A doubtful Cuyp is unbearable. How-

ever, I don't want to be too hard on Nature. I wish the Channel,
especially at Hastings, did not look quite so often like a Henry
Moore, grey pearl with yellow lights, but then, when Art is more
varied, Nature will, no doubt, be more varied also. That she imitates
Art, I don't think even her worst enemy would deny now. It is the
one thing that keeps her in touch with civilized man. But have I
proved my theory to your satisfaction?

CYRIL. You have proved it to my dissatisfaction, which is better. But
even admitting this strange imitative instinct in Life and Nature,
surely you would acknowledge that Art expresses the temper of its
age, the spirit of its time, the moral and social conditions that sur-
round it, and under whose influence it is produced.

VIVIAN. Certainly not! Art never expresses anything but itself. This is
the principle of my new æsthetics; and it is this, more than that
vital connection between form and substance, on which Mr. Pater
dwells, that makes music the type of all the arts. Of course, nations
and individuals, with that healthy, natural vanity which is the
secret of existence, are always under the impression that it is of
them that the Muses are talking, always trying to find in the calm
dignity of imaginative art some mirror of their own turbid passions,
always forgetting that the singer of Life is not Apollo, but Marsyas.
Remote from reality, and with her eyes turned away from the
shadows of the cave, Art reveals her own perfection, and the wondering crowd that watches the opening of the marvellous, many-
petalled rose fancies that it is its own history that is being told to
it, its own spirit that is finding expression in a new form. But it is
not so. The highest art rejects the burden of the human spirit, and
gains more from a new medium or a fresh material than she does
from any enthusiasm for art, or from any lofty passion, or from any
great awakening of the human consciousness. She develops purely
on her own lines. She is not symbolic of any age. It is the ages that
are her symbols.

Even those who hold that Art is representative of time and place
and people, cannot help admitting that the more imitative an art
is, the less it represents to us the spirit of its age. The evil faces of
the Roman emperors look out at us from the foul porphyry and
spotted jasper in which the realistic artists of the day delighted to
work, and we fancy that in those cruel lips and heavy sensual jaws

we can find the secret of the ruin of the Empire. But it was not so.
The vices of Tiberius could not destroy that supreme civilization, any
more than the virtues of the Antonines could save it. It fell for
other, for less interesting reasons. The sibyls and prophets of the
Sistine may indeed serve to interpret for some that new birth of
the emancipated spirit that we call the Renaissance; but what do the
drunken boors and brawling peasants of Dutch art tell us about the
great soul of Holland? The more abstract, the more ideal an art is,
the more it reveals to us the temper of its age. If we wish to understand a nation by means of its art, let us look at its architecture
or its music.

CYRIL. I quite agree with you there. The spirit of an age may be best
expressed in the abstract ideal arts, for the spirit itself is abstract
and ideal. Upon the other hand, for the visible aspect of an age, for
its look, as the phrase goes, we must of course go to the arts of
imitation.

VIVIAN. I don't think so. After all, what the imitative arts really give
us are merely the various styles of particular artists, or of certain
schools of artists. Surely you don't imagine that the people of the
Middle Ages bore any resemblance at all to the figures on mediæval
stained glass or in mediæval stone and wood carving, or on
mediæval metal-work, or tapestries, or illuminated MSS. They
were probably very ordinary-looking people, with nothing grotesque, or remarkable, or fantastic in their appearance. The Middle
Ages, as we know them in art, are simply a definite form of
style, and there is no reason at all why an artist with this style
should not be produced in the nineteenth century. No great
artist ever sees things as they really are. If he did, he would
cease to be an artist. Take an example from our own day. I know
that you are fond of Japanese things. Now, do you really imagine
that the Japanese people, as they are presented to us in art, have
any existence? If you do, you have never understood Japanese art
at all. The Japanese people are the deliberate self-conscious creation
of certain individual artists. If you set a picture by Hokusai, or
Hokkei, or any of the great native painters, beside a real Japanese
gentleman or lady, you will see that there is not the slightest
resemblance between them. The actual people who live in Japan
are not unlike the general run of English people; that is to say,

they are extremely commonplace, and have nothing curious or extraordinary about them. In fact the whole of Japan is a pure invention. There is no such country, there are no such people. One of our most charming painters went recently to the Land of the Chrysanthemum in the foolish hope of seeing the Japanese. All he saw, all he had the chance of painting, were a few lanterns and some fans. He was quite unable to discover the inhabitants, as his delightful exhibition at Messrs. Dowdeswell's Gallery showed only too well. He did not know that the Japanese people are, as I have said, simply a mode of style, an exquisite fancy of art. And so, if you desire to see a Japanese effect, you will not behave like a tourist and go to Tokio. On the contrary, you will stay at home, and steep yourself in the work of certain Japanese artists, and then, when you have absorbed the spirit of their style, and caught their imaginative manner of vision, you will go some afternoon and sit in the Park or stroll down Piccadilly, and if you cannot see an absolutely Japanese effect there, you will not see it anywhere. Or, to return again to the past, take as another instance the ancient Greeks. Do you think that Greek art ever tells us what the Greek people were like? Do you believe that the Athenian women were like the stately dignified figures of the Parthenon frieze, or like those marvellous goddesses who sat in the triangular pediments of the same building? If you judge from the art, they certainly were so. But read an authority, like Aristophanes for instance. You will find that the Athenian ladies laced tightly, wore high-heeled shoes, dyed their hair yellow, painted and rouged their faces, and were exactly like any silly fashionable or fallen creature of our own day. The fact is that we look back on the ages entirely through the medium of Art, and Art, very fortunately, has never once told us the truth.

CYRIL. But modern portraits by English painters, what of them? Surely they are like the people they pretend to represent?

VIVIAN. Quite so. They are so like them that a hundred years from now no one will believe in them. The only portraits in which one believes are portraits where there is very little of the sitter and a very great deal of the artist. Holbein's drawings of the men and women of his time impress us with a sense of their absolute reality. But this is simply because Holbein compelled life to accept his conditions, to restrain itself within his limitations, to reproduce his type, and

to appear as he wished it to appear. It is style that makes us believe
in a thing — nothing but style. Most of our modern portrait painters
are doomed to absolute oblivion. They never paint what they see.
They paint what the public sees, and the public never sees anything.

CYRIL. Well, after that I think I should like to hear the end of your
article.

VIVIAN. With pleasure. Whether it will do any good I really cannot say.
Ours is certainly the dullest and most prosaic century possible.
Why, even Sleep has played us false, and has closed up the gates
of ivory, and opened the gates of horn. The dreams of the great
middle classes of this country, as recorded in Mr. Myers's two bulky
volumes on the subject and in the Transactions of the Physical
Society, are the most depressing things that I have ever read. There
is not even a fine nightmare among them. They are commonplace,
sordid, and tedious. As for the Church I cannot conceive anything
better for the culture of a country than the presence in it of a
body of men whose duty it is to believe in the supernatural, to per-
form daily miracles, and to keep alive that mythopœic faculty which
is so essential for the imagination. But in the English Church a
man succeeds, not through his capacity for belief but through his
capacity for disbelief. Ours is the only Church where the sceptic
stands at the altar, and where St. Thomas is regarded as the ideal
apostle. Many a worthy clergyman, who passes his life in admirable
works of kindly charity, lives and dies unnoticed and unknown; but
it is sufficient for some shallow uneducated passman out of either
University to get up in his pulpit and express his doubts about
Noah's ark, or Balaam's ass, or Jonah and the whale, for half of
London to flock to hear him, and to sit open-mouthed in rapt
admiration at his superb intellect. The growth of common sense in
the English Church is a thing very much to be regretted. It is
really a degrading concession to a low form of realism. It is silly, too.
It springs from an entire ignorance of psychology. Man can believe
the impossible, but man can never believe the improbable. However,
I must read the end of my article: —

"What we have to do, what at any rate it is our duty to do, is to
revive this old art of Lying. Much of course may be done, in the way
of educating the public, by amateurs in the domestic circle, at
literary lunches, and at afternoon teas. But this is merely the light

and graceful side of lying, such as was probably heard at Cretan dinner parties. There are many other forms. Lying for the sake of gaining some immediate personal advantage, for instance — lying with a moral purpose, as it is usually called — though of late it has been rather looked down upon, was extremely popular with the antique world. Athena laughs when Odysseus tells her 'his words of sly devising,' as Mr. William Morris phrases it, and the glory of mendacity illumines the pale brow of the stainless hero of Euripidean tragedy, and sets among the noble women of the past the young bride of one of Horace's most exquisite odes. Later on, what at first had been merely a natural instinct was elevated into a self-conscious science. Elaborate rules were laid down for the guidance of mankind, and an important school of literature grew up round the subject. Indeed, when one remembers the excellent philosophical treatise of Sanchez on the whole question one cannot help regretting that no one has ever thought of publishing a cheap and condensed edition of the works of that great casuist. A short primer, 'When to Lie and How,' if brought out in an attractive and not too expensive a form, would no doubt command a large scale, and would prove of real practical service to many earnest and deep-thinking people. Lying for the sake of the improvement of the young, which is the basis of home education, still lingers amongst us, and its advantages are so admirably set forth in the early books of Plato's *Republic* that it is unnecessary to dwell upon them here. It is a mode of lying for which all good mothers have peculiar capabilities, but it is capable of still further development, and has been sadly overlooked by the School Board. Lying for the sake of a monthly salary is of course well known in Fleet Street, and the profession of a political leader-writer is not without its advantages. But it is said to be a somewhat dull occupation, and it certainly does not lead to much beyond a kind of ostentatious obscurity. The only form of lying that is absolutely beyond reproach is Lying for its own sake, and the highest development of this is, as we have already pointed out, Lying in Art. Just as those who do not love Plato more than Truth cannot pass beyond the threshold of the Academe, so those who do not love Beauty more than Truth never know the inmost shrine of Art. The solid stolid British intellect lies in the desert sands like the Sphinx in Flaubert's marvellous tale, and fantasy *La Chimère,* dances round it, and calls to it with her false, flute-toned voice. It may not hear her now, but surely some day, when we are all bored to death with the commonplace character of modern fiction, it will hearken to her and try to borrow her wings.

"And when that day dawns, or sunset reddens how joyous we shall all be! Facts will be regarded as discreditable, Truth will be found mourning over her fetters, and Romance, with her temper of wonder, will return to the land. The very aspect of the world will change to our startled eyes. Out of the sea will rise Behemoth and Leviathan, and sail round the high-pooped galleys, as they do on the delightful maps of those ages when books on geography were actually readable. Dragons will wander about the waste places, and the phœnix will soar from her nest of fire into the air. We shall lay our hands upon the basilisk, and see the jewel in the toad's head. Champing his gilded oats, the Hippogriff will stand in our stalls, and over our heads will float the Blue Bird singing of beautiful and impossible things, of things that are lovely and that never happened, of things that are not and that should be. But before this comes to pass we must cultivate the lost art of Lying."

CYRIL. Then we must certainly cultivate it at once. But in order to avoid making any error I want you to tell me briefly the doctrines of the new æsthetics.

VIVIAN. Briefly, then, they are these. Art never expresses anything but itself. It has an independent life, just as Thought has, and develops purely on its own lines. It is not necessarily realistic in an age of realism, nor spiritual in an age of faith. So far from being the creation of its time, it is usually in direct opposition to it, and the only history that it preserves for us is the history of its own progress. Sometimes it returns upon its footsteps, and revives some antique form, as happened in the archaistic movement of late Greek Art, and in the pre-Raphaelite movement of our own day. At other times it entirely anticipates its age, and produces in one century work that it takes another century to understand, to appreciate, and to enjoy it. In no case does it reproduce its age. To pass from the art of a time to the time itself is the great mistake that all historians commit.

The second doctrine is this. All bad art comes from returning to Life and Nature, and elevating them into ideals. Life and Nature may sometimes be used as part of Art's rough material, but before they are of any real service to art they must be translated into artistic conventions. The moment Art surrenders its imaginative medium it surrenders everything. As a method Realism is a complete failure, and the two things that every artist should avoid are modernity of form and modernity of subject-matter. To us, who live in the nineteenth century, any century is a suitable subject for art except our own. The only beautiful things are the things that do not concern us. It is, to have the pleasure of quoting myself, exactly because Hecuba is nothing to us, that her sorrows are so suitable a motive for a tragedy. Besides, it is only the modern that ever becomes old-fashioned. M. Zola sits down to give us a picture of the Second Empire. Who cares for the Second Empire now? It is out of date. Life goes faster than Realism, but Romanticism is always in front of Life.

The third doctrine is that Life imitates Art far more than Art imitates Life. This results not merely from Life's imitative instinct, but from the fact that the self-conscious aim of Life is to find expression, and that Art offers it certain beautiful forms through which it may realise that energy. It is a theory that has never been put forward before, but it is extremely fruitful, and throws an entirely new light upon the history of Art.

It follows, as a corollary from this, that external Nature also imitates Art. The only effects that she can show us are effects that we have already seen through poetry, or in paintings. This is the secret of Nature's charm, as well as the explanation of Nature's weakness.

The final revelation is that Lying, the telling of beautiful untrue things, is the proper aim of Art. But of this I think I have spoken at sufficient length. And now let us go out on the terrace, where "droops the milk-white peacock like a ghost," while the evening star "washes the dusk with silver." At twilight nature becomes a wonderfully suggestive effect, and is not without loveliness, though perhaps its chief use is to illustrate quotations from the poets. Come! We have talked long enough.

NOTE ON ILLUSTRATIONS: GROUP IV
Numbers 47 to 63

The essence of Stylism was the creation of a pattern of behavior which shall be independent from the situation in which it is used. One aspect of it was Aestheticism, the slogan of which was "Art for art's sake." This motto can be used for any number of purposes, but the Stylist flourished it in order to claim his freedom from all social demands; and this freedom he symbolized in his art by creating an aesthetic surface, the interest and charm of which was wholly independent of the subject of the painting or the function of the building. Moreau (Number 47) is the Swinburne of painting. The next three paintings show what happened to Impressionism. It is clear that the original Objectist program of Impressionism has been abandoned, and a technique originally developed to represent the light of the natural world has come to be manipulated in its own right. The aim is no longer to give scientifically valid information about the Object, but on the contrary, to present the Object only as an excuse for displaying the style or artistic surface. The development of Abstract Expressionism has made this much more obvious, as the revival of interest in the late Monet has shown. This manipulation of surface led logically to a reduction of interest in representational accuracy and consequently to distortion, which begins to emerge in Cézanne and Gauguin and becomes quite obvious in Seurat (Numbers 51 to 53). The extremely free sketch by Moreau, far less free than some of his other sketches, had as its primary purpose the establishment of a color scheme for a finished painting. That is, Moreau here is interested in the symbolic function of color, and this links him to Redon and also to Mallarmé. "Symbolism" in this late-nineteenth-century sense was concerned with symbolizing the otherwise inexpressible, or rather, the inexpressibility

310

of the inexpressible; the silence, the nothingness, the absence in which the Self was conceived as existing, or which was its mode of existence. In relatively weak minds and personalities, like that of the young Yeats, this desire to separate the Self entirely from the phenomenal world, to redeem the Subject utterly from involvement with the Object, led to a curious interest in Spiritualism and Theosophy. There is something of this in Moreau and Redon.

Similarly in architecture, the extreme expressivity of Objectism was abandoned. The Red House *(Number 56) has something of the Objectist simplification of Daumier, but its elegance and restraint point to the future. Richardson's Stylism appears in the re-emergence of the wall, as in Webb's building. Objectist architecture did everything it could to deny the existence of the wall; hence its interest in Baroque ideas. Stylist architecture, for the most part, particularly in its earlier stages, renews the wall or screen; as in painting and poetry, the surface is manipulated for its own sake. But the emphasis upon the wall or screen turns a building into something of a fortress; and the Allegheny County Court House is, in fact, a fortress. The next three buildings (Numbers 59 to 61) are enchanting examples of the elegance which the more conservative branch of Stylism achieved. It is the equivalent of the Parnassian poetry of France. This tradition continued to be capable of producing historically idiomatic buildings of the utmost elegance and beauty until the 1930's. At the same time, however, another tradition was developing, which culminated in Art Nouveau, the equivalent of representational distortion in painting, and Symbolism, as defined above, in painting and poetry. (This is the spirit of the intransigent young Stephen, in Joyce's* A Portrait of the Artist as a Young Man.) *This other architectural tradition is represented here by an early work by Gaudi and a later and mature masterpiece by Mackintosh (Numbers 62 and 63). Like all Stylistic work there is still a strong reference to the past, and the various sources of Art Nouveau are quite apparent. They are meant to be. The manipulative tradition of nineteenth-century architecture here achieves a climax, and the cultural situation is now ready for the breakthrough into Modern art.*

47. Gustave Moreau, *The Unicorn*.

48. Claude Monet,
Rouen Cathedral, 1894.

49. Edgar Dégas,
Après le Bain, 1883.

50. Auguste Renoir, *Seated Nude*, 1916.

51. Paul Cézanne, *Still Life with Apples*, 1890–1900.

52. Paul Gauguin, *Tahitian Landscape*, c. 1891.

53. Georges Seurat,
*Young Woman
Powdering Herself,*
1889–1890.

54. Odilon Redon,
Mystery.

55. Gustave Moreau, *Thomris and Cyrus.*

56. Philip Webb, *The Red House*, Bexley Heath, Kent, 1859.

57. Henry Hobson Richardson, *Watts Sherman Residence*, Newport, 1874–1876.

58. Henry Hobson Richardson, *Allegheny County Court House,* Pittsburgh, 1884–1886.

59. Richard M. Hunt, *Biltmore,* Asheville, 1896.

60. Richard M. Hunt, *The Marble House*, Newport.

61. John Carrère and Thomas Hastings, *Hotel Ponce de Leon*, St. Augustine, 1885–1888.

62. Antonio Gaudí, *Casa Vicens*, Barcelona, 1878–1880.

63. Charles Rennie Mackintosh, *Glasgow School of Art,* 1897–1899.

The Triumph of Romanticism

The weakness of Stylism — or Aestheticism, as it is traditionally named — lay in its pragmatism, its expediency. That is, it was a deliberately created illusion of the alienated Romantic with his passionate need to assert the antithesis of Self and role. But a deliberately and consciously self-created illusion is, after all, only an illusion, and it classifies the Romantic with those non-Romantics — most individuals — who live in the illusion of the role. It was an attempt to give stability to what in fact has no stability. The Self is not a metaphysical entity, something that really exists, but is only the sense *of identity, the* sense *of Self-hood.* Thus value is not something which the Self creates. Value is the Self. *The mere feeling that life is worth the trouble it takes to live it is what we are talking about when we use the word "Self." Alienation, then, is the feeling that value cannot be derived from Society, nor from Nature, but only from the joyful encounter with Society and the World. The attempt to create the Self as a continuity must fail, as the collapse of Stylism had revealed. We enter the world, we manipulate the world, only in terms of roles:*

*even the inaction of alienation is a form of action. Aliena-
tion is, at best, an anti-role, and thus a role. It is only by
surrendering to roles, and then by the free transformation of roles, that the Self, eternally recurring, can emerge
as the sense of value and meaning in existence.*

Beyond Good and Evil

FRIEDRICH NIETZSCHE

(1844–1900)

This "Preface to a Philosophy of the Future" was published in 1886. The whole Romantic tradition moves irresistibly towards Nietzsche. And it is Nietzsche who was the great liberator and releaser for almost every creator of modern art and culture.

WHAT DOES "DISTINGUISHED" MEAN?

257.

Every heightening of the type "man" hitherto has been the work of an aristocratic society — and thus it will always be; a society which believes in a long ladder of rank order and value differences in men, which needs slavery in some sense. Without the *pathos of distance* as it grows out of the deep-seated differences of caste, out of the constant view, the downward view, that the ruling caste gets of its subordinates and tools, out of its equally constant exercise in obeying and commanding, in keeping apart and keeping a distance — without this pathos of distance there could not grow that other more mysterious pathos, that longing for ever greater distances within the soul itself, the evolving of ever higher, rarer, more spacious, more widely arched, more comprehensive states — in short: the heightening of the type "man," the continued "self-mastery of man," to take a moral formula in a supra-moral sense. To be sure, we must not yield to humanitarian self-deception about the history of the origins of an aristocratic society (in other words, the presuppositions for the heightening of the type "man"): the truth is hard. Let us tell ourselves without indulging ourselves how every superior culture on earth got its *start!* Men whose nature was still natural, barbarians in every frightful sense of the word, men of prey, men still in possession of unbroken strength of will and power-drives — such men threw themselves upon weaker, better-behaved, more peaceable races, possibly those engaged in commerce or cattle-raising, or else upon old hollow cultures in which the last life powers were flickering away in flashing fireworks of intellect and corruption. The distinguished caste in the beginning was always the barbarian caste; their superiority lay not primarily in their physical but in their psychic power; they were more whole as human beings (which on every level also means "more whole as beasts").

258.

Corruption is the expression of the fact that there is anarchy which threatens to spread among the instincts, and that the basic structure of the passions, called "life," has been shaken. Types of corruption are radically different from one another, depending on the life-structure in which they show up. When for example an aristocracy, such as that of France at the start of the Revolution, throws away its privileges with a sublime nausea, and sacrifices itself to an extravagance of its moral feelings, that is corruption. It was really only the final act of that century-long corruption in the course of which the aristocracy yielded step by step its ruling prerogatives and lowered itself until it was a *function* of royalty (and in the very end merely its ornament and crowning glory). But the essential nature of a good and healthy aristocracy is that it does *not* feel it is a function (whether of royalty or of the community) but its meaning, its highest justification. Therefore it accepts with a clear conscience the sacrifice of an enormous number of men who must *for the sake of the aristocracy* be suppressed and reduced to incomplete human beings, to slaves, to tools. It must be aristocracy's basic belief that society exists *not* for the sake of society, but only as the foundation, the skeleton structure, by means of which a select kind of creature can raise itself to a higher task, a higher level of *being* — like those sun-seeking climbing plants in Java, called *Sipo Matador,* which cling to an oak so long and so often until finally they unfold their crowns in the open air, displaying their bliss high above the oak but supported by it.

259.

To refrain from wounding, violating, and exploiting one another, to acknowledge another's will as equal to one's own: this can become proper behavior, in a certain coarse sense, between individuals when the conditions for making it possible obtain (namely the factual similarity of the individuals as to power and standards of value, and their co-existence in one greater body). But as soon as one wants to extend this principle, to make it the *basic principle of society,* it shows itself for what it is: the will to negate life, the principle of dissolution and decay. Here one must think radically to the very roots of things and ward off all weakness of sensibility. Life itself is essential assimilation, injury, violation of the foreign and the weaker, suppression, hardness, the forcing of one's own forms upon something else, ingestion and — at least in its mildest form — exploitation. But why should we always use such words which were coined from time immemorial to reveal a calumniatory intention? Even that body to which we referred, the body within which individuals may treat each other with equality (and it is so in any healthy aristocracy) — even this body itself, if it is alive and not dying off, must do to other bodies all the things from which its members refrain; it will have to be the will to power incarnate; it will have to want to grow, to branch out, to draw others into itself, to gain supremacy. And not because it is moral or immoral in any sense but because it is *alive,* and because life simply *is* will to power. But there is no point at which the common consciousness in Europe today is less willing to lean than just here; everywhere today, and even in the guise of science, there is grandiose talk about future social conditions where there is to be no more "exploitation." To my ears that sounds as though they promised to invent a kind of life that would refrain from all the organic functions. "Exploitation" is not a part of a vicious or imperfect or primitive society: it belongs to the *nature* of living things, it is a basic organic function, a consequence of the will to power which is the will to life. Admitted that this is a novelty as a theory — as a reality it is the *basic fact* underlying all history. Let us be honest with ourselves at least this far!

260.

Wandering through the many fine and coarse moralities which have hitherto ruled on earth, as well as those which still rule, I found certain features regularly occurring together and bound up with one another. Finally they revealed two basic types to me, and a basic difference leaped to my eye. There is *master-morality* and *slave-morality:* I add immediately that in all higher and mixed cultures there are also attempts at a mediation between these two, and even more frequently a mix-up of them and a mutual misunderstanding; at times in fact a relentless juxtaposition even within the psyche of a single individual. The moral value-differentiations arose either among a ruling type which was pleasantly conscious of its difference from the ruled — or else among the ruled, the slaves and dependents of all kinds. In the first case, when the rulers determine the concept "good," it is the elevated and proud conditions of the psyche which are felt to be what excels and determines the order of rank. The distinguished human being divorces himself from the being in whom the opposite of such elevated and proud conditions is expressed. He despises them. One may note immediately that in the first type of morality the antithesis "good vs. bad" means "distinguished vs. despicable"; the antithesis "good vs. evil" has a different origin. What is despised is the coward, the timid man, and the petty man, he who thinks in terms of narrow utility; likewise the suspicious man with his cowed look, the one who humiliates himself, the dog-type who lets himself be mistreated, the begging flatterer, and above all the liar: it is the basic faith of all aristocrats that the common people are liars. "We truthful ones" the nobles called themselves in ancient Greece. It is obvious that the moral value-characteristics are at first applied to *people* and only later, in a transferred sense, to *acts.* This is why it is a sad mistake when moral historians begin with questions like "Why was the compassionate act praised?" The distinguished type of human being feels *himself* as value-determining; he does not need to be ratified; he judges that "which is harmful to me is harmful as such"; he knows that *he* is the something which gives honor to objects; he *creates values.* This type honors everything he knows about himself; his morality is self-glorification. In the foreground is the feeling of fullness, of power that would flow forth, the bliss of high tension, the consciousness of riches which would like to give and lavish. The distinguished man, too, helps the unhappy, but not — at least not mainly — from compassion, but more from an internal pressure that has been built up by an excess of power. The distinguished man honors himself in the mighty, including those who have power over themselves; those who know when to talk and when to keep silent; those who take delight in being rigorous and hard with themselves and who have respect for anything rigorous and hard. "Wotan placed a hard heart in my breast," says an old Scandinavian saga: this is the proper poetic expression for the soul of a proud Viking. Such a type of man is proud *not* to have been made for compassion; hence the hero of the saga adds a warning: "Whoever has not a hard heart when young will never get it at all." Distinguished and courageous men with such thoughts are at the opposite end from that morality which sees the characteristic function of morality in pity or in doing for others or *désintéressement*. Belief in oneself, pride in oneself, basic hostility and irony against "self-lessness" is as sure a part of distinguished morality as an easy disdain and cautious attitude toward the fellow-feelings and the "warm heart." It is the powerful men who *understand* how to accord honor: that is their art, the domain of their invention. Profound respect for old age and for origins: their whole law stands on this twofold respect. Faith in and prepossession for one's ancestors and prejudice against the future ones is typical of the morality of the powerful. Contrariwise, when men of "modern ideas" believe almost instinctively in "progress" and in "the future" and have less and less respect for the old, that alone reveals clearly enough the undistinguished origin of their "ideas." But the point at which the morality of rulers is most foreign to current taste and most painstakingly strict in principle is this: one has duties only toward one's equals; toward beings of a lower rank, toward everything foreign to one, one may act as one sees fit, "as one's heart dictates" — in any event, "beyond good and evil." The ability and the duty to sustain enduring gratitude and enduring vengefulness — both only toward one's equals; subtlety in requital and retaliation; a subtly refined concept of friendship; a certain need to have enemies (as outlets for the passions: envy, quarrelsomeness and wantonness — basically, in order to be capable of being a good *friend*): all these are typical marks of the distinguished type of morality which, as I have indicated, is not the morality of "modern ideas" and hence is difficult today to empathize with, and equally difficult to dig out and uncover. — The situation is different with the second type of morality, the slave-morality. Assuming that the violated ones, the oppressed, the suffering, the unfree, those who are uncertain and tired of themselves — assuming that they moralize: What will they have in common in their moral evaluations? Probably a pessimistic suspiciousness against the whole situation of mankind will appear; perhaps a judgment against mankind together with its position. The eye of the slave looks unfavorably upon the virtues of the powerful; he *subtly* mistrusts all the "good" that the others honor — he would like to persuade himself that even their happiness is not real. Conversely, those qualities are emphasized and illuminated which serve to make existence easier for the sufferers: here compassion, the complaisant helping hand, the warm heart, patience, diligence, humility and friendliness are honored, for these are the useful qualities and almost the only means for enduring the pressure of existence. Slave-morality is essentially a utility-morality. Here is the cornerstone for the origin of that famous antithesis "good vs. evil." Power and dangerousness, a certain frightfulness, subtlety and strength which do not permit of despisal, are felt to belong to evil. Hence according to slave morality, the "evil" man inspires fear; according to master morality, the "good" man does and wants to, whereas the "bad" man is felt to be despicable. The antithesis reaches its sharpest point when ultimately the "good" man within a slave morality becomes the logical target of a breath of disdain — however slight and well-meaning, because he is the *undangerous* element in his morality: good natured, easily deceived, perhaps a little stupid, *un bonhomme*. Wherever slave morality preponderates, language shows a tendency to reconcile the meanings of "good" and "dumb." A final basic distinction is that the longing for *freedom,* the instinct for happiness and the subtleties of the freedom-feelings belong as necessarily to slave morality as skill and enthusiasm for reverence, for devotion, is the regular symptom of an aristocratic manner of thinking and evaluating. — This enables us to understand easily why love *as passion* (our European specialty) must be of distinguished origin; we know it was invented by the Provençal knightly poets, those magnificent inventive men of *gai saber* [1] — to whom Europe owes so much, and almost itself.

261.

Vanity belongs among the things which are hardest for a distinguished man to comprehend; he is tempted to deny it where it is painfully obvious to another type of man. His problem is that he cannot imagine creatures who seek to stimulate a good opinion of themselves in others — an opinion which they do not share and hence do not "deserve" — and who then *believe* in that good opinion. To the distinguished man this seems partly such bad taste and lack of respect for oneself and partly so baroquely irrational that it is easier for him to think of vanity as an exceptional state and to doubt its presence in most cases where others see it. He will say, for example, "I can be wrong about my worth and yet demand that it be recognized by others in the terms in which I announce it" — this is not vanity, however, but conceit, or, more frequently, what is known as "humility" or "modesty." Or he can say, "I may rejoice in other people's opinion for many reasons: perhaps because I love and honor them and rejoice in any of their rejoicings; perhaps because their good opinion echoes and supports my own good opinion; perhaps because the good opinion of others, even when I do not share it, is useful to me or promises to be useful — but all this is not vanity either." The distinguished man has to compel himself, with the help of history, to realize that since time immemorial the common man in any dependent strata of mankind *was* only what he *was taken for*. He was not accustomed to pose values of his own, and he never estimated himself to be of any value other than that accorded him by his masters. (For it is the intrinsic *right of masters* to create values.) One may consider it the consequence of an enormous atavism that the ordinary man even today *waits* for an opinion of himself and then instinctively subordinates himself to it — by no means always a "good" opinion, however; just as likely a bad or an unfair one. (Think, for example, of the majority of self-ratings and self-underratings that pious women learn from their father confessors, and pious Christians in general from their church!) Thanks to the slow rise of the democratic order of things (which goes back to a mingling of master and slave) the originally distinguished and rare impulse to ascribe one's own value to oneself, to think well of oneself, is in fact more and more encouraged and spread out. But at all times it has working against it an older, broader, and more thoroughly imbedded tendency — and in the phenomenon of "vanity" this older tendency masters the new. The vain man is just as pleased with *every* good opinion about himself that he hears (quite aside from any utility and any truth or falseness involved) as he suffers from every bad opinion. For he subordinates himself to both; he *feels* himself dependent on them, out of that ancient instinct of dependency that breaks out in him. — It is the "slave" in the blood of the vain, a remainder of slave-like slyness (how much of the "slave" is still reactionary-active in women, for example!) that seeks to *seduce* others to have good opinions about him; it is likewise the slave who immediately falls down before those opinions just as though he had not called them forth. — To say it once more: vanity is an atavism.

262.

A species, a *type* originates, and grows firm and strong, in a long struggle with essentially constant but unfavorable conditions. Conversely, we
know from the experience of breeders that species which get superabundant nourishment and generally more protection and care tend very
strongly to variations in type; they are rich in miracles and monstrosities
(including monstrous vices). Now let us look at an aristocratic community
(an ancient Greek *polis,* for example, or Venice) as though it were a
voluntary or involuntary institution for the purpose of breeding: there
are men in it, intermingled and dependent on one another, who want to
propagate their type, mostly because they *must,* or because they are in
some terrible danger of being exterminated. Here all favoritism, all
abundance, all protection is lacking with which variations are furthered;
the species needs itself as a species, as something which can only assert
itself and make itself last by means of hardness, monotony of form, and,
in general, simplicity. For they are in constant battle with their neighbors
or their subordinates who are rebelling or are threatening to rebel. All
sorts of experience teaches them to which of their qualities in particular
they owe their continuous existence, the whole line of their victories in
spite of all gods and men. These qualities they call virtues; these virtues
alone breed greatness into them. Aristocratic morality acts harshly; it
wants hardness; it is intolerant — in the education of youth, in the disposition of woman, in marriage customs, in the relations between the
generations, in the primitive laws (which are directed solely toward the
ones who threaten to vary from the type). Aristocratic morality counts
intolerance itself among the virtues, calling it "justice." A type with few
but strong characteristics, a kind of rigorous warrior-like cleverly silent,
closed off and reserved man (who, being such, has a very subtle sense for
the charm and nuances of sociability) is in this fashion stabilized beyond
the changes from generation to generation; the constant struggle with
ever constant unfavorable conditions, as I have said, is the reason why a
type becomes solid and hard. But finally some day there arise favorable
conditions; the enormous tension slackens; perhaps there are no more
enemies among the neighbors; the means for living and even for the enjoyment of life are suddenly superabundant. All at once the bond breaks,
the compulsion of the old discipline no longer feels itself as necessary,
as determining men's very existence. If it wants to endure beyond this

point, it can do so only as a form of *luxury,* as a *taste* for the archaic. Variety (whether as variation into higher, subtler, rarer forms, or as deterioration and monstrosity) suddenly appears on the scene in great abundance and magnificence; the individual dares to individuate himself. At these turning points of history there shows itself juxtaposed and often completely entangled with one another a magnificent, manifold, jungle-like growing and striving, a sort of *tropical* tempo in rivalry of development, and an enormous destruction and self-destruction thanks to the egoisms violently opposed to one another, exploding as it were, battling each other for sun and light, unable to find any limitation, any check, any considerateness within the morality at their disposal. It was the morality itself which had accumulated power to the point of enormity, which had so dangerously tensed the bow: now, at this moment, it is "outlived." The dangerous and uncanny point has been reached where a greater, more complex, more extensive life *lives beyond, out-reaches,* the old morality. The "individual" stands ready, needing a set of laws of his own, needing his own skills and wiles for self-preservation, self-heightening, self-liberation. Nothing but new "wherefore's," nothing but new "wherewith's," no longer any communal formulas; a new alliance of misunderstanding and mutual disrespect; decay, vice, and the most superior desires gruesomely bound up with one another, the genius of the race welling up over all the cornucopias of good and ill; a fateful simultaneity of spring and autumn, full of new charms and misty veils that adhere to the young, the still unexhausted, unwearied perversion. Again there is danger, the mother of morality — great danger — but this time displaced onto the individual, onto the nearest and dearest, onto the street, onto one's own child, one's own heart, one's innermost and secret recesses of wish and will: what will the morality philosophers who emerge now have to preach? They discover, these keen observers and Little Jack Horners, that the end is rapidly approaching, that everything around them is approaching ruin and making for ruination, that nothing will last till the day after tomorrow except one type of man: the incurably *mediocre.* Only the mediocre have prospects for continuing and reproducing their kind; they are the men of the future, the sole survivors. "Be like them! Become mediocre!" — is now the sole morality that makes sense, that find ears to hear. But it is hard to preach it, this morality of mediocrity! For it can never admit what it is and what it wants. It must talk about measure and dignity and duty and love for one's neighbor — it will have trouble *hiding its irony!* —

263.

There is an *instinct for rank* which is, more than anything else, the sign of a *high* rank; there is a delight in nuances of reverence which reveals distinguished origin and habits. The subtlety, goodness, and elevation of a soul is dangerously tested when something of first rank passes by it, without being guarded as yet by the shudders of authority from importunate touchings and grossness; something which goes along its way, unmarked, undiscovered, experimentally — perhaps intentionally — shrouded and disguised, like a living touchstone. Someone who makes it his task and exercise to probe souls will make use of this knowledge in many ways, in order to determine the ultimate value of a soul, its immovably inborn order of rank. He will test a soul for its *instinct of reverence. Différence engendre haine:* the meanness of some natures suddenly splashes up like dirty water when some holy vessel, some precious object out of a locked shrine, some book with the signs of high destiny imprinted upon it, is carried past them. Some, on the other hand, become involuntarily silent, hesitant of eye, quiet of gesture, and thereby express that their soul *feels* the proximity of an object worthy of deep reverence. The manner, on the whole, in which reverence for the *Bible* is still preserved in Europe is perhaps the best part of discipline and refinement of behavior that Europe owes to Christianity; such books of depth and ultimate significance need the protection of an external tyranny of authority, in order to gain those millenniums of *preservation* which are necessary to exhaust them and read all their riddles. Much is gained, when the feeling is finely bred into the masses (the flatheads and runny-guts of all sorts) that there are some things they may not touch; that there are sacred experiences in the presence of which they are to remove their shoes and keep their dirty hands to themselves: this is almost their highest possible approximation to humanity. Conversely, nothing is so nauseating in the so-called cultured intellectuals, the believers in "modern ideas" as their lack of shame, their complaisant impudence of eye and hand with which they touch, lick, and finger everything. It is possible that among the common people, on the lowest levels, particularly among peasants, there is more relative distinction of taste and tactfulness of reverence today than among the newspaper-reading *demi-monde* of the intellect, the educated intellectuals.

264.

It cannot be erased from a man's psyche what his ancestors liked best and did most; whether they were diligent economizers, part and parcel of a desk or a cash-box, modest and bourgeois in their desires and modest also in their virtues; or whether they lived from early till late accustomed to giving orders, fond of rough entertainment — and of even rougher duties and responsibilities besides; or finally whether they at some time sacrified old privileges of birth and property in order to live wholly for their belief, their "god," as men of an inexorable and delicate conscience which blushes at any mediation. It is simply not possible for a man *not* to have in his body the qualities and predilections of his parents and ancestors, no matter what appearances seem to be against it. This is the problem of race. If one knows something of the parents, one can permit oneself some conclusions about the child. A certain repulsive incontinence, a dog-in-the-manger enviousness, a boorish desire to be always right (these three together having composed the genuine rabble-type at all times) — such things must be transferred to the child as surely as contaminated blood. With the help of the best education and cultivation one will only manage to *deceive* others as to the child's heritage. — And what else do education and culture want today? In our very popularly-minded, i.e. rabble-minded times, education and culture *must* essentially be the art of deception — as to one's origin, one's inherited rabble in body and soul. An educator who today would preach truthfulness above all, who constantly admonished his charges to be "true," to be "natural — be what you are" — even such a virtuous and well-meaning ass would learn shortly to grasp that *furca* of Horace's, in order *naturam expellere*. With what result, however? "Rabble" *usque recurret.* —

265.

At the risk of displeasing innocent ears, I propose the following: Egoism belongs to the nature of a distinguished soul. I mean that immovable faith that other beings are by nature subordinate to a being such as "we are"; that they should sacrifice themselves to us. The distinguished soul accepts this fact of its egoism without any question mark, and also without any feeling that it is hard or oppressive or arbitrary; rather as something which may be founded in the basic law of all things. If it were to look for a name for its feeling, it would say, "This is justice itself." It admits, under certain circumstances which at first make it hesitate, that there are other souls who are its equals as to rights. As soon as it clarifies for itself this question of rank, it moves among its equals with the same sureness in modesty and delicate respect that it has toward itself, according to an inborn stellar mechanism which the stars understand well. It is a *further* aspect of its egoism, this subtlety and self-limitation in intercourse with its peers — every star in the sky is this sort of egoist. The soul honors *itself* in its peers and the rights it yields to them; it never doubts that the exchange of honors and rights is the very *nature* of human intercourse, belonging to the natural order of things. The distinguished soul gives, as it takes, from the passionate and sensitive instinct for requital which lies at its very bottom. The concept of "mercy" has no meaning, no good odor, among equals; there may exist some sublime manner of taking gifts which drop like a gentle rain from above, and of sucking such droppings thirstily, but the distinguished soul has no talent for this skill or posture. Its egoism hinders it; it doesn't like to look "up" anyway, but prefers to look ahead, horizontally and slowly, or to look down. *It knows that it is on a height.*

266.

"One can truly honor only those who do not *seek* themselves." — Goethe to *Rath* Schlosser.

267.

The Chinese have a proverb which the mothers teach even to their little children: *siao-sin,* "make thy heart *small.*" This is the essential basic inclination of late civilizations; I do not doubt that an ancient Greek would first find out the self-belittlement among us Europeans of today. In this alone we should run "counter to his taste." —

268.

What, ultimately, is commonness? — Words are sound-symbols for concepts; concepts, however, are more or less definite image-symbols for frequently returning and concurring sensations, for sensation-groups. To use the same words is not a sufficient guarantee of understanding; one must use the same words for the same genus of inward experience; ultimately one must have one's experiences in *common.* That is why the people of one nation understand each other better than members of several nations even when they share a language; or rather, when people have lived with each other for a long time under similar conditions (of climate, soil, danger, needs, work), then there *arises* something from them that can "come to an understanding," i.e. a nation. A similar number of frequently returning experiences has gained the upper hand in everyone's psyche over those that occur more rarely; regarding them one comes to a more and more rapid understanding (the history of a language is the history of an abbreviation process); upon this rapid understanding one feels more and more closely allied. The greater the danger, the greater the need to agree quickly and easily on everything necessary: not to misunderstand one another in time of danger is what men cannot dispense with in their intercourse. It is a test that each friendship and each love-affair also undergoes. Nothing of this sort can endure as soon as the parties find out that one of the two using the same words feels, means, wishes, fears different things with them. (Fear of "eternal misunderstanding" is the well-meaning genius which often keeps persons of different sex from the over-eager attachments to which their senses and their hearts prompt them — *not* some Schopenhauerian "genius of the species"!) Which groups of sensations within a given psyche awaken most quickly, which ones come to expression, come to command — this is what decides the total order of its value, this is what in the end decides its table of goods. The value-estimates of a human being reveal something of the *structure* of his psyche, something of the way in which the psyche sees its basic conditions for life, its essential needs. Assuming now that need has always brought only those people together who could express similar needs and similar experiences with similar symbols, then we shall find, all things considered, that easy *communicability* of need, which means ultimately the experiencing of merely average and *common* experiences, must have been the most powerful of all the forces that have ever ruled mankind. The more alike and the more ordinary people were, and always are, at an advantage; the more select, subtle, and strange, those who are harder to understand, may easily remain alone; due to their solitary position they easily meet with accidents, and seldom propagate themselves. One must call upon enormous oppositional powers in order to contend against this natural, all-too natural *progressus in simile,* the continuous progress of man toward similarity, ordinariness, the average, the herd-like, the *common!*

269.

The more a psychologist — a born, irrepressible psychologist and soul-diviner — turns his attention to the more select cases and human beings, the greater becomes the danger that he will choke on compassion. He *needs* hardness and gay serenity more than other men. For the perishableness, the destructability, of superior human beings, of the rarer psychic types, is the rule: it is horrifying to have such a rule always before one's eyes. The psychologist who, at first once and then almost always and throughout history, discovers this destructability, the whole inner incurability [2] of the superior man, his everlasting "too late" in every sense, suffers a complex martyrdom which some day may cause him to turn against his own fate and attempt to destroy himself — to "perish." In almost every psychologist one will find a revealing inclination toward and pleasure in dealing with everyday, well-ordered human beings. What he reveals with this is that he always needs healing himself, that he needs a kind of escape and forgetting, away from the burdens that his insights and incisions, his "trade," have placed on his conscience. He is characterized by a fear of his own memory. He easily becomes silent when he hears the judgment of others; with an unmoved face he listens to them honoring, admiring, loving, and transfiguring something that he has *seen* — or else he hides even his silence by expressly agreeing with some foreground-opinion. Perhaps the paradox of his position goes so far toward the gruesome, that the masses, the educated people, the enthusiasts, learn their great reverence just where he has learned his great compassion plus his great contempt — the reverence for "great men," for the rare creatures for whose sake one blesses and honors one's fatherland, the earth, all human dignity, oneself; toward whom one guides and educates the youth. . . . And who knows whether the same thing did not happen in all the great cases thus far: the masses adored a god, and the "god" was only a poor sacrificial animal. Success has always been the worst of liars and even "works" are a form of success; the great statesman, the conqueror, the discoverer are all disguised by their own creations to the point of unrecognizability; the "work" of the artist, the philosopher, really invents him who created it — who is supposed to have created it; the "great men" as they are honored are small poor fictions after the fact; in the world of historical values it is counterfeiting that rules. These great poets, for example, these Byrons, Mussets, Poes, Leopardis, Kleists, Gogols (I don't dare mention the greater names but I mean them) — such as they are and perhaps have to be, are men of the moment, enthusiastic, sensual, child-brained, equally irresponsible and precipitous in suspiciousness and confidence, the owners of souls that usually contain some kind of a fissure, often avenging in their works an inner defilement, often seeking release from an all too faithful memory, often lost in the swamps and almost in love with the swamps until they become like will-o'-the-wisps and can *pretend* to be stars — the people then call them idealists — often struggling with a long-lasting nausea, with an oft-returning ghost of unbelief that makes them cold and forces them to pant after "glory" and to eat "faith in themselves (and as such)" out of the hands of ecstatic flatterers — what a torture are these great artists and superior men in general for one who has found them out! It is so easy to understand how they receive those outbreaks of boundless and utterly devoted *compassion* from women — women being clairvoyant in the world of suffering and unfortunately possessed of a mania for helping and saving that which is far beyond their actual power to help and save. The masses, particularly the masses who honor and respect the artist, do not understand this phenomenon and overwhelm it with inquisitive and self-complaisant interpretations. The compassion of women is regularly deceived in its powers; they would like to believe that love can do *anything* — it is their characteristic *superstition*. Alas, whoever knows the human heart guesses how poor, helpless, pretentious, and blundering even the best and deepest love is — it destroys more easily than it saves! It is possible that beneath the holy fable and disguise of the life of Jesus there is hidden one of the most painful instances of the martyrdom that comes from *knowing about love:* the martyrdom of the most innocent and greedy heart that never ever got enough of human love, the heart that *demanded* nothing other than love, than being loved; who turned hardness, insanity, and frightful explosions against all who denied their love; the history of a poor unsated and insatiable creature of love who had to invent hell in order to send those who didn't *want* to love him there — who finally, after he had become knowing in human love, had to invent a God who is entirely love, entirely *able* to love, who takes pity on human love because it is so wretched, so unknowing! Whoever feels this way, whoever *knows* love in this fashion — *seeks* death. But why ponder such painful matters? Assuming that one does not have to. . . .

270.

The spiritual arrogance and nausea of every man who has suffered deeply (*how* deeply men can suffer almost determines the order of rank)

— the gruesome certainty, which thoroughly imbues and colors him, that by virtue of his suffering he *knows more* than the shrewdest and wisest can know, that he has been familiar with, and at home in, many distant, dreadful worlds of which *"you* know nothing" — this spiritual arrogance of the sufferer, this pride in being of the elite of insight, one of the initiate, one of the almost sacrificed, needs all forms of disguise in order to protect itself from contact with importunate and compassionate hands, and in general from everything that is not its equal in suffering. Deep suffering makes one distinguished; it draws distinctions. One of the most subtle forms of disguise is Epicureanism, along with a certain ostentatious courageousness of taste, which takes suffering lightly and takes a defensive stand against everything sad and profound. There are "serene men," who make use of serenity because they are misunderstood on account of it — they *want* to be misunderstood. There are "scientific men," who make use of science because science appears serene and because the scientific mind leads one to the conclusion that the scientist is concerned with the surface of things — such men *want* to lead us to a false conclusion. There are free brash spirits which would like to conceal and deny that they are broken, proud, incurable hearts (the cynicism of Hamlet — the case of Galiani); and occasionally it is folly itself that is the mask for an unhappy, all-too-knowing knowledge. From which it follows that it behooves a more subtle humaneness to have reverence "for the mask" and not to practice psychology and curiosity in the wrong place.

271.

What separates two human beings most deeply is their differing sense for degrees of cleanliness. What is the use of decency and mutual usefulness, what is the use of all good will toward one another, if in the end they cannot "stand each other's smell!" The highest instinct for cleanliness places the one who has it into the strangest, most dangerous solitude, as though he were a saint. For this *is* saintliness: the highest spiritualization of the above-named instinct. Some sort of knowledge of an indescribable wealth of the joys of bathing, some sort of ardor and thirst that constantly drives the soul out of the night into the morning and out of the gloom, the "gloominess" into the light, the glowing, the deep, the delicate. Such an inclination *separates* as much as it characterizes — it is a distinguished and distinguishing trait. The saint's compassion is compassion with the *filth* of the human, all too human. And there are degrees and heights where compassion itself is felt to be defilement, filth. . . .

272.

Signs of distinction: never to think of lowering our duties to be duties for everyman; not to yield, not to want to share, one's own responsibility; to count one's privileges and one's exercise of them among one's *duties.*

273.

A man who strives for great things regards everyone whom he meets on his way as either a means or a delay or an obstacle — or as a temporary bed to rest on. The highly developed *goodness* toward his fellowmen which is characteristic of him is not possible until he has reached his height and dominion. His impatience and his consciousness that he is meanwhile sentenced to be a character in a comedy (for even war is a comedy and hides something, just as every means hides its ends) spoil all his relations with other people; this type of man knows solitude and its worst poisons.

274.

The Problem of Those Who Wait: Lucky accidents and all sorts of incalculable things are necessary for a superior man in whom the solution of a problem is dormant to reach his action at the proper time — for his action to "break out," one might say. On the average it does *not* happen; in all corners of the earth there are human beings sitting and waiting, hardly knowing to what extent they are waiting and even less aware that they are waiting in vain. Occasionally the call to awakening, the accident that "permits" action comes too late — when their best youth and power to act has been used up by sitting; how many have found to their horror when they "jumped up" that their limbs were asleep, their spirits too heavy! "Too late," they tell themselves, having lost faith in themselves and being now forever useless. It is not possible in the realm of genius that some "Raphael without hands" [3] (taking the expression in its widest sense) is perhaps the rule rather than the exception? Perhaps genius is not so very rare at all; but rather the five hundred *hands* that it needs to tyrannize over the *kairos,* the "right moment," to seize chance by its forelock!

275.

Whoever does not *want* to see what is high in a man looks all the more sharply at what is low, and in the foreground. Thus he gives himself away.

276.

The lower and coarser soul is better off in cases of any sort of injury and loss than the more distinguished one. The danger of the latter must be greater. The probability that it meets with an accident and perishes is, in fact, enormous, because of the complexity of the conditions necessary to its life. In a lizard a finger that has been lost will grow again; not so in a man.

277.

Too bad! Once more the same old story! When we have finished building our house we realize that we have inadvertently learned something which we should have known before we ever started to build. This everlasting baleful "too late!" — The melancholy of all that is *finished!* . . .

278.

Wanderer, who are you? I see you going your way, without scorn, without love, with unfathomable eyes, damp and sad like a plummet which has returned to the light from every depth without finding satisfaction. What was it seeking down below? I see your breast which does not heave, your lips that hide their nausea, your hands which are slow to touch anything — who are you? What were you doing? Come rest here; this place is hospitable for everyman; regain your strength! Whoever you may be, what would you like? What will serve to refresh you? Just name it: I offer you all that I have. "To refresh myself? To refresh myself? Oh you inquisitive man, what are you saying? But give me . . . please give me. . . ." What? What? Tell me! "Another mask! A second mask!" —

279.

Men of profound sadness give themselves away when they are happy. They have a way of seizing happiness as though they wanted to crush it and choke it — out of jealousy. Ah, they know only too well that it will run away from them!

280.

"Bad! Bad! Look — isn't he going backward?" Yes, but you misunderstand him if you complain of it. He is going backward like someone who is about to take a great leap. —

281.

"Will people believe me? — But I demand that they believe me: I myself have never thought well of myself and about myself; I have thought of myself only in very rare cases; only when forced; always ready to digress from 'myself,' always without faith in the result — thanks to an irresistible distrust against the very possibility of self-recognition. It has led me so far as to sense a contradiction in terms in even the concept 'immediate self-knowledge' that the theoreticians permit themselves. This whole fact is almost the surest thing I know about myself. There must be an unwillingness in me to *believe* any definite thing about myself. Is there a riddle in that? Probably, but fortunately not one which I have to solve. Perhaps it reveals the species to which I belong — but not to me; and I like it that way. — "

282.

"But what has crossed your path?" "I don't know," he said hesitantly. "Perhaps the Harpies flew over my table." — It occasionally happens nowadays that a mild, moderate, reserved man suddenly flies into a rage; he smashes the plates, overturns the table, screams, raves, insults everybody — and finally withdraws, ashamed, furious with himself. Where is he going? What for? To starve in solitude? To choke on his memory? Whoever has the appetites of a superior discriminating soul but only rarely find his table set and his meal prepared runs a great danger at all times. But today the danger is extraordinary. Flung into a noisy plebeian epoch, unable to eat from its dishes, he can easily perish of hunger and thirst or, in case he finally "takes a bite," of sudden nausea. All of us have probably at some time sat at tables where we did not belong, and those of us who are most intelligent, most difficult to nourish, know that dangerous dyspepsia which arises out of our sudden insight into and disappointment with the food and the others sitting at table — the *after-dinner nausea*.

283.

There is a subtle and at the same time distinguished self-control in praising — if one wants to praise at all — only where one does not agree. Otherwise one would be praising oneself, which is not in good taste. It is a self-control, to be sure, which offers an excellent opportunity and provocation to be constantly *misunderstood*. To be able to afford this genuine luxury of taste and morality, one cannot live among idiots of the intellect; rather one must live among people whose misunderstandings and blunders afford delight in their very subtlety, or else one pays far too heavily for this pleasure! "He praises me, *hence* acknowledges that I am right." — This asinine inference ruins half our life for us anchorites, for it gives us asses for our neighbors and friends.

284.

To live in an immense and proud serenity: always "beyond" — to have and not to have one's passions, one's pro's and con's arbitrarily, to lower oneself to them, but only for hours at a time; to "sit down" on them, as though they were horses — often donkeys; for one must know how to utilize their stupidity as well as their fire. To preserve one's three hundred foregrounds; to retain one's dark glasses, for there are cases where no one should look us in the eye, much less into our motives. And to choose for one's company that roguish and joyful vice: courtesy. And to remain master of one's four virtues: courage, insight, fellow-feeling, and solitude. For solitude is a virtue in us, a sublime bent and bias for cleanliness that guesses how unavoidably unclean things get when human beings come in close contact, in "society." Any communion in any way, anywhere, at any time, makes for "commonness."

285.

The greatest events and thoughts (and the greatest thoughts are the greatest events) are comprehended most slowly. The generations which are their contemporaries do not experience, do not "live through" them — they live alongside them. What happens is similar to what happens in the stellar universe. The light of the remotest stars reaches men last; while it has not yet reached them, they *deny* that there are stars there. "How many centuries does it take before a mind is fully comprehended?"

That is also a standard for creating an order of rank, a protocol, such as is needed — for minds as well as for stars. —

286.

"Hier ist die Aussicht frei, der Geist erhoben." [4] But there is also an opposite type of human being: those who are also on a summit and have the prospect free — but are looking *down*.

287.

What is distinguished? What can the word "distinguished" still mean to us today? What reveals, how does one recognize, the distinguished human being beneath today's sky heavily overcast by the beginnings of a plebeian rule that makes everything opaque and leaden? It is not his actions by which he can be proved: actions are always ambiguous, always unfathomable; neither is it his "works." Among artists and scholars there are many to be found today who reveal through their works a drive, a deep desire, for distinction. But precisely the need *for* distinction is fundamentally different from the needs of the distinguished soul. It is in fact the most persuasive and dangerous mark of what they lack. It is not works but "faith" that here decides, that determines the order or rank — to reactivate an old religious formula in a new and deeper sense. There is some kind of basic certainty about itself which a distinguished soul possesses, something which cannot be sought nor found nor perhaps lost. *The distinguished soul has reverence for itself.* —

288.

There are people who have "intelligence" in an unavoidable way; they can turn and twist as they wish; they can cover their treacherous eyes with their hands (as though hands couldn't betray!), but in the end it appears again and again: they have something they wish to hide: intelligence. One of the subtlest means for deceiving others at least as long as possible, for successfully appearing dumber than one is (which, in ordinary life is as desirable as an umbrella) is called *enthusiasm,* including what goes with it — virtue, for example. For Galiani, who should knows, said *vertu est enthousiasme.*

289.

If one listens to the footsteps of an anchorite, one can always hear something of an echo of desolation, something of the whisper and the fearful vigilance of solitude. In his strongest words, in his shriek even, there resounds a new, a more dangerous type of silence, of silent concealment. Whoever has sat alone with his soul year-in, year-out, day and night, in confidential discord and discourse, whoever became a cave-bear or a treasure seeker or a treasure guardian, a dragon, in his lair (which might be a labyrinth or a gold-mine) — in the end his very concepts will take on a unique twilight-color, an odor of depth as well as of mold, something incommunicative and repulsive that blows cold on anyone who passes by. The anchorite does not believe that any philosopher (assuming that all philosophers were once anchorites) ever expressed his essential and ultimate opinions in a book. On the contrary, one writes books in order to conceal what is concealed in one! He will doubt, in fact, that a philosopher *can* ever have an "ultimate and essential" opinion. He will suspect behind each cave a deeper cave, a more extensive, more exotic, richer world beyond the surface, a bottomless abyss beyond every "bottom," beneath every "foundation." Every philosophy is a foreground-philosophy: this is an anchorite's judgment. There is something arbitrary in the fact that the philosopher stopped *here,* that he looked back and looked around, that *here* he refrained from digging deeper, that he laid aside his spade. There is, in fact, something that arouses suspicion! Each philosophy also *conceals* a philosophy; each opinion is also a hiding place; each word is also a mask.

290.

Every deep thinker fears being understood more than he fears being misunderstood. His vanity may suffer from the latter, but his heart, his fellow-feeling suffers from the former. For it always says, "Why, oh why, do *you* want to have as hard a time as I do?"

291.

Man, a complex, lying, artificial, and inscrutable animal, weird-looking to the other animals not so much because of his power but rather because of his guile and shrewdness, has invented the clear conscience, so that he might have the sensation, for once, that his psyche is a *simple* thing. All of morality is a continuous courageous forgery, without which an enjoyment of the sight of man's soul would be impossible. From this point of view, the concept "art" may be much more comprehensive than one commonly believes.

292.

A philosopher: a human being who constantly experiences, sees, hears, suspects, hopes, and dreams the extraordinary; who is struck by his own thoughts as though they were external to him, as though they struck him from above and from below, who is struck by *his* type of events as though by lightning; who is himself perhaps a thunderstorm pregnant with new lightning flashes; a fateful man around whom there is a constant grumbling and rumbling, sudden illuminations of gaping abysses, and all sorts of uncanny mysteries. A philosopher: alas, a creature who often runs away from himself — but so inquisitive that he always "comes to" again, to himself.

293.

A man who says "I like this; I take it for my own; I will protect it and defend it against everyman," a man who can plead a cause, carry out a resolution, remain faithful to an idea, hold a woman, punish and lay low a transgressor; a man who has his anger and his sword, to whom the weak, the suffering, the oppressed, and the animals as well like to belong, and by nature do belong — in short a man who is a natural *master* — when *such* a man feels compassion, then such compassion is worth something! But of what use is the compassion of those who suffer? Or even worse, of those who *preach* compassion? Almost everywhere in Europe today there is a pathological sensibility and sensitivity for pain; also a repulsive excess of lamentation, a weakness which would like to pretend with the help of religion and philosophical bric-a-brac that it is a superiority: there is a regular cult of suffering. The *unmanliness* of that which is called "compassion" in such circles of devotees is in my opinion only too obvious. One must resolutely and fundamentally taboo this type of bad taste; for protection against it, I wish one might wear the good amulet *"gai saber"* around one's heart and neck (*Fröhliche Wissenschaft* — to make it plainer to the Germans)!

294.

The Olympian Vice. In spite of that philosopher (Hobbes) who, as a genuine Englishman, sought to ruin the reputation of laughter, claiming that it is a terrible infirmity of human nature which every rational mind should seek to overcome, I should permit myself an ordering of the ranks of philosophers according to the quality of their laughter — all the way up to those who are capable of *golden* laughter. And if the gods, too, philosophize (a conclusion to which I have often been driven), I do not doubt that they also know how to laugh in a superhuman and original fashion — and at the expense of all serious things! Gods like to mock; it seems that they cannot refrain from laughter even in the presence of holy acts.

295.

Genius of the heart: as it is possessed by that great Hidden One, the Tempter-God and born Rat-Catcher of the Conscience, whose voice can climb into the underworld of any psyche, who never speaks a word or looks a look in which there is not some hind-sight, some complexity of allure, whose craftsmanship includes knowing how to be an illusion — not an illusion of what he is, but of what constitutes one more compulsion upon his followers to follow him ever more intimately and thoroughly — *genius of the heart* which renders dumb all that is loud and complaisant, teaching it how to listen, which smooths rough souls and creates a taste in them for a new desire: to lie still like a mirror so that the deep sky might be reflected in them — *genius of the heart* which teaches the bungling and precipitous hand to hesitate and handle things delicately, which guesses the hidden and forgotten treasure, the drop of goodness and sweet intelligence beneath layers of murky, thick ice: which is a divining rod for every speck of gold that lies buried in its dungeon of deep muck and sand — *genius of the heart,* upon whose touch everyone departs richer, not full of grace, not surprised, not enriched and oppressed as though by strange goods, but richer in himself, newer than before, cracked wide open, blown upon and drawn out by a spring wind, more uncertain now perhaps, more delicate, fragile, and broken, but full of hopes that have no names as yet, full of new will and flow, full of new ill will and counter-flow — but what am I doing, my friends? Of whom am I speaking? Did I forget myself so far as not to tell you his name? Unless you yourselves have guessed who this questionable spirit and God is; who it is that demands such praise! For, as happens to everyone who from his early years has been a wanderer and an exile, many a strange and precarious spirit has run across my path. Foremost of all of them, and again and again, the one I was telling you bout, no less a one than the God *Dionysos,* that great Ambivalent One and Tempter-God, the one to whom I once, as you know, in all secrecy and all reverence, sacrificed my first-born [5] (having been the last, it seems to me, to sacrifice anything to him, for I found no one who understood what I was doing at that time). Meanwhile I learned much, all too much, about this God's philosophy by word of mouth, as I have said — I, the last disciple and initiate of the God Dionysos. It is really time, therefore, to give you, my friends, a small taste of this philosophy, insofar as I am permitted. *Sotto voce,* as is proper, for it is a matter of many things that are mysterious, new, exotic, strange, uncanny. Even that Dionysos is a philosopher and hence that gods philosophize seems to me a piece of precarious news, designed to create suspicion among philosophers. Among you, my friends, it is probably safer to tell it — unless it is told too late or at the wrong time — for you no longer like to believe in God or any gods nowadays, as you tell me. Furthermore, I may have to be more frank in my tale than the stern habits of your ears will like. In any event, the God in question always went further, a great deal further, when *he* held such discourses; He was always many steps ahead of me. . . . If it were allowed, I should accord him, as is the human custom, many beautiful solemn titles of pomp and virtue, much extolling of his explorer's and discoverer's courage, of his daring candor, his truthfulness, his love for wisdom. But a God such as he does not know what to do with such respectable clap-trap and pomp. "Keep it," he would say, "keep it for yourself and whoever is like you, whoever else needs such stuff! I have no reason to cover my nakedness!" One may easily guess that this type of divinity and philosopher lacks modesty. Once, for example, he said, "I love mankind under certain conditions" (alluding to Ariadne who was there at the time), "man seems to me to be a pleasant, courageous, inventive animal who has not his likes on earth; he can find his way around any labyrinth. I wish him well; I often contemplate how I might advance him, how I might make him stronger, more evil, and deeper than he is." "Stronger, more evil, and deeper?" I asked, shocked. "Yes," he said once more, "stronger, more evil, deeper, and also — more beautiful" — and saying this he smiled his halcyon smile, this Temper-God, as though he had delivered himself of an enchanting courtesy. One sees at once that it is not only modesty which this divinity lacks. . . . There are good reasons, in fact, for supposing that all the gods could learn from us men in several respects. We men are more — humane. . . .

296.

Alas, what are you in the end, my written and painted thoughts? Not long ago you were so brightly colored, so young and wicked, so full of thorns and secret spices that you made me sneeze and laugh — and now? You have taken off your newness; some of you, I fear, are ready to turn into truths, so immortal do you already look, so heart-breakingly decent, so boring! And was it ever otherwise? What sort of thing do we copy down, we mandarins with our Chinese brushes, we immortalizers of the things that *can* be written? What are we able to copy down? Only, alas, what is about to fade and lose its fragrance! Only departing and exhausted thunderstorms, alas, and belated yellow feelings! Only birds, alas, who flew till they were weary and lost their way, who can be caught in the hand — in *our* hand! We immortalize what has not long to live, what can no longer soar — tired and hollow things! It is only your afternoon, you my written and painted thoughts, for which I have the right colors — perhaps many colors, many bright-colored tendernesses, fifty yellows and browns and greens and reds. But no one could guess from these how you looked during your morning, you flashing sparks and miracles of my solitude — you old beloved *wicked* thoughts of mine!

[TRANSLATED BY MARIANNE COWAN]

NOTES

1. Gay learning. Nietzsche used the phrase for the title of a previous work, *Die fröhliche Wissenschaft. Translator.*

2. Nietzsche uses the word *Heillosigkeit* (from German *heilen*, heal) which suggests not only incurable (English "heal") but also lack of salvation (*Heil*-salvation; compare English "holy") and lack of wholeness (*heil* — English whole, hale). *Translator.*

3. The implication is similar to that of Gray's "some mute inglorious Milton." *Translator.*

4. The prospect here is free; the mind looks upward. (Goethe, *Faust*, Part II.)

5. Nietzsche alludes to his first work, *Die Geburt der Tragödie. Tr.*

The Twentieth Century

The solution to the Romantic problem lies not in attempting the impossible, not in trying to stabilize the Self, but in continuous self-transformation, in continuously transcending tragedy, and comedy, and good, and evil. The Self is the rainbow, an illusion made up of ever-changing substance, which hovers above the cataract of the tears of things. It is an illusion, but compared to it, the world we know is but the illusion of an illusion. With Nietzsche, Romanticism got to the root of its problem and found a stable solution to its difficulty in instability itself, in conceiving of life as the eternal possibility for continuous self-transformation. And that continuous self-transformation and renewal of Self which is the distinguishing mark of the twentieth-century artist, scientist, and philosopher is the triumph of Romanticism.